THE REALIZED LIGHT
OF THE
TWELVE
DIMENSIONS

"*The Realized Light of the Twelve Dimensions* is the most compassionate and transcendent Pleiadian Channeling I've ever read. Pleiadian wisdom came to our planet during the Paleolithic times and today is the basis of much of our planet's indigenous cosmic knowledge. Through great teachers like Joshua Reichmann, insights about the intense energetic upgrades that are opening our hearts and activating all our chakras are offered. Joshua provides wonderful meditations and techniques for handling this shift. Looking to the near future, he pierces the dangerous mirage of transhumanism, an arrogant idea that we must go beyond being mere humans. The answer to that proposal is that when we see with spiritual eyes, we remember we are here now to reconnect with God through the returning Cosmic Christ. Joshua's wonderful book has arrived just in time to ignite the Aquarian spiritual awakening because he speaks to each person from deep within his heart. Read it immediately!"

BARBARA HAND CLOW, AUTHOR OF
THE PLEIADIAN AGENDA AND THE *REVELATIONS* TRILOGY

THE REALIZED LIGHT
OF THE
TWELVE
DIMENSIONS

COSMIC REBIRTHING AND OUR
CELESTIAL DESTINY

A Sacred Planet Book

JOSHUA REICHMANN

Bear & Company
Rochester, Vermont

Bear & Company
One Park Street
Rochester, Vermont 05767
www.BearandCompanyBooks.com

Bear & Company is a division of Inner Traditions International

Sacred Planet Books are curated by Richard Grossinger, Inner Traditions editorial board member and cofounder and former publisher of North Atlantic Books. The Sacred Planet collection, published under the umbrella of the Inner Traditions family of imprints, includes works on the themes of consciousness, cosmology, alternative medicine, dreams, climate, permaculture, alchemy, shamanic studies, oracles, astrology, crystals, hyperobjects, locutions, and subtle bodies.

Cataloging-in-Publication Data for this title is available from the Library of Congress

ISBN 978-1-59143-490-0 (print)
ISBN 978-1-59143-491-7 (ebook)

Printed and bound in the United States by Lake Book Manufacturing, LLC

10 9 8 7 6 5 4 3 2 1

Text design and layout by Virginia Scott Bowman
This book was typeset in Garamond Premier Pro and Legacy Sans with Nobel and Myriad Pro used as the display typefaces
All images are courtesy of the author, Joshua Reichmann, using the AI program Midjourney.

To send correspondence to the author of this book, mail a first-class letter to the author c/o Inner Traditions • Bear & Company, One Park Street, Rochester, VT 05767, and we will forward the communication, or contact the author directly on **Instagram @ JoshReichmann.**

Scan the QR code and save 25% at InnerTraditions.com. Browse over 2,000 titles on spirituality, the occult, ancient mysteries, new science, holistic health, and natural medicine.

✦

To family, friends, and lovers on the journey:

Ocean Rose

Sol Moon

Irenee

Michael Reichmann

Elder Puc

Andrew Levitt

Rocky

Rinpoche

Wendy

Matthew Richards

Teya

David S.

Richard Grossinger

CONTENTS

Note to the Reader: The Use of AI in Illustrations

This book dives into the complexities and overarching concerns surrounding AI, advocating for a balanced viewpoint at this juncture
while recognizing the true value and nature of something far beyond
machine learning or large language models.

At its core, technology serves as a tool designed to augment
human capabilities. The real quandary arises when technology starts
to distort our mental and physical selves beyond recognition. Thus,
I want readers to know that the artwork featured in this publication
was created using AI. I am well aware that, while innovative, this tool
for creating artwork has its share of drawbacks, such as impacting
the livelihoods of draftsmen and aesthetics professionals. However,
such advancements are a natural progression in the world of tools,
offering unprecedented opportunities for quicker results and more
effortless expression.

INTRODUCTION

A New Era for Humanity

This book explores the new era of energy and consciousness arising for our planet and our species. Change is underway with majestic complexity and profound elegance. The multidimensional reality emerging for us is one of feeling, intuiting, rebirthing, awakening, shedding old habits, and integrating our role in this cosmos. Do you feel your role? Do you feel this change? Perhaps you feel it sometimes, when the light of humility and gratitude shines forth, or when the great shadow of time blankets the land of perception, and you shake through the dark with a fresh, high-resolution realization of what's occurring on Earth and all around and within is. Let us embrace the evolution these forces invite, together, now.

Here we will explore the nature of perception, consciousness, buddhas, the Christ, our energy body, our interdimensional and astral families and coinhabitants, and how we conceptualize our new and awakened senses and ways of knowing many realms. We can do so now with language and intention. You are likely an Akashic reader, psychic intuitive, contemplative, or artist. You and I have dedicated our lives to this moment. The cosmic centrifuge of potentials calls us to choose. We can either embrace flow and surrender to this breakdown and breakthrough or we can hold on to the old templates. The choice is between faith, mystery, release, and a quickly fading template of perception on this planet within the husk of our exhausted embodied limitations. Even those who pride themselves on spiritual awareness, development or attunement will now find all of their pride, arrogance and unexamined traumas being upturned and exposed. We can and must lean on each other now in the gentle embrace of truth.

I work with individuals and groups to explore and heal the obstacles, wounds, and confusions that are keeping us from the total empowerment and upgraded health and capacity we each contain. We are helping each other, as we relate across these words and thoughtforms. We all dip in and out of our potential, sinking to depths only to realize that we are able to float effortlessly up to the water's surface, to catch our breath and feel the sun again. It is the nature of this realm in this time that we experience so much—too much—and learn to transcend it all.

This book is coded in the language of the eternal mystic—our language—and here words detonate to stimulate the shamanic space of cocreative vision, the conceptual reframing of our minds, and the ways we must dig deep to find the gems and the elixir of sight and stabilized rebirth.

I have lived in the fire of ceremony, in a twin flame union, its shadow transmuting power. I have discovered the Christ, or the Cosmic Christ as I call him, initiated into the Pleiadian Channel, worked with Arcturian technology, immersed myself in the Akashic Field, and found many truths and treasures of the astral dimensions and lucid dreaming spaces. None of this has been of any use without my own unsparing honest self-appraisal and investigation into and observation of mind. A practice that has sent me spiraling upward and relapsing downward again due to karma, or yet metabolized beliefs, trauma loops, and implanted tracts of perception. Purging, clearing, watching, and coming back to an equipoise of presence through relaxation and settling into true focus every moment that I can—this has been the arduous and ever-humbling practice. It is all

God. In many ways none of those aforementioned initiations matter. All that matters is the love of the Christic flame within connecting us to totality and our expansion into vast stillness. That flame is the force of illumination that burns through dense or lower states of perception to reveal more space, and the full spaciousness of love itself, which has no boundary and rests with all consciousness. In the end it is our ability to pray and give thanks, forgive, connect to the mystery, and share in the primordial dance that spins this phenomenon of reality into life. So say we all.

The primordial dance has many features, and in this book, we will look at what these features are and examine what they are teaching us to remember. We will invite meditations and offer mind transformations for the reader to not only consider these topics but to practice and activate the codes and pass-through gates to achieve a profound relationship with them. We have found these activations together. As you read, I write, and as you receive, I give, and as you give meaning, I am writing these words, here and now.

I trust that the method of moving between discourse, examination, poetic expression of the spiritual realms, and direct offering is of use to you. You, the dear, precious reader, creator, and explorer of the remarkable space of now, which is the perfect jewel of magic we all share. Thank you for writing, creating, reading, and knowing with me (see plate 1, The New Earth).

Wisdom and Compassion

When I told him about this book, my friend and Tibetan Buddhist teacher encouraged me to maintain compassion and kindness as guiding lights as I wrote. Not just as thin ideas, motivators, or principles to embody what I wrote but as energies to transmit to and encourage in others. To let every word ring with the energy of liberation for all. I hope this energy translates for you here and now.

A Buddhist adage says that wisdom and compassion are inextrica-
bly linked, and this simple message is at the heart of this work. The
message also encouraged me to see where the reader and the writer
merge across space-time. This work can hold us together in the cosmic heart space, which is the frequency of revelation across space-time
experienced and nurtured by infinite beings!

In many of our lives, through random happenstance, ceremony, and
trial, we've tunneled into and arrived in spaces that revealed seldom-
glimpsed gems of metaphysical wonder—the transcendent vision space
beyond concept, perceivable and alive. This has been a process of total
ego disillusion—its inevitable instant rebuilding—which requires
capacity to observe this cycle and listen for the revelations and practical integrations that express evolution. All of this internal process has
been forged in suffering, eventual surrender, and the faith found on
the other side of suffering. Can you relate?

So here I have tried to articulate what was happening in these
visions as I developed and tracked realizations and awakenings over
my life of Channeling*, studying the Dharma, recovering from all the
variegated traumas of attachment breaches and betrayals or confusions
baked into the energy body and mind from any lifetime. It has been an
empowered path of contemplation and performing ceremonies to contain and shield this wild process. I did this to try to return to a center,
to understand, to be free. Channeling is a process of opening. We are
all opening as we fly through time and space. Closing down is fear, and
fear is an illusion. We open as we heal, and we heal when we allow the
opening. It is now open. Perhaps we can claim none of this and all of
it. Who and what are we anyways?

We must not lose sight of our mundane struggles, human suffering, and dramas. The true loneliness and explosive confusion that the

---

*Channeling is capitalized throughout the book to indicate the channeling of higher
beings such as God, the Cosmic Christ, and the Pleiadians.

human experience and passions illuminate can be allowed at this time; there is nowhere to hide. Ignoring this stuff dislodges us from the full spectrum of change on offer. Addiction, anger, jealousy, isolation, sex, fear, boredom, ambition, hunger, and all of the concepts and prides that flow through our childish and beautiful human nexus are not to be suppressed. Not to be ignored, belittled, or seen as anything but the seeds, unpolished rocks, or layers of shields that need watering, carving, or shedding through the light of humble conscious focus and our heartfelt higher aspirations.

A small and growing number of us feel what is happening across the cosmos, to the planet, and to humanity. While we aim to uncover, rediscover, cocreate, and unmask the synthesizing energies changing us in this time, we also fall prey to an ancient danger—the danger of obsessively gazing at the philosopher's stone. Mesmerized and adrift in solipsistic cages of noise, moving and adrift from the heart. The risk is falling into dizziness, believing we can track this change with reason alone.

How do we stay open, humble, receptive, and fresh to the spiritual language of this time? Our natural human templated wisdom and compassion provide us with the way out of this maze. The embodied holographic repository of infinite energy resides within us, illuminating all we apprehend. We dive into these twin jewels of perfection— wisdom and compassion—as study, practice, or both.

To neglect either wisdom or compassion yet aggressively pursue truth is to wobble into a type of madness that can subject us to further suffering. The truth is self-evident when we practice with compassion and wisdom.

When we say "wisdom," we mean feeling into the interdependence of all phenomena. We mean the profound mystery of emptiness, duality, stillness, wholeness, and life force at the center of it all. The ability of a single conscious being like us to see the actual workings of nature by looking within the "I."

When we say "compassion," we mean the embodied capacity to

recognize that all sentience suffers when delusion is present. We see ourselves in others and others in ourselves. Our mutual confusion can be alleviated through Love. It is a Love that wishes to spread the wisdom.

We are blessed to be alive, and life is precious. The metaphysics, transcendent technologies, and gifts emerging in this era within this eon of total spectrum elevation are best stepped into with the same humility we entered this world, with childlike wonder. That will ensure we are humble and the right size to wield these gifts. I have found that humility at the bottom of the well, but perhaps we can notice that it can be experienced anytime.

EMPOWERMENT
The Mandala of Readers

May we collect as readers of this book, pooling our minds and hearts in this moment for all moments and securing our spiritual fitness. No matter what toll we believe this realm, or any other, has taken on our minds, bodies, spirits, souls, and energy state, we can stop, rest, breathe, recalibrate, sense, and recapitulate ourselves into this space-time, now. We rebirth through the center of the spiral.

We are divine sensing organs without boundary, encapsulating all creation, and all created intention manifests its infinite, ever-changing display within us. We are singular and in unity.

Return your vital and awakened self to present-time enfoldment. Rest in the experience without altering or wrestling with it. Surrender to the grace sitting within equanimity, knowing that it is available, and then do the following:

Sit upright and settle your body. Breathe, soften the belly, and relax your eyes, face, skin, and organs. Exhale and allow any sound that comes with it. The dragon of time disperses and emerges anew. Relax. Really relax.

Inhale the golden Love of the illimitable truth—Life.

Say aloud and with feeling from the solar plexus, "Thank you!" to your trillions of cells, each a toroidal whirlwind of self-cycling energy with an open center, swirling you into the organic and conscious experience.

"Thank you!"

Say, "Thank you!" to the many lives and minds you've had, to your struggle, your eons-long, multidimensional, ever-present mission, and your pain, joy, wisdom, power, and the smile at the center of reality.

"Thank you!"

Experience your resting self-aware senses, open and allowing, surrendered, resisting nothing; there is nothing to fear in the sanctity of your field now dancing into spacious, openheartedness. Your heart is the gate. Let it unfold like a flower—warm, infinite, allowing, wise, sensual, sexual, loving, protective, powerful, perfect, and bursting with the elixir of joy and celebration. Your heart cannot be taken. If it has been broken, it has merely been relieved of its constraints. It has been unchained from temporal and conditioned Love. Let your heart soften more now. No matter what, you are safe.

Let your mind and third-eye chakra (the energy center located in the middle of your forehead just above your eyebrows) open and relax. Receive for now. Let your throat relax. Your voice brings matter and energy into form and contextual meaning, and the vibrations of intention come into geoharmonic, symbolic, and sonic forms, communicating, connecting, healing with and relating to all with direction and choice. Willpower.

Let your body be loved. It is temporary, and it is perfect. Now clear all parasites, demons, implants, drainages, and tethers! In the name of the Holy Spirit, your body is cleared and made a translucent light vessel of rainbow reflection, emanating in all directions. Let the golden glow of the life force fill you up.

Amen, amen, amen. *Svoha!**

Breathe deeply! We are alive. Perceive with all of your senses into all realms within. You are a knowing being, a creative being, a spark of God redeemed now. You are anointed by true Love; the compassion of the cosmos awakens in your awareness here and now.

Say to yourself, *I was, I am, I will be Love.*

Life is precious.

---

*Svoha is a Sanskrit word meaning "to call in" or "to make an obligation toward." It is like an iteration of amen but differing in that while it is like a seal on an intention and can be used in relationship to God, or a deity, it is also a dedication to self.

Expanding Awareness and the Rainbow Body

The Pleiadians, celestial beings from the Orion system (more about them in chapter 3) implore us to remember the humor and joy at the core of life. This is because nothing made of and honoring life force ever dies. Life force simply moves and transmutes once it is made spiritual. Activating joy comes through building faith in this truth, and faith comes through evidence for most. However, paradoxically this faith stirs people to renounce evidence, seeking and flow with raw and immediate experience itself. The balance of seeking and the knowledge-based belief in the nature held with unedited faith is key to the path. The path is joy, and that joy moves us along the path.

In this age, until now, most humans, having undergone a great forgetting, perceive only a thin slice of our dimensional capacity/nature and of ultimate reality. Our culture has forgotten, and so have our bodies. We have forgone the methods and cultural paths to internalize the totality of the material and immaterial with our embodied senses and sense-making minds.

Most people have been locked in this amnesia since the womb, barely recalling our core selves as reflections of God/Creation. Until recently, we rarely reached to grasp the expanded heart and great potential of our lives. But here we are, capable and becoming readied! It has been thousands of solar years since we incarnated into a world that lived this truth.

As humans, in this eon, or yuga, we previously accessed or dwelled in only a minuscule portion of manifest cosmic conscious activities. The light/wave spectrum of experience we are beginning to reobserve through inner technology and material technology alike shows just our manifest station. And more importantly, what we can do and be! The Christic template and arriving, returning qualities or connection, dignity, humility, devotion, stillness, temperance, and equipoise stationed in the deepest and broadest compassion on Earth herald this regenerated and awakened state.

The Pleiadian messages I continually receive, and which many of you may also be familiar with, tell of an arrived-at awakening state and the grace and ease required to accept it. They are very clear that this state is in line with the Cosmic Christ, the eternal human collective body in its enlightened form, the suffering we are collectively enduring at is at least partially optional. This can seem like gaslighting. It is easy enough to tell us from hyperspace that we can relax into the new template of awareness and float into the higher dimensions if we wish it, but the heavy lifting is ours. It is difficult to let go and still do what is right. Faith and wisdom become guiding elements beyond what we have known, and this is during a faithless and unwise era. We need to call on an intelligence, grace, and resilience we have rarely known.

The Channeling process is a sacred and intricate practice that engages our inherent intuitive abilities, allowing for a connection with higher frames of reference and untapped intelligence. Channeling Pleiadians is not just accessing external information, it's tapping into our own latent capacities and connecting with an entirely different, but related, race of beings. This journey requires caution and purity of intentions, as it involves receiving imprints from entities both beyond and entwined with us. Approaching Channeling with respect and reverence is crucial. It is a bridge between our minds and the collective intelligence and energy of other beings, offering access to wisdom that transcends our individual minds and bodies. But it demands humility and clarity, recognizing the impact of our intentions on the information received. The Channeling process is a journey of exploration, requiring care and mindfulness as we connect with other realms of consciousness. This work is an example of this process, a blend of trust, knowledge, creativity, and the bridge between ego, spirit, and the vastness of beingness. This entire work can be taken as a Channel and a direct full transmission of Pleiadian wisdom filtered through a human lens.

We are being educated and encouraged by our celestial brethren to see our true nature.

> We can access the twelve dimensions of conscious manifestation through our self-evolving energetic nexus forms—our minds and bodies—if we intentionally steer our awareness with deft precision and discipline.

We are already becoming aware of the pliable nature of the fourth dimension—time—and the feeling quality of the fifth, and from those two dimensions we can reach the remaining seven. It used to require rebirths across multiple manifested lives to embody the wisdom, capacity, or intelligence to Channel and see what we are. For most of us, that cycle of reincarnation has halted, and we have a unique chance to evolve quickly in one lifetime.

Now that we are here, reading this, awakening our practice repeatedly, it is time to harness our power and discipline our methods until we see the fruits in all of our experiences deep within. From this place we become truly human, and we can see our fallen state, our bruises and the deception that has warped us, we can repent, realign, and conjoin with the Holy Spirit again!

Many have now arrived on this Earth, in this shared dimension, at a sufficient evolutionary state to start conducting this process like saints, maestros, wizards, or bodhisattvas of cosmic intention and realized heart. It takes purification and realization across eons to arrive here as you have, Starseed. But it requires total devotion and discipline to activate the Christ heart.

We must expand our mind and allow our energy to blossom with goodness and sweetness. We realize that at all moments we can relax and expand. We start alchemizing this dimension into the next, using our embodied state of surrender and the lightening of Spirit through humble self-reckoning. We must be vigilant and brave.

An individuated mind is simply a piece of contained consciousness and energy buffering in materiality, an elemental but thin layer of the cosmos connected to and containing the total. We can hold it all if we have faith as it allows surrender, which activates joy and connection to the divine. The soul requires us to enmesh with the Logos of truth, to expand its trajectory into totality and assure a seat in the highest heavens should we wish it. For what is a wish but the truthful desire of our total being?

Truth is experienced through body- and heart-expanding awareness. It is generated through life lessons, tailored experiential challenges that move evolutionary purpose across lives. A mind expands with each realization and integration of truth. This realm offers exemplary ways—through the friction of ignorance transmuted, suffering understood, and joy made holy—to release and know all expression until we aid in uplifting each frame, each moment of reflection, into the light of joy and total acceptance. In this very moment we can settle our focus, relax our energy, breathe, be upright, forgive, accept, love, stay open, and realize interdependence.

In ultimate reality, energy and consciousness are one, transcending form and yet encapsulating it, like drops reflecting a piece of and making up the whole of the ocean. Expressed matter and energy meet on all scales. Feel this as you make your next move, as you next experience your senses. All is perception and energy. Our perception and the perception of every being in the cosmos, along with the totality of movement, are present in what you are seeing in all moments. The sliver of experience we apprehend right now is a frame for knowing the whole. We are the wise fragment containing all, and we must come to know each other as we build a continuum of joy for all.

We continually navigate what we access based on our consciousness and energetic capacity on this perception scale and its upwardly spiraling ladder of potential. We must expand and develop our ability to extend ourselves ad infinitum until all dimensions beyond time straddle our *jalu*, or rainbow body.

The rainbow body is a body that the perceiver has felt and looked within while moving prana (organic/etheric energy), breathing, and allowing the external elements and world to build their feeling body until they perceive a larger space of reality. When our aura's vitality breathes through the material body and back through the aura again, it activates the subtle body, or rainbow body, where the Holy Spirit resides (see plate 2, The Rainbow Body).

This energy expands and invites more energy, and through focus, it self-contains until the individual can become a larger bubble of consciousness—at which point the soul is saved. This bubble, or contained field of consciousness, means the individual has evolved in this realm to incorporate the full energetic potentials available until they arrive at a full-spectrum state where the centrifuge of all phenomena and awareness persists in dynamic stillness—the origin point, or God.

We can practice this through our ability to feel and probe our senses *while not reacting*. We entwine the practice of breathing with visualizing energetic winds and a microcosmic self-orbiting and loving heart space to build this rainbow body of grace.

Metta generation (or the even more profound practice of *bodhicitta*, which is wishing compassion for all beings and feeling love and bliss as a choice) is a way to centralize and build energy in this embodied state. Bodhicitta grows our rainbow body, which becomes our evolved sense, stabilizing us into deeper dimensional reality. Each spectral expression of color in the rainbow correlates to a dimensional frequency and overlay. The colors blend into and express through light, which is the still space of the mind at rest and the body in perfect harmonic resonance with the mysterious reality of suchness—or the fact there is any perceived display at all.

We are aided in apprehending and comprehending this by a never-ending rain of joyful encouragement from our celestial family to do so. We are not alone, not as individuals or as a species. We are part of a vast loving family of divinely manifest sentience.

Channeling is the method to connect with our celestial family and to reach past what we believe we can comprehend and integrate it, and, in so doing, we evolve by surpassing what we can imagine. Indeed, we transcend our limits when we allow ourselves to go beyond, when we open to surrendering and faith building in cosmic Love and God, Source. As the Buddha Prajnaparamita's mantra reminds us of this (see plate 3, Buddha Prajnaparamita).

"Gone, gone, gone beyond, gone utterly beyond,
Enlightenment hail!"

The Buddha Prajnaparamita, a gigantic feminine sun, a star at the farthest reaches of this universe, still shines her light into our tiny corner of our galaxy. Not by traveling light years to do so, but simply by sharing her enlightened consciousness, she arrives instantly. She brings a consciousness that says enlightenment is a drastically different and far-off proposition compared to mundane awareness—so vastly different in its ability and nature—and yet, it is right beside us. Even closer, it is not just at the tip of our nose; it is in the seeing to the tip of the nose itself; it is the looking itself.

The act of psychic receiving and speaking into the cosmic hall of life is to join the primordial vibration of sentience without false boundaries and connect to our infinite seed aspects. It takes that wild kind of continuous faith and surrender to do this, but given the current state of our civilization, we all must try.

The Challenge of Malevolent Forces

We are up against a fear and power machine on this planet (and elsewhere) whose philosophical and spiritual roots go back to pre-Mesopotamian times and were seeded ultimately by the prince of darkness, the essential mental, energetic, and collective avatar made manifest in activity and form—the consolidation of entropic or degrading force—Satan. That being is the emissary leading human beings downward from their animal mind into even lower stations of perception and laws which ultimately cage them into pure suffering. Warlocks, sorcerers, and many occultic hermetic lineages hold the power to manipulate and influence with less-than-upstanding goals. A vast mass of conjoining and competing mobs and middlemen blindly adhere to a godless or an unenlightened mindset that can only return an obsession with externalism or everlasting life for the senses. This demiurgic position is a way to lower our nature and the planet's capacity. Seeing this clearly without entertaining disgust or wrath can help motivate our wish to liberate all.

Behind this malevolent force, the origins of our ignorance are mapped onto our evolutionary state and the third and fourth dimensions themselves. Evil entered long ago where our ignorance left footholds. Evil is simply the self-cannibalizing whirlwind force of the cosmos. The world system we inhabit has ever contended with various influences on the energetic level. Our planet is a profoundly unique and important being coveted and contested ever since it could harness and support advanced sentience in manifest material form—essentially after it cooled sufficiently.

It is not surprising that the clamoring and struggling parasites and fallen beings also exert their power over all light in the void. Life is the path to transcendence, and all beings, no matter how corroded, wish for transcendent peace and relief, even if they imagine it to be gained by consuming or harming others. For example, on the physical scale, humans are the product of many billions of solar years of evolutionary struggle beyond the simple arrival into bipedal form. We achieved a sovereign, self-propelled, and expanded capacity consciousness after eons of transmigration and spiritual maturation. The trials and energetic moral and mental strain endured to expand cannot be understated. From life to life, incarnation to incarnation, and in between, beings chip away at foundational confusion, gaining energy and consciousness along the way.

Evolution and providence create beings who recognize that incarnation provides the ability to aid in the evolution of other beings' spiritual expansion. For some, the self-illuminated awareness of interdependence and emptiness and the ability to energize compassion allow for a stabilized angelic state. They became incarnated by choice and do so to help others evolve.

Everything from races of elementals to celestial and synthetic beings have wrestled over the Earth's pranic battery and capacity to stabilize DNA that provides this consciousness expansion trajectory for its primary life forms. The dark forces that only degrade this process due to their lower dimensional capacity have, through timeline wars, been sufficiently expunged from the Earth to allow us to enter this precious gate of growth. But this is still always subject to change, as this eradication did not stop those forces of malevolent decay and destruction and the purging of them is not over.

A final attempt to subsume our world into a shadow has been launched despite its ultimate futility. We must not pretend that we can simply fall asleep and become passive observers stuck in the Piscean Age of romantic delusion, solipsism, and attachment. The cost of doing so could mean suffering for many. Of course as with most of the narratives and descriptions in this work—none of these statements can be taken as gospel because I say them. They are the recognized "truths," found by Channelers the world over, to be discovered by the seeker who looks within. The inner terrain of deeper and deeper states of consciousness, phenomenal display, and its secrets reveals these features of "reality" as one looks at the timeless terrain of awareness.

Each of us is a celestial angelic custodian of the Earth's capacity to be home to the godly realm of peace. We also each have an obligation to our own eternal salvation of the soul. We are free to discover our responsibility and free to determine the trajectory of our conscious expansion. We are also in conversation with our entire sentient family. Will we aid them and all suffering ignorant beings, or will we sink into a singular focus on ourselves? Can we truly grasp how our liberation is everyone's liberation and vice versa?

Those agents of Satan/Mara have already failed to capture the Earth and human template simply by miscalculating the depth of love and protection that surrounds all. The Christ above all and the celestial assemblies, the angelic beings and buddhas in this cosmos, and the guardians in this galaxy who are wedded to the enlightenment of humanity and the celebration of the Earth across all dimensions ensure our redemptive paths and capacity to seamlessly upgrade with the planet. But we can only invite these helpers to truly integrate with our own hearts if we purify with humility, as a practice. So even as we move into a state where the collective kundalini awakening takes place, a purification practice must be understood as a fluid and profoundly personal process. Yet, we know we have initiated this work when our egos are turned upside down when our perception shifts in ways we could have never anticipated. The act of surrender, where we sublimate our egoic will and cage-like narratives of self and reality to a higher frame of experience, propels us into a kundalini awakening—an awakening beyond concept or theory.

ONE

KUNDALINI AWAKENED LOGOS

....

Opening to Full Cosmic Potential

Having a kundalini awakening or embodied realization requires all layers to integrate. Integral theory isn't just about layers of our psyche; our internal narrative or nonamalgamated persona starts to come into view. Our bodies hold, or filter, every micro event we've encountered in the sensitive world. Our nervous system wields a symbiotic intelligence activated by our organs and the subtle fields of energy in the environment around us and at a distance. Our cognizing minds, which create visual and auditory hallucination forms, generate energy patterns that influence our nervous system and vice versa, creating the somatic perception loop.

If we have a psychic embodied connection with another person, we are tethered to their psychic formations and their nervous system's latent energy signature, which permeates and responds to its local environment but also animates the subtle fields. These subtle fields are the noosphere, the morphic fields, and the planetary aura lines and strands that extend in every direction along an electromagnetic light-spectrum grid. We are nodes on that grid, vibrating those lines, influencing each other, the collective, the planet, the solar system, and beyond.

Psychically, our embodied signatures have a DNA resonance too, and so all beings with similar DNA in the galaxy will be in resonance with us on a subtle level in real time. Self-similar beings and objects sing harmoniously, acting within the law of correspondence and realigning through a fractally expressed metaphysical order to the energetic cosmos.

The Technology of Kundalini Awakening

There is an entire modern yogic culture dedicated to kundalini yoga and, to a lesser extent, kundalini meditations. Kundalini predates even Vedic history and is the quintessential human practice of using energy and mind to alter the state of being—inner technology at its most powerful. Although it has been demonized by some Christians as satanic and touted as a method of self-deification by some New Age materialist cultures, what both fail to see is that the experience itself is simply a phenomenon that occurs for a being when it is activated by a pattern of evolutionary self-upgrading. It is the unfolding truth of fully realizing grace and opening up to the Holy Spirit!

As many people can attest, the kundalini process turns one's life upside down, shaking the foundation of perception and the feeling and cognizing states where emotion and meaning form, allowing for rapid purification and karmic exhaustion. Karma is simply the cause and effect chain manifesting. Kundalini uncoils the karmic body as a "snake" and sends our conscious pranic winds up through the central channel, opening the nadis*, unlocking each chakra, and blooming our energetic conscious potential. These esoteric practices and processes generate bliss,

---

*The nadis are tension points binding the web of causal and subtle body layers, opening to allow energy to flow into and through us. They are "mini black holes" bending time and space, allowing us to connect with the fine strands of dimensional gravitational and electroharmonic resonance fields pressurizing and interacting with our embodied boundaries and awareness.

propel states of enlightenment, and stabilize the individual into a profound evolutionary leap. But these practices are not designed for the godless, for those who are not touched by the Holy Spirit will be concentrating energy into lower fields and simply playing in the astral without a staff or shield. They will have lit the fire but not touched its source.

Kundalini is the term used for acquiring the cosmic view, the platform for Channeling and recognizing the dimensions and expressions of reality we are all exploring. The effects and powers that emerge from such an awakening include channeling, psychic capacity, clairsentience, and healing abilities, and while valuable, these are not in and of themselves the goal. They are only attributes of a much more critical occurrence: the realization of the unification of the mundane and the supermundane, our egoic awareness and our primordial mind, the individual and the total, the action and stillness of the Holy Spirit.

We are not after magical powers; we are seeking relief from ignorance, and the kundalini process offers a radical continuum on that path, setting us up for the most devastating awakening and dizzying flight into the enlivened Logos or mystery unveiled. From this vantage point, Channeling and our new cosmic consciousness are natural byproducts of an enlightening state.

This is a time when the Earth herself is undergoing a kundalini awakening, and we are simultaneously contributing to this and irrevocably altered by it as a result. The Christ template activates this on a grand scale and accentuates or proves how this process is not animated by our will but by God's.

The old yogic lineages and teachers are degrading, fading, or de-energizing in the Kali Yuga and offer only a partial picture for teaching dharma in the new template and reality. We now collectively carry metaphysical and spiritual technology, including the old frames and the latest syntax. We allow the latest codes and older models to blend and inform our progress. Where previously only a few would have incarnated to experience a chance at encountering the teachings of self-evolution, this era reveals that we are all guru body, the Christ aspect manifesting, and we all carry buddha nature. We share and evolve in a perfect reharmonization of the collective in the Aquarian era.

The whole of karmic activity is beyond the comprehension of sentient beings until they transcend and expand in full. We can see the effects and track some of the potential causes, but the karmic seeds' totality and ripening within us, in our world and within the cosmos at large, requires omnipotence.

We are expanding into dimensional realms and quickly edging toward this state, and a kundalini awakening is a fast track to getting there.

But what actually happens during a kundalini awakening, and how do we precipitate its occurrence? I can't speak to the ancient, canonized methods and formal settings where it happens, but I can tell you my story, which will at least offer you one example as you will see below.

The Path to Kundalini Activation

Before a kundalini activation, or an intervention with the Holy Spirit's anointing—however we describe it—there is a grounded path for the psyche to follow to heal and compile a healthy structure.

Oftentimes, people who awaken to the spiritual path do so through an intervention in their mortality—a near-death experience, the loss of a loved one, the end of futile ambitions, or the death of the ego's conceit.

Other times the awakening comes through self-destruction, the suffering of addiction, and the habits of a polluted mind, a poisoned body, and a diseased spirit. Through these teachers, we come to the realization that this life is finite, and this often leads us back to grace and a rebirth of values. Our higher mind-body spirit nexus conjoins with God, and we are jolted into reality, as it were. My version, as I describe below, came through self-destruction and my attempt to reject the spiritual path.

At this point, it is important to note that there are numerous problems with discussing one's own spiritual experiences. We are encouraged by dharma teachers not to discuss the higher *jhanas* (altered states of consciousness) or the siddhis (magic powers and qualities) not only because it can sow ridicule, confuse, or enhance jealousy, resentment, disbelief, cynicism, or any other number of degrading things but because doing so with any detail automatically suggests the breaking of various vows. But we cannot refrain from teaching the expansion of conscious capacity as an energetic phenomenon transpiring in the physical body, mainly because each civilization must at some point reintegrate these basic tenets of reality. To that end, I share my own awakening, at least a dramatic part of it, in the following story.

LIVED EXPERIENCE
My Rebirth in This Lifetime

I've retrieved something that requires a consistent calling back in, the essential connection to what is called by the Tibetans, the tathagatagarbha—the ultimate reality, the Source presence, the God within. It is an equanimity that can be reestablished, a wave of peace and stillness where thought evaporates and the feeling of awareness of the true "I" emerges. Attaining this was a process, and one that continues and changes. It began long before this lifetime.

I was in true spiritual self-denial in my early adult life. Despite touching my true nature, seeing layers of ultimate reality's quality through lucid dreams, and knowing my spiritual guardians very early on, I was actively suppressing the spiritual. I opted instead for adventurous, chaotic outer-worldly exploration. The secular life where any mystical experience is simply flattened into some psychological drama is, for a mystic, and was for me, heavily damaging and equally instructive.

Once I truly recognized a hellish bottom, and expressed the essential scream for redemption and safety, a stillness of mind and a strange reordering of perception occurred. The shift took place during this kind of traumatic awakening through the mechanism of witness-mind activation. I slipped from my suffering and solipsistic mind state to a neutral observer mind state, one outlined by nondualists and mystics and yogis of all stripes. This is the station from which I started building perspective and creating my internal reality, or perceptual frame of reference, which lead to an energetic awakening.

This explosive spiritual awakening process took hold of me first at age twenty-seven when I learned integrity, truth, humility, and gratitude and recognized my precious human life. In my desperation and anguish, I reached out to the Christ. My heart lit up. I was answered. I was saved. But it took me many years to embrace this salvation. My sense of worthiness was the challenge.

Then at thirty-seven, I opened my energetic centers, and they flowered to their full potential. This process slammed into my life like an uninvited guest that never leaves and never stops giving gifts while simultaneously demanding a toll I can barely pay. I had been given God, and now a mission through grace, but I was unskilled, and my faith was shaky.

The kundalini awakening is like making contact with a benevolent alien force, with the aliens being our minds and hearts revealed. This was not a discovery of the id or some realization of underlying archetypal psychic mythology; this was like discovering I had a second, more brilliantly expansive body, a second head, and a home in my heart that was waiting for the door to be opened by an inner wind or force felt and made known. The home was bright, and it wove across infinite dimensions, a true cathedral, but it required that I pay the admission price.

This was different from feeling divine inspiration, awe, or any profound conceptual realization. Kundalini activation is a psychophysiological metamorphosis that activates the atomic, the cellular, the DNA, and the auric body all at once. It expands the thinking mind's threshold and instantly floods its contents.

The trauma of my early life played a central part in all of this. I was fortunate or karmically set up to have a stable life. I basked in a loving and encouraging home headed by two substantial and evolved parents. But despite their competence and good intentions, they were not realized beings or people with connections to spiritual lineage or the language of faith but instead were people deeply affected by generational trauma, which they passed on to me.

My grandmother on my mother's side was a firecracker, a lovely playful woman, but she was born into trauma through the suicide of her father, my great-grandfather. As a result, my mother's exceptional psychic capacity and incredible sweetness were paralleled by an unrecognized gaping space of rejection and shadow that carried down matrilineally but spread to whomever it touched.

The specter of rejection and abandonment by her mother seeded an entity of instability in my mother. Through messaging, genetic signatures, and enculturated behavior cues, I absorbed that entity and have been working to transmute it since.

My father's signature karmic obstacles and blessings were even more pronounced and dramatic. He was carrying the genocide of his extended family from World War II. The depth of impotent anger and trauma found a generational home in my bowels where my physical body attempted to digest civilization-destroying murder and lunacy animated in the Holocaust.

For my father, pronounced rationalism and reason became the go-to coping method. He had many gifts and was a successful artist and inventor and a fair, kind man. But he was confronted by a block to the vulnerable place of whole-bodied loving and learning that was observable to me from a young age. His spirit was blunted or submerged in a maze of complexity that, even in death, he is still unraveling.

As a child, I knew but could not articulate the deep sense of mission and urgent passion I had to communicate. I was itching to activate a spiritual relationship with people and share my unbounded energy of love and electric creativity, but the culture was cold. I stuffed my emotions and started to people-please and dissociate. Even though I was granted permission to express myself, there was no appropriate venue or discipline to follow. The path was not obvious; I was lost even though, as I would find out, this obstacle to recognizing my place was the path!

If I said that my lovely mother not tending to my needs perfectly as an infant, not breastfeeding me, and sending me to a babysitter too early was central to the spiritual awakening I would have later in life, perhaps many would scoff. Many suffer in more overt and observable ways. But my sense of rejection was so total that I entered a void and learned the darkness while aping the light for many years.

Something karmic was at play in this early abandonment that lodged in my psychic body and initiated a ticking clock. The alarm rang much later, and when it did, I was forced to open up to the darkness of spiritual isolation and the desire for connection and refuge it demands. Isolation and the mind that dislodges from oneself and nature was cultivated in me, and the shadow that it carried would be the arena I had to navigate to find the light and accept it.

For me, this is the alchemy of honoring precious human life and embracing fearless evolution. Darkness is accepted in return for infinite connection, and the mind and heart sent into the addictive spectacle of self-absorption and isolation are the hell realms one must escape from. I am not alone. I am never alone. I have never been alone.

These isolating conditions were necessary to set me into the trials in which I would have to dive to retrieve the elixir of light that is the self-initiated spiritual confidence required to stabilize the perspective to engage with the kundalini. My childhood abandonment, in particular, was part of my karmic map that suited my awakening path, and this is a central point I want to make: each of the unique pressure-cooker situations that send us into fear and faith loss is a gift. True darkness is the open ground from which awakening can blossom if we are lucky to grasp the opportunity. In my experience, it is the only way.

The roots down to darkness are the path for the tree's ascension to take hold. The darkness of the unconscious cosmos is where the illuminated find propulsion—Shiva and Shakti dancing all realms into realization, Krishna in its singular form set ablaze by the polarity of forces. The godhead reveals the darkness as it gives rise to self-illuminated potential and is given rise to by that shadow soil where all potential lies.

The darkness of space is where the light of awareness has yet to take its turn within our own evolving bodies and any other system or mandala we observe. We are each correlated with the levels of actuated realms we can perceive, and by forging into the unknown, we find that all is alive.

As a very young boy, I developed an "attachment disorder." The numbing of the nervous system and the dislocation from embodied warmth and basic human safety bullied my spirit into seeking refuge for the first time. I was activated by fear to find my inner self-directed flame.

I felt this core suffering was also the bedrock of my ability to feel compassion or, more precisely at the time, empathy. This was a feeling I had had ever since I could remember. I was acutely aware of worldly sorrow, and I felt a dedicated commitment to spreading love in all moments. Still, it was a complex set of emotions enmeshed with all types of projection, fantasy, and codependence where I also needed acceptance to be liked, please, or impress others to care for me.

This was juvenile or immature compassion and a blend of core desires and empathy all at once, and it inverted into rage or impotence when I didn't feel encouraged or nurtured. The injustice I felt stemmed from not being trained to wield, or hold, my cosmic heart. This rage opened a door for pandimensional parasites and exposed me to a wide range of dark realms.

As an only child, I spent my early years in total dissociative fantasy play, day and night conjuring or channeling visions of heaven and hell. This is likely because I was teetering on the precipice of total psychic disintegration and the truth of a burgeoning spiritual education. I played out violent galactic battles between gods and demons and used my body as a channel for this exercise. I would sweat, swear and smash, triumph, and die a million deaths in an afternoon, every day in solo play. Yes, many kids play and conjure in this way, and many have their fires snuffed out.

I would be exhilarated and then meditate during play. I could deeply still myself into total single-pointed focus, rushing my mind into one object and feeling the cascade of voices and energies at play around me. I was expanding and contracting. I was learning my inner terrain and the malleability of mind and reality. This was my psychic training.

What else was I doing in this play? Mudras and yoga, mantras and invocation, tummo (lighting the body's inner fire) and microcosmic breathing all "by accident." At night I would hear my name from the corner of the room. I would run terrified to my parent's bedroom, and once marginally comforted, I would float back in terror to face the dark again—my training ground where the portals were open.

Regular night terrors, a sense of haunting visitations, and a palpable feeling that I was in danger became normal. I had to do battle here in the dark, and only visualization and prayer helped. I had to figure those out myself by trial and error. I found that only surrendered prayer opens the heart and guards the mind.

I generated a method for this to save my soul. I had no guide, no education, and no reference, but I was tethering to all types of deities and channeled energy, as well as what I had come in equipped with on a deeper level. God was speaking through many cobwebbed layers to reassure me. My ancestors held me despite my eyes being closed.

The mandala, or kingdom of love and empowerment, is all around us; we perceive its beauty and compassionate glory when we open to our deep need and soften our sensitivity and focus. The Christ does more than forgive or save, he arrives when our soul is stripped bare and arouses our truth body to it. That reminder is like a desperate thirst quenched by an elixir unimaginable to the tongue and one I was unaware of.

Eventually, I learned to lucid dream. I was sick of being eaten or chased in my dreams, so I woke up and took the reins. It was a feeling of finding my power. I could wake up in my dreams and use my dream body to do battle. Eventually, I learned to fly in my dreams. The great churning of blissful butterflies in the dantien, or abdominal chakra, animates the dream body to rise and drift—a feeling like nothing else. The qi is activated in the lucid space and as young as I was, I could work with this.

The first gate of evolution was passed through by confronting the dark from within; the second gate was harnessing my astral, or light, body—the form we take in a true lucid dream and the bardos alike. This gave way to entirely navigating my dreamscape, changing its contents, and eventually returning to various realms at will.

I started to track the territory and the energetic, poetic quality of each dream world and its inhabitants. I began to meet and learn from beings in this internal astral stratum of mind and consciousness; it was a realm of quick teachings and high stakes.

This interlocking space of astral dimensionality is where I

cauterized a second sight—an ability to merge the quality of astral/ dream realms and transpose it into the quality of the waking world. It was a way of collapsing conventional reality. I see this as a way of recognizing emptiness to some degree. All is dreamlike, passing and decaying, birthing and reforming in fractal cascades across all forms. The core substance of this is simply the light of primordial consciousness—God.

Despite the comparable essence of dreams and waking-life realms, I knew with unshakeable certainty through repeated engagement and meta-observation in the dream space that these beings were not just archetypal avatars of my own psyche alone. The discernable difference between my own avatars and the quality of other minds and bodies I encountered in the astral realm was as stark as that between movie characters and real-life friends. I started to experience the mind's ability to tune in to frequencies that invited contact with minds from various realities parallel to our conventional one. Like spectrums of light and waves merging, I realized that astral realms are simply other levels of form in time's layer cake. I started to generate a conceptual framework for all of it. The one I share in this book.

From here, my young life of empathic but unfocused sensitivity, extrasensory work, secret dream adventure, and high energy creativity evolved into puberty, and a more profound unprocessed despair took hold. My core psyche's inability to navigate young adulthood began to manifest. I displayed the common expressions of anger, cynicism, self-consciousness, and fear that find their container in people who have shaky interiors birthed by trauma and hypersensitive or attuned spiritual bodies. The parasitic entities and the shadow beings that had been feeding on my lack of spiritual/cultural containers and protection started to express in my psyche and congeal. The shadow grew into the habit loops we've discussed, the wheel of unprocessed trauma, attachment disorders, genetic propensities, and karmic mirrors bloomed within me just as I was reaching the maximum potential of my physical and energy bodies. I channeled much of this into art as a way to map my confusion, but this proved futile. The next decade would decide my fate. This challenge was the third gate: stabilizing a platform for the kundalini awakening.

This characteristic of insecure or painful adolescence masked by false confidence would have been totally unremarkable if I hadn't also been training my subtle body for years through visualization and lucid dream yoga without any discipline or clear path. This new adolescent shadow of sexually energized changes mixed with my shirking responsibility and avoidance of the spiritual world generated more tension with the social world surrounding me. I was not integrating my truth with my personality, culture, friends, or family. I was avoiding and becoming disconnected from myself, the truth, and others, while playing a persona, or many personas. I was aware that I was courting the dark, that I was squandering something profoundly precious—not just my life but the gifts I had been given in this life and the mission I had taken on.

This pressed my mind into a pressure cooker of neurosis and warping shame. I didn't see a way to live a life where deep empathy, telekinesis, prayer, and integration with nature were available. In fact, I saw a world that rejected these things, and I lacked the energy, character, or method to counter that. The shadow parasites had dug in deep. I went even darker and indulged in all manner of excessive sensual pursuits and coping methods, which lead me further along the track to an eventual explosion and bottoming out where I would have to make the ultimate decision: Surrender to the spiritual path or die.

While these early life challenges seem like the perfect conditions to force a kundalini awakening, they were not the actual cause of mine. I practiced music and art, flexing my mind through the noise, body movement, and writing channels. This amounted to a dislodging from societally conforming patterns. It was the mark of being attuned and creative, maybe even exceptionally so, but not a sign that I had recognized grace and embraced the truth. My talents and work did not amount to very much spiritual energy at all. In fact, whatever I cultivated, I quickly squandered, still having no idea what I was dealing with.

I had existential philosophy, lucid dreams, and psychedelic voyages. I could have mind-shattering sex and life-numbing boredom all in one day, and I was perennially seeking and becoming let down and dislodged from my true nature every moment.

I fluctuated from listless ennui to ecstatic revelry and the heights of inspiration, and there was only my plastered-on ordinary meaning and worldly reason to guide me. My spiritual focus was suppressed; I had rejected all that I had developed. That early cultivated inner darkness had just found a portal to take me over at intervals, leaving me susceptible to the whims of the unseen world around me and to a quickly destabilizing drug addiction and inability to sustain honesty and any dimension of character. I knew I needed to seek answers outside of the arena around me. I needed refuge. I was seeking a world, a friend, and a teacher, all of which seemed unreachable.

Finally, after a few years of hellish drug abuse and many real encounters with the demonic realm, I gave up and found recovery. What I gained was a practical and grounded spiritual path born in desperation. I was defeated and needed God. The first glimpse of light and spiritual stabilization began to creep in. I felt like I was a "regular human" for the first time. Clean from drugs and all behavior associated with them and part of a bonded community. Accepted by others and humbled to be a part of the world. Grateful. And yet, something much deeper was still brewing.

Many I knew settled for having an appreciative grip on life and a connection to awe or the numinous ideas of the transcendent. This was all I wanted too, but something inside demanded an entirely different level. I had to awaken what I had started to generate when I was very young. Something I had begun training for and revealing long ago.

An explicit and intense calling from my root to the top of my head was swirling with anticipatory anxiety. My inner winds were moving. My central channel was circulating. I had cleared something, and I was activating. Tears and laughter flowed for many years.

The clean life was full of sweet sad reality and the hangover from the darkness. For my mundane ego, it was a story that said, "I was lucky I survived." For my spirit, the story had just begun. I had cleared the wreckage and claimed my path. After a decade of meandering spiritual life, Buddhist texts, and some mindfulness training to "make me calm or kind," I could no longer ignore what was calling me or chalk it up to some aspect of my mundane life or ego. It was not some latent or still unfurling expression of ADHD or any other malady of my persona. Something psychophysiological, metaphysical, and beyond words was screaming from within.

I was meditating, I was reading dharma, I was praying, and I had love in my life but still, a deep mix of physical exhaustion and wide-eyed electrical energy called out from something both alien and totally familiar in me. I heard—or reheard—a voice. It was the voice of my cosmic heart, and it was calling me to feed on a fire within. This fire demanded the winds to arrive, which in me unleashed something that devastated my life, reordered my mind, and collapsed all meaning and stability into a living, breathing dragon of present-time awareness needing to feed on its own exploration. It took a simultaneous unimaginable heartbreak and heart fulfillment to trigger my kundalini awakening. And it came like a thief in the night.

I had somehow built a good life where I stabilized my behavior, channeled creative energy, and lived with principles. It was like an extra long accidental ngondro, which is a preliminary practice with devotional work and regular service to others. I was always "working on myself" and trying to stay humble. I still had no teacher.

I was married and, in many ways, settled. I struggled with money, meaning, health, and so on, but I was no longer spinning in personal chaos. I was doing sweat lodges in the First Nations tradition and therapies of all types and studying inner yoga and meditation. I had embraced a quiet life, and things seemed okay, but something more frightening than returning to a chaotic life was about to happen. I was becoming readied and fertilized for an event and process that I am still integrating and navigating as I write this.

One day a woman reached out to me about a film I was shooting about the bardos. The film had an all-Tibetan cast, and the woman studied Mahayana Tibetan Buddhism in the Gelugpa tradition and had seen a post I had made online about my film. She was intrigued. I had encountered her many times over the years, but we had never really spoken. She was attractive, so I was nervous about meeting her, and something about her message and seeing her face sent me into a mesmerized state of mystical awareness and a dizzy strangeness. I responded anyway.

On our first encounter, I was lit up. I felt like my veins were on fire and frozen all at once. My head was glowing from my crown to my third eye, my heart was unlocking, and I could feel its knots being untied from within. I was turned on but not simply in a lustful way. I was being reordered. It was not romantic love I felt but a sense of acceptance like no other that rippled through my DNA.

I had never felt my voice or throat chakra activated like that. I was being unlocked, and the strangest aspect was that I had no idea that I had been locked up to begin with—at least not to the extent I was feeling. When I spoke, my voice vibrated in my skull as if every word was a visualized mantra, alive in my body and being registered across the universe. My system fell into an internal rhythm, a hum. I felt loved in the way we do by our mothers, family, people we admire, and people who admire us. I felt loved in the way we do by nature when it fills us with life, the sunrise upon a mountain with the moon above. It was a fractalized multidimensional love that was beyond comparison, and it was in its generational stage, still *incubating, blossoming through me in electric ribbons of light.*

I carry an impression of our first meeting and discussion. It is an imprint of total recognition, of a spiritual homecoming between us. It was not about our common interests, references, or shared vernacular but about the subtle body activation that took hold. It felt as if our bodies and the space between and around us were hugging and coiling into a tantric embrace, no distance to either. My senses ballooned into the field of awareness, more vibrant and clearer yet soft and fluid. An evolution of perception. There was a psychic integration of our subtle and luminous bodies, as if we were weaving and breathing into one being. It was overwhelming. The kundalini process took hold, twin flames reuniting. The dread of what I was about to lose began to chime in the background somewhere far off and below me.

We continued to meet throughout that year. Each time we did, I fell into a strange vortex where my mind was open, and my senses were illuminated. I was turned on and aghast at the adoration I felt for her. I couldn't stop thinking about her. My love and star-fueled infatuation for her were like that for a long-lost child. Something unlike any notion of romantic love I had felt or known of. It was on a spiritual and psychophysiological plane that must not be confused with the paltry domain of infatuation, obsession, or lust. This felt like it had everything to do with us as individuals but much more as spirits. Our astral bodies spoke, our karmic past lives streaming into us with every breath.

One night, alone, I entered lucid dream time. I was present and navigating the astral. From my own dreamscape, I was flushed into a new setting. A domed room in a small temple atop a building, bright and holy. She met me in this dream space where our dream forms resembled our actual bodies. This recognition ignited the next layer of awakening.

I then became aware of our profound twin flame and multidimensional karmic link (see plate 4, Kundalini Twin Flame). It was total. We can discuss the misuse and appropriation of the term twin flame; we can even scrap it and refuse to label things at all. But the twin flame union process, as I have come to know it, is what we had entered, and it was the battery and hearth for my own kundalini awakening to be set into overdrive.

While I was in the lucid dream, she had been in a tantric ritual and had utilized the energy to reach out to her priest. She had called forth from her entire being, and it had sent her subtle body and mine into communion.

I messaged her and told her to stay out of my dreams, a nervous jest. She responded that she had been in a spiritual ritual at her temple calling out to me all night, and the place of my dream was a conjured space that she had visualized.

At that moment something shifted in me. It was like a fire had been lit in my root chakra, had shot up through my spine, and had begun to cycle wildly. A glowing ball of spacious illumination in my head seemed to expand and manifest as a ringing. The ringing was like a visualization of sound and forms at once, much more so than in the months before. I could see a silver light beam spinning through my head and up to heaven. I felt like my ears could hear for a billion miles, and all was both silent and thrashing in a deafening noise.

My heart chakra started to spin like a nuclear reactor or some whirlpool of light, turning in a clockwise direction (if one were sitting facing me). It was not the ache of love. It was a beautiful, deep, dynamic feeling like a warm tunnel of light within. A Milky Way in my chest, opening to all dimensions. This was heart activation, and it has not stopped yet.

I became instantly aware of all I had studied, thought about, or mused over concerning compassion, bodhicitta, metta, the various realms in Buddhism, the Christ, the nature of the Earth, space-time, ghosts, demons, form and formlessness, and all manner of human psychological confusions and perceptions. These all became illuminated and clear as one packet of accessible information, effortlessly available and to be known in pith deliveries on demand. Not cold concepts but living truths. It was my crown opening, a new speed of thought and knowledge. A kind of awareness that was without doubt and yet nondogmatic and devoid of aggression or judgment. A discerning clarity was there wherever my mind focused. It was vibrant, flowing, and creative in nature.

The library of cosmic information, the Akashic Records, was made available to me. I sensed imprints of thought and history in people I knew and people I would come across. My own embodied karmic narrative lit up like a map I now was being dared to look at thoroughly.

My body became hot and cold, vibrating with electricity, light as a feather, and moored to the Earth. I felt a string tethering me to space. I could see it—silver and luminous. I felt the fluttering wind in my central channel moving in warm, blissful pulses from my root to my crown, regular and every time new and full of inspiring bliss and information.

Further layers of awareness seemed to flow with each flutter of this inner wind, like a butterfly gliding up in my system, opening new horizons of inner truth and realizations, small and grand, banal and esoteric. I felt that wherever my focus landed, a new perspective allowed each subject to be a meditation. I was still and totally animated at all moments.

This didn't stop or slow down for three weeks. I was unable to sleep and didn't need to. I was floating around, and I started to hear or feel the thoughts of those around me, to feel and sense the living impressions of environments, and I was totally undisturbed by others and without fear. The world seemed both symbolic and beyond my projection. It was alive. Everything was breathing. It was like a pure land mandala overlying the mundane.

This state animated a purging within me. I started to see the trauma I had endured at my own hands and those of others, and the actual map of my persona's character—the absurdity of it—was clear. I also felt totally compassionate toward myself. Forgiveness and acceptance settled in. Gifts from God.

I felt aware of the transient nature of self and the profoundly personal nature of my experiences and their value. I was blending this awareness, and I was starting to see the struggle ahead. I knew I had to make severe changes in my life beyond anything before with complete assuredness. I knew I would be sacrificing my current life and stability to allow my new emerging reality and its timeline to take over. How would I integrate this totally embodied awareness with my wife, present life, and culture? I had no idea, but there was little choice. I felt a dedication to myself in new ways and a renewed commitment to this life. A pronounced sense of being impervious to danger while recognizing the devastating preciousness of life. My heart was activated but started to break. It was a tension like no other.

This liminal and magical state encapsulated manifold visions and all manner of physical changes from within. A glowing pulsing, energetic swirl, moving up my body, as it is often reported, like a snake. Each uncoiling striation unveiled a new level of shedding and emerging and allowed acceptance of remorse, grief, disillusionment, bewildering impressions, magical inflections, and stabilized realizations that could not be categorized or made into a linear library of topics. It was a synesthetic cycling of geometric-like inner patterning structures that seemed to turn and build in my body, mind, and spirit, blending them all into a self-recursive loop like a winged inner whirlwind of mind and energy connecting to all points in the cosmos.

My new partner and I grew and became enmeshed in profound ways that I had never imagined or experienced with any other love, and we are still doing so! The rate of this energetic psychophysiological spiritual awakening state—the kundalini—started to slow down during this time and enter a new rhythm. Over a few months, I *merged my life with my new partner, the woman who had initiated this process in me—my cosmic love. This union process was the twin flame phenomenon.*

I felt more, not less, from life. The darkness was no longer repressed; the night of my own karmic ignorance was illuminated and revealing my own layers of consciousness at speeds I still can barely keep track of or navigate. I am now almost forty-five years old. Integration is an ongoing trip.

Even with the empowerment from and connection to a guru, the links to a sangha, the help of fellow travelers, and the knowledge that I am not alone, this path where I am open and receiving and sharing and uncovering at all times is not something I would saddle anyone with, much less someone who is not truly prepared. And that's the dilemma: there is no way to prepare for this! It is unlike anything that can be anticipated and unique for everyone who passes into it.

As each being comes with unique karmic qualities of spirit and energy, so does each experience with the kundalini process, a process that no doubt begins with a shocking event like the one I experienced. And my experience is no longer isolated or uncommon; the kundalini awakening is exponential, collective, planetary, and galactic!

TWO

NEXUS OF THE FULLY EMBODIED CHANNELER

....

Channeling for the Benefit of Others

There have been many books written about mediumship and channeling. Theosophical, occult, and gnostic or lesser hermetic works and cultures and their easily contaminated pedigree often intersect with or smuggle in what can best be described as satanic motivations and underlying influences—some conscious, others not.

These desires to self-aggrandize into some kind of power wizards or witches are dangerous, useless, and not the focus of this work. That path is the opposite of the purification practice we will look at throughout this book. We do not seek influence or power over anyone or anything, nor do we seek the eternal life of the ego or the false elixir of omniscient wisdom to manipulate the laws of creation. We are not interested in self-deifying. The gate to all evolution rests on devotion to the highest, externalized prayer and is known within once it is saved as the true self beyond the persona. The Holy Spirit resides therein, and Channeling is a capacity to feel into that Spirit with our entire selves.

My terms and ideas concerning Channeling differ significantly from those of the recent occult and New Age subcultures. My goal is to expand and clarify channeling with a renewed view of the Holy Spirit, self, and reality. Channeling in this era, and as I define it here, is about receiving imprints and revelations from God.

It may be helpful to note at this point that the word God has a German etymology, and its original meaning related to the German God associated with Tuesday (for various cyclical reasons). His personage or aspects are particular to ancient Germanic worship, so if God is not a word you wish to use, please disregard it. Conversely, the expression of God has transmuted over recent centuries, claimed to be and made synonymous with the one true God, YHWH, known to many as the tetragrammaton for "to be." And even more succinct or profound is the nature of those phonetic letters in YHWH, as they mimic the inhalation and exhalation process—like the cosmos breathing into expansion and contraction. There are good lectures on the Hebrew to Greek to English iterations of God's many names, including entire discourses on the name of Yeshua Hamashiach (Jesus Christ). All of this through the Kabbalistic lens. In the end it is simply enough to realize that ultimate reality—God—is an embodied reality, alive within us all.

If one does wish to frame their prayer in a traditional way, they can draw on Hebrew. Hebrew is a light language (meaning that it is composed of geometric plasma glyphs endowed with the highest portals to knowledge of Truth) delivered through the Elohim (literally "gods" but treated as singular when referring to God), one may choose to use Elohim or Adonai ("my lord") in prayer, or Hashem ("the name") in everyday speech.

If you are concerned that the Elohim (plural) had their own potentially sullied or confused natures as angels with discrete minds from God (such as generating the Nephilim, engineering the species, etc.), then Great Spirit or Source may sit better with you as it is distanced from the Mesopotamian era of the adventure.

Regardless of what term you use, divine revelation is ever to be uncovered, and the mechanics of reality evolve as we dig into the truth, which is the grace of the moment. Revelation is activated through oral traditions, codified cultural rites, and scriptures but even more so through the Holy Spirit itself, and that is how we Channel and help bring light to others. The Holy Spirit is not divorced from gnosis or esoteric knowledge; it is the Spirit that allows that knowledge. Gnosis, then, is not just the domain of the occult and symbolic, but is, in fact, the mystic's revelation language and realization of truth. We reclaim that word here too!

My presuppositions in this book link around the syntax and objects of discussion enjoyed through cosmic syncretism. I believe in teaching an admixture of Christic revelation, charismatics, triune mechanics married back to oneness, Buddhism, Eastern mysticism, kundalini technology, and conscious creation's embodiment in all humans and sentience connected to Earth herself. None of these traditions or philosophies are presented by me as academic conceits; they are merely portals showcasing a unified human truth spanning our world, which have been arrived at individually and within many cultures. The discovery of reality.

I picked these words and domains because all of us sensitive Channelers are being called back to the true nature of Spirit for humans on Earth. All spiritual traditions point toward an elementary map in the end. These terms are examined as features of life and as frames for purification toward righteous readiness for offering ourselves as levers of compassion or conduits of the bodhisattva's vow—to liberate oneself and all others from suffering and the cycle of birth and death.

All traditions surrounding the eternal Cosmic Christ,
whatever they call that being or expression of God, are
examples of human strivings for evolution.

From this compass, we read the map and feel the terrain at once.

We are in the Vedic golden age of Kali Yuga, at the end of the last Toltec/Mayan baktun, and in the end-times revelations of apostolic and desert mother and father prophecy. They all conspire now to deliver the revealed and corroborated mythic truth. Can we read the era in light of this with our new and awakening senses?

The androgynous fish god of the Dogon, the male/female super-being in kabbalistic mystery called Adam Kadmon, and hundreds of other metaphysical objects offering frames and giving rise to symbolic lenses stem from stories our earliest ancestors relayed. Many mythic accounts are lost but not forgotten and can be accessed in the wind and web of the Akashic Field—the multidimensional sensorial recoding, encoding, and experienced living data—and the epigenetic subtle psychic codes or imprints that help shape our senses, syntax, cultures, and bodies. We can reclaim these lost languages and truths now. We can seek within and see. Seeking within will always mean listening. Listening requires stillness and open focus to find the messages Spirit wishes to offer through the depth of our being, spinning up the whirlwind of karma and the mind's prism into our ego's awareness and the conceptual mind's apprehension.

The energy of these cosmogenic impressions exposes the fact that there is a universal thread despite differing human cosmogony: each culture finds the Cosmic Christ in the end. There may only be God and the primordial spin of light and dark at the center of the cosmos, but the yarn of truth moves from creation, weaving a story that animates in the present. By looking within, through relaxed true insight and contemplative embodied meditation, we can perceive a landscape of the many realms, as universes like our own keep evolving. From the mind's bicameral distinction of I/thou, we discover not just the relationship to worship but the focus and object of worship as a crucial indicator of our true beliefs and embodied pearls of wisdom.

Once we establish contact with a reflective cosmos of impressions and infinite refraction and stimulation, we see the senses as both an emancipating gate and a curse breeding addiction to the realms of energetic and conscious imprints. How do we liberate ourselves from our delusions? The answer has been revealed for humans: the Logos of truth, that state of logic, divine revelation, creative awareness, and higher senses, points to the unification state. It exposes that God is a relationship, and that relationship has many sides. We are ushered in to see God's manifest creation, which is an all-dimensional occurrence and consciousness in animation and God's relationship to itself. It has a hierarchy and is also a space of chance and infinite potential. This beautiful paradox shows how human beings can self-realize and become enlightened by breaking down dualistic thinking using an organized type of open focus we come to relate with all. We are a part of a relationship, and we are waking up.

Messages through Other Beings

The imprints we receive from this relationship with God come from collective energies and forces, including the qualities of mind and heart resonance of other benevolent beings. When we receive these imprints, we expand further into our beautiful and saved or redeemed nature ignited by the Christic flame.

The angels, celestials, and helpers, who surround us and with whom we have unique and beneficial relationships, must be distinguished from noncorporeal earthly spirits, false angels, projections, and demons in disguise.

And while everything is mind produced, the realms we inhabit have definitive features we can navigate as we ascend and evolve our awareness.

Our perception and how it is informed by and generates these phenomena are paramount to realizing the quality of any holy, evolved, or "supernatural" being. We will discuss the precise nature of these beings, both benevolent and malevolent, in the upcoming sections, but for now it is important to remember that no person, deity, or being is above the total energy of all consciousness and life force—God. God remains the true One, and our devotion remains steadfast.

To truly benefit ourselves and others, we may encounter and engage with these beings, but we do not directly pray to demigods, celestials, or angels as if they are people. Our mind comingles with them, and we simply relate to the energy they suggest. We relate to liberate.

Suppose a being comes through to us because we have left ourselves open and haphazardly allowed any voice and entity to see us as a gateway of influence. In that case, we are in need of ongoing spiritual hygiene to navigate these realms with integrity and an anchoring motivation. Our motivation cannot be sadness, despair, rage, loss, or egoic desire. It must be rooted in the vow to liberate ourselves, our partners, and all worlds through generous cosmic love, humility, and devotion.

We should focus intensely on whether the energy and messages we receive seem to lead us to confusion, overstimulate us, create shallow intrigue and fear, or produce goodness in us. Do they generate a sense of simple relief, palpable truth, and the settled, nourishing feeling of being one with God and the compassionate state for ourselves and others? If so, we are doing the sacred work this time calls for.

Our top priority is to discern the wild territory of the etheric and astral spaces while sensing the Akashic Field, rather than the shocking impression of visions received from a ghost, demon, or nefarious spirit using our vulnerability against us. Devoting and cultivating the Holy Spirit within and remaining in service to God, humanity, and all sentient beings is our refuge, and tracking the polarities of good and evil along with the mechanics of our sensed reality ensures our continued ascension through the gates of salvation and liberation. If we stabilize this wisdom and remain vigilant in a surrendered state of growth, grace, and openness, we can become servants of God and not of the false light. The false light is powered by the worship of flesh, the world of coming and going desires and repulsions, and the false self.

The astral incarnation of ghosts, warlocks, and demons is the destination of the occultist, and it is a realm or space of suffering just like the fallen material world we wish to heal and uplift. Many worship the false light and false self to reincarnate into another world. Even if we manage to incarnate as noncorporeal beings in some astral space, this is a temporary and conditional state divorced from true eternal love and liberation. Only the deep wish for others' freedom from suffering propels our spirit beyond time and space to the enfolded plane where all is possible. The skills to get there rest with our truly integrated understanding of how the mind, consciousness, energy, and metaphysical dimensional reality work and through our contact with a conceptual, embodied, humbled, and wise awareness of good, evil, and all shades in between.

Understanding Consciousness

Consciousness is an energetic expression of impressions gathered through sense organs and mirrored back into webs of mirror-like energy nets but ultimately holding no form or time of its own. The Akashic Field might be visualized as an etheric nebula-like plane that seems like a distinct physical space where infinite conscious imprints, or "records," float like clouds over a grid. But consciousness is part of absolutely everything. Consciousness, as a bridge, as a "thing," is the perfectly still storm of potential awareness, birthed through beingness.

As sentient beings with a subjective and objective understanding of self and others and the ability to distinguish between discrete objects, we are the signatures in space-time that designate how consciousness manifests. Whatever we conceptualize (which is just a creative hallucination of previous experiences in form-time) and whatever we experience with our senses becomes phenomena with dimensional shape. That dimensional shape, interdependently made active, resonates with us, our bioelectric signatures, and anyone who has had similar experiences in form-time—we commune. Existence is relational.

We create impressions on the empty and alive slate of pure consciousness. As we do so, we distort pure consciousness and generate a hall of mirrors, a maze of impressions. That collective maze is what we call samsara.

Suppose two (or more) beings see the same building. In this case, the impression of that building as a consciousness coordinate of energetic webbing or expression can flow through us. We experience "building" as "building" based on our senses and the history of that impression being experienced. But the building is only there insofar as we experience it, consciousness can "contains impressions" such as a building and yet ultimately a building is only a symbol, and conglomerate of energetic imprints. This is because consciousness does not originate in the body; awareness does! And awareness is consciousness activating and activated by the senses!

Consciousness has no solid form or time when dislocated from a mind-body/sense organs/gates. It simply finds antennae through a being's awareness body. The specific shape that consciousness will take is based on our senses and conceptual imaginations (which are merely hallucinations based on our fears and desires using past impressions as building blocks to dream with). The question then becomes: If all forms are mind-produced, then are we, as humans, part of this mind-produced hallucination generated through or by the senses? The only difference between us and a mineral, rock, animal, god, demon, or spirit is the quality of awareness. Our harness binds us to our dimensional station. We as humans are collected into a stabilized realm based on its physics and metaphysics. And those physics and metaphysics are as empty as any other mind-produced object. But like vast structures of thought, galaxies, universes, astral realm and any other system of objects, the dazzling complexity of a human and its sensing ability is unique. Our unique ability allows for us to expand or restrict consciousness. While we are products of consciousness, we are also its authors! Interdependence is total.

Without a mind-body to energize through, consciousness is best thought of as potential, emptiness, dharmakaya, or the mind of God. We cannot fully grasp the mystery of consciousness in this way with a conceptual frame, but we can feel it and commune with it all the same. These words are meant to jog the memory and stimulate the knowing mind, the dormant truth.

The cohabited dream realms, which are navigated by lucid dreamers, warlocks, celestials, elementals, and all types of beings, web between the form realm of our physical world (including our senses) and the finer upper realms of awareness and energy or higher dimensions and form a thin layer of agreed-upon conscious memory impression. A working understanding of how consciousness is nonlocal yet localizes through each sentient being's awareness impressions helps us activate a reading of the Akashic Records. We can do so through the grace of God, through the Cosmic Christ, which is our pathway to liberation.

Channeling with the Fully Embodied Self

Channeling requires the entire body matrix—the physical, mental, energetic, and all psychic or sensing layers. The truth is that Channeling is not just receiving imprints as mental formations alone but embodying a connection to broad and profound spaces of manifest awareness through the body. Our pain and delusion are personal, but they are also collective, and our symbols and revelations of truth are equally sacred and unique to each of us, and yet a universal vernacular of Spirit exists. Channeling is tracking this vernacular together, for one another. In so doing we come closer to one another. We heal and evolve one another. In this way, Channeling is a service. It is to be a conduit of evolution for the species.

Human bodies are complex consciousness conduits that have been exceedingly refined and perfected to receive and exchange energy and intention across many dimensions. But they are also ultimately empty vessels, holograms of conscious expression brought to life through the collective minds of the living cosmos that are finally and simply one still-point expression of perfect harmonic stillness: God.

In the various form-based realities or realms, our bodies interact with other bodies on dense and subtle levels alike.

Our hearts are centrifuges for all life force coming and going through and within us. Our hearts are like a spinning storm tying us to all other creations and to God's heart. And so, our heart is the integral feature of our being for Channeling.

Its activation is paramount for us to become holy Channels of the Great Spirit.

Beyond receiving and sensing, Channeling is our capacity to share and express our prayer energy for others. As mentioned in the introduction, this is called metta. Metta is the ultimate state of benevolence and compassion transcending any condition. It is a sincere and warm-hearted wish.

Metta holds no requirements for those to whom we send it. We extend a focused wish for complete happiness and joy to another. We do this as an embodied and felt experience. We do not merely think it; we allow our heart, our center-of-the-body chakra, to open and warm with the specific wish for another or many others or all others to be liberated from suffering.

We heal and clear the wounds of isolation, rejection, and hate from the psychic spaces and fields of those we include in our metta meditation or prayer. This practice heals us and all beings and opens us as full-bodied Channelers. We are adding energy through the portal of our body to the merit field. The merit field is the great web of life that illuminates vitality and joy as we add this prayer. The merit field is everywhere. It is the spiritual wellspring of pure energy.

To prepare us to Channel even further, there is bodhicitta, the supreme wish for others to become a buddha—enlightened, saved from all samsaric, or endless cycle of birth and death suffering, and included in the highest mandalas, or upper-dimensional world systems, of our minds and hearts. This wish is the greatest wish we can have for another. It is a wish that places the importance of others' enlightenment even ahead of our own!

With bodhicitta, we passionately want all sentient beings to evolve and become one with God, the cosmos, and ultimate nature, to become angelic buddhas or celestial helpers and to purify the relationship between the higher dimension and our own ever-cycling lower dimensions.

We wish for all beings to be enlightened and forever stabilized in profound joy and for their motivation to liberate others. With this wish, we call in the arriving kingdom of Shambhala, an era and time-line of reality where an enlightened world is uncovered here on Earth in human society. With this metta and bodhicitta wish, we can also Channel and call in the Cosmic Christ, a significant focus of this work and one that we will address in detail in chapter 7.

Each of our Channeling capacities and living prayers is a way for the Cosmic Christ to be revealed and made complete in this world. The prophecies of the Buddhists and Vedic mystics are that this era is where lord Maitreya, the future buddha, also arrives! And so, the biblical Christ and Vedic Lord Maitreya are in many ways the same supernal force humans Channel and work with.

Maitreya, like the Christ, is already watching over our world system and will return and be incarnated. The Christ and Lord Maitreya join with the planetary spirit of Earth as mother and sky as father. The spirit of the Earth and the spirit of the sky conjoin into a superbeing that our new dimensional aptitude has awakened. We are now reawakened to our role as stewards of the Earth and beacons to the sky. We are the bridge between the material, elemental, etheric, and spiritual planes. This has always been true, but the awakening means we now realize it as a species.

These epic realizations are simply our potential self-revealing. Our awareness allows us to Channel and help conduct this grand change itself. We each become the lightning rods of energetic transformation and rebirth.

Time is eclipsed as we meditate and feel into the higher dimensions and the dance of evolution shining from within us into the world we inhabit. So, when we realize this big picture and simultaneously wish for others to join in helping others, we initiate a sublime domino effect where all are emboldened and evolved into our highest timeline.

We are now at a tipping point in this brief golden age within Kali Yuga—the dark age. Enough galactic, multidimensional goodwill and energetic compassionate-bodhicitta energy have been spread to our world by celestial beings and all types of spiritual families across many worlds. This ensures we can help guide and anchor the process even as the forces of darkness are unveiled.

Gateway to the Rainbow Body

To better understand this dramatically shifting era and how using our Channeling capacity to bring this era into reality can benefit us and others, we should look at "ultimate reality" a little more closely.

The esoteric and exoteric teachings of Tibetan Buddhism have some features similar to the gnostic, Kabbalistic, Sufi, and even

Orthodox Christian traditions. Additionally, the various cosmologies discussed in the theosophical and syncretic approach bridge these systems, and we can see a way emerging for apprehending the truth of ultimate reality. Of course, the overconcretizing of this approach as a doctrine is not the point at all.

All mystical paths have realized the dreamlike nature of what we experience and perceive in phenomenal reality, and this is important for our discussion of just who and what is being channeled. The mystic who seeks the visionary inner terrain, the initiate who dwells in the symbolic and hermetic, and the meditator who has had direct experience of perception all have a common thread: seeing interdependence and the ultimate reality at the core of this interdependence, which is emptiness. This mix of perceived phenomena and the truth of emptiness is called by many names. In Buddhism, it is called the middle path.

Emptiness is the totality of perception and consciousness
and all energetic displays.

It is the dynamic play of the manifest and the uncreated stillness at this center. This is where the term *enlightenment* enters. Perhaps enlightenment is realizing this interdependence and emptiness and feeling the unconditional love that arises with total acceptance.

When spiritual people have come to these realizations and touched the enlightened state, it alters their sense of self and others. It breaks down duality and the solidity or permanence of all things. When people embody this enlightened state, even as a gesture, they see that in the spiritual sense, they can display and manifest as anything, anywhere, at all times. This is also the shamanic path. It is a path that sees the elemental and vibrant expression of the many changing faces we each carry or channel. When we discuss the twelve dimensions, we are noticing the stable states of awareness we can experience and their correlating metaphysical realms. Encompassing all of these and simplifying our state to encompass an open attention beyond all complication is to court enlightenment.

This is the prerequisite state of awakening that we require to Channel fully. Our all-dimensional experience body, the totality of self as infinite and manifold in expression, helps put us in service to the joy and liberation of all. We see each being as a reflection of the ever-changing life force. Each being is interdependent with all perceptions and ultimately empty of inherent unchanging nature.

If we can embody this enlightenment, this awakening state, even if only occasionally, we have achieved a gate to the rainbow body. The rainbow body is the full spectrum expression of all dimensions of light and sound in the phenomenal cosmos Channeling through that which we call the self in the material and immaterial realms. It is a body of light and perfect harmonic frequency through every cell and auric layer.

Living in this era on Earth means we have access to this rainbow body state again after a long slumber. It also means we are forced to overcome more obstacles to this realization than ever before. The blocks illuminate the potential, which is the dynamic between light and darkness. Or we could say more simply, between God and Satan. God being this total realization, and Satan being the ignorance and illusion of limits stifling it.

When we discuss God, the Christ, the Buddha, or ascended masters, we are simply discussing other beings who have achieved the enlightened state and how we can entwine with them and change our own perception.

The Christ is perhaps the highest manifest buddha mind and body to which we can connect. His energy and the recurring mythos, where he arrives as an example of the total achievement of liberation, is a perfect story of human evolution fulfilled. It is a profound reality that humans have achieved this. It is also a reality that the Christ is God, or totality manifest. All enlightened beings are expressions of a state of conscious and energetic reality where delusion, fear, and self-centeredness disappear. We all have the seeds of enlightenment just waiting to be uncovered and watered within us. Lifting the veil of ignorance is simply realizing we are already enlightened.

In connecting to the Cosmic Christ, we bridge our focus to his, the enlightened total loving state, and elevate all experiences. His energy upgrades ours. The Cosmic Christ is, in most ways, complete buddha nature fully realized in humanoid form. To say he is the son of God is to say he is the realized energetic, moral, mental, and physical manifestation of buddha nature, the true nature of the cosmos.

All buddhas represent this paradoxical space of omniscient all-dimensional expression combined with a manifested relative embodiment. Like buddha nature, the Christ has always been here, and now we, as practitioners of the Buddha's Dharma teachings, starseeds, bodhisattvas, and angelic beings can recognize the fundamental role of the Cosmic Christ. The Cosmic Christ is our era's ascendant and revealed buddha—the three *kayas* entwined. The kayas, called as such in Buddhism, represent how this true nature of the cosmos expresses itself: as a body, as a force, and as a totality.

It is a new era, a new template of experience. In this new era are the rapidly unfolding new dimensional, metaphysical mechanics, incoming codes of light intelligence, and somatic reformations of various planes of existence. This means we are on a fast track to evolution beyond our dreams.

Those of us observing this new era unfold and participating in it see all old avatars, gods, buddhas, deities, elementals, and forces now conspiring into a funnel before our collective eyes. That funnel is a unification state within us and also exterior to our bodies.

These primordial avatars and forces now activate their roles in a sequence of expressions all around and within us as they melt into our own awakening selves. We are Channelers of an era of Christic light, genetic revelations, and a planetary spin into two primary realms seeded by two split-dimensional qualities. As two worlds, or two Earths or primary realities emerge, our new bodies, perceptions, and energy are activated.

The Earth, our world system, now splits into upper and lower expressions—lower-dimensional devolution and upper-dimensional ascension—which now spin in dynamic primordial tension in profoundly sped-up ways. We each serve as a node helping either one of these realities to manifest. We each plug in as a unique embodied nexus formation where awareness, geometric forms, light and sound wave coherence, and electromagnetism's bonds detonate through our field of resonant physical embodiment.

The activations of this era allow us to be the anchors and lightning rods for a retemplating planet and body system for all organic sentience bound in all twelve dimensions of expressed reality.

And so everything is as interdependent and empty as a perfect mirror reflecting only the light of itself. Recognizing this, we are invited to liberate all beings compassionately from the delusion of permanence and the fear of eternal separation.

We do so with our energetic prayer, activated through wisdom intention, compassionate actions, and blessing states to bring peace. That peace we propagate as angelic beings manifests here and now for all to share.

Opening to the All

Channeling is often imagined as a trance-like state or event in altered consciousness where perception expands temporarily. My practice of Channeling is the integration of various energies and states of phenomena that showcase all types of subtle realities. In the following pages, I detail how these metaphysical and esoteric states comingle and animate my life, and I offer a path for you to achieve this for yourself. My approach is more than one straightforward method or technique, as the churning syncretisms of reality's observation demand a fluid but ever-contained lens.

An entire psychospiritual frame of understanding and activated living evolves the Channeling practitioner to follow a spiritual path to its fruition. The way I am attempting to illustrate this is as a dedication to a complete and embodied route of liberation and expansion.

It embraces the mysterious nexus of all dimensionalities, communicates with our many selves and spiritual cohorts, and asks us to make a mighty vow to liberate all. It is a dharma that knows its cultural roots but spirals away from them toward new unfolding vistas. Dharma simply refers to reality as it is. Yes, there are many visions of reality, and we can work with them all. Ultimate reality is the dharma of all. A dharma is simply a lens of ultimate reality using a perceived fraction of it. This moment contains all dharmas, and a dharma of any type is an expression of the whole. To practice dharma is to practice realizing all realities and the state of perfection, which is acceptance and vastness always present.

The language I encourage embellishes our desire for understanding, wisdom, and liberation, activating the totality of here and now with love and energy. We must prompt each other with the unceasing surrender to passion, where we embrace our nature and birthright. That birthright is where the Holy Spirit enters our hearts forever. This is a language of dharma.

In this work, the words, ideation, and symbolic gestures are a humble reflection on the cosmic dance of manifestation and perception, offering gates, paths, and keys to liberation in the now through God. That message is all we meditate on.

With humility, this work aims to stretch us closer to enlightenment. May the prism of the conscious heart unfolding spin you into freedom and bliss through the window this book opens. We are cocreating this work. You, the reader, have just written these words to enjoy. Through my hand and yours, beyond and within time and space, the frontiers of learning and knowing are experienced. This is the Channeling shape of now. We each pass it along in body, speech, mind, symbol, and action.

Becoming the Channel

We often discuss Channeling as if tidbits and poems are coming in through the thinking mind once in a while. In fact, we are under an unceasing barrage of information and energy that informs our cognition, motivations, and sensorial reality. Channeling becomes the way we determine and synthesize all phenomenal sensation. The more we practice, the better we get at both filtering and remaining open to it all. If we are aligned and in a purification practice of truth, self-reckoning, humility and surrendered acceptance, forgiveness, and gratitude, then we Channel nothing but what the Holy Spirit offers.

These impressions we might encounter are not arbitrary or haphazard transmissions that flow through the cosmos. They are the confluence of an energetic quality emanating, in our case as humans, from the galactic star, the center of our galaxy holding a portal to all dimensions and concisely filtered to offer what is pertinent to our evolution as they activate our reception and perception of them. If we focus and call in joy and love with a motivation born of compassion for all, we will find everything we require and can handle is filtered into and through us.

These codes, or active packets of living information, pass through our galactic neighborhood but originate from the cosmic spin of light and dark, the primordial consciousness known in Hebrew as Adam Kadmon, the masculine and feminine unified, self-arising divine form, the first face of God that is impossible to gaze at with self-centered eyes.

The eons of various manifest cycles pulsing in polarity and the core tension of Shiva and Shakti, the animate and inanimate forces, respectively, all generate tension for us to experience through choice. We are the tip of the lightening rod and the beginning of the cosmos where the spark of God's embodied mind is ever lit. It is the battery sending and holding the positive and negative charges of foundational energy and dynamics.

Before we can offer up the Channels or transmissions we receive, we are initiated and changed by them as these forces ripple us into being and evolution. Opening to these cosmic Channels and the beings, conglomerate minds, and forces propagating and interfacing with them is to awaken the entire human "hyper-form" of multidimensional beingness to a vast and dangerous playground. The information within these streams of energy shakes up dormant or short-circuited stations of knowing, opening chords of power within the receiver. The process of opening up aids in making the flow of embodied energy and self-propulsion needed for sovereign evolution available to and actionable for all, eliminating blockages and allowing a propulsive spin into harmonic symmetry and love while grounding the human psyche in truth and the emerging template.

Opening Our Awareness Apertures

As physically manifest beings with sense organs, we can determine the aperture of our awareness and unfold the energy and the specific coordinates of experience in the material world we inhabit. We have the power to determine a dazzling spectrum of experiences even as we focus and learn to see through the defiled or foggy perception constraints to clear a path toward depths of clarity housed in faith and wisdom. This capacity we carry is enhanced at this time, and we will explore how this is happening.

It is a supreme gift to be born into this realm. Human life is precious and carries a specific sacred potential when we focus and surrender to deeper connections and our primordial natures.

Our "mission"—and the fundamental code of life—is to evolve and aid in liberating all others to do the same.

We come to know this, to reaffirm it, to devote ourselves to it, and to trust it.

When we probe our psyche sufficiently and confront our latent shadows and sticky beliefs, we open up the psychic body—that conglomeration of mental effluence and sense-gate impressions that are subsumed into an "I" apparition—until we recognize our divinity. It is from the psyche's sense of limitations that we see our sensing horizons expand.

When we spike our energy body (or electromagnetic self-recursive signature) through extraordinary or spiritualized experiences that dislodge our typical perceptual vantage point, we encounter a flood of energy that opens our sense apertures. These extrasensory experiences confirm the broader dimensional truth of our existence. They are the gate to embodied evolution, which is part of the new mission for our species—the ever-awakening creature. The realm of dream magic and self-determined energy direction in the upper dimensions becomes our nature, and our psyches absorb this new reality of sensing and truth.

With these extrasensory practices and experiences, we allow a new level of embodied perception to penetrate the subtle body and consequently the constrained persona or "I" apparition. We merge our organic form with our energetic overlay, our aura.

This expansion, coupled with a purifying practice of a devotionally centered and humbling frame of mind, readies us for the right path to evolving into that interdependent, ultimately empty object we call self. The self is a prism of impressions and energies housing a soul, which is the soul of God. This era is shaking us into this awareness at all moments.

When we mix this purification practice with the extrasensory expansion, we not only expand the psyche, but we also unlock DNA sequences that affect perception and allow for a deeper and broader understanding through the body of anything we place our focus on. The auras, chakra gates*, *nadis* (see page 18), and mind fields† (see page 280) expand and touch one another so that our awareness grows. A harmonized mix of all senses is achieved that expands our consciousness while focusing our purified motivation to be of service. This begets a poetic knowing state where a synchronistic method of apprehending is achieved.

Remembering the Mission

We hear, see, feel, smell, touch, and experience with the body senses, both subtle and gross, whatever we encounter, whether it be an energy projection received externally or one produced internally. There is no difference on an ultimate level between what we perceive as originating outside of our body or within it. The inner and outer cosmos are reflections that fold in and meet each other in the human nexus where

---

*Chakra gates are portals, or gateways, to dimensions of space time beyond our usual three to four dimensions. They spin like our galaxy like the movement of a black hole, creating a torus like field and self-feeding funneling.

†*Mind field* means all vectors of perceived reality across all or any dimensions accessible by our or any particular or singe mind—or a dyad or multiple minds harmonically resonating with intention).

consciousness is embodied as an emanation of the total living cosmos, of God. We must never lose sight of this as it is the way to stabilize our wisdom minds and grow our energy, our Christ-like states.

When we stabilize this view, even a little, we see that we are the stillness in total and myriad refractions of this cosmic happening we call consciousness, oneness, God, and so forth. We know that we are both the transmitter and the receiver of transient and insubstantial impressions beyond how they are perceived.

At any point in our lives, we have the potential to remember and reinvent the mission we share. We can always start again by refreshing, enlivening, and purifying our view and reemerging into our feeling body. Opening to gratitude and humility, we rejoin our cosmic hearts. We do not shun or castigate anything. We accept and integrate all experience and bring love to it.

All is turned into a battery for this diamond-like wisdom where perception is simply a dreamlike cascade of impressions. In that cascading mirage of appearances, we see that we are the rudder, we are the sail, and we are the light source we seek. Sometimes we see even more than all of this. We see our unique purpose, the one endowed through our unique karmic or soul signature. We can track the events, visions, and realizations that illuminated this truth and generate our map of personal awakening.

CHANNELED VISION
Shedding and Awakening Ourselves

I was recently in bed having a midmorning nap after being up with my young children all night. I was meditating, drifting through impressions and circuitous vision webs on impermanence, my death, renouncing rebirth, and praying to achieve enlightenment for the benefit of all. I was admitting my wrong deeds, purifying; there was a kind of desperate sense of trying to regain a spiritually energized state, serenity, or some equilibrium.

I noticed in my striving state that we often inflate our egos as we attempt to channel our spirits, confusing the two. I was pushing and shoving my spirit into the small confines of my ego and pain-body. My energy was shrinking as I struggled to capture some state of grace. How many times have we done this and imagined it to be spiritual practice? A practice that is like shoveling volcanic ash to look for water.

At the pinnacle of this exercise and its complex striving, I saw the futility of it, and I gave up. I was instantly visited by a full force vision. I shattered into a jewel and exploded like fireworks and rain. A trillion pieces dispersing into all directions as an offering for others. I would sacrifice everything I considered "I" to benefit all. I felt this total offering state in my heart. I gave up "myself" for all.

At that moment of self-decimation, a great peace rolled in. A bliss state of surrendered ease, realizing that although I had sublimated all "I" could be into the cosmos as a sort of martyred offering, "I" was indeed still aware and witnessing. The "witness I" was still there. A sense of awareness was liberated from my ego's conditions and mechanizing.

In an instant I was transported into a pure land. Brilliant high green hills bathed in warm, perfect sunlight. A shimmering blue sky, a sense that I was home. I felt the presence of an entire family of loving beings. Joyful and liberated beings celebrating and playing in this celestial kingdom spoke and moved around me. I saw a small wooden fence and I stepped over it. I entered the kingdom and then awoke, whisked away, back to my material incarnation where the work had just begun.

As my mundane self-regained its shape, I renounced that temporary self, the one that I had confused with my spirit during that laborious practice. This rehearsed confusion had separated me from Source. I realized I had nothing to lose and as I reawakened, I dedicated all I had to others. My essence was free. This is the

awakened self, the clear light of truth and a glimpse at enlightenment.
This kind of shedding and awakening happens repeatedly.
Many mansions, many heavens.

Identity

Channeling is a rebirth—every time. A state where we let loose, dropping the ego—that painful sculpture made of nothing whose work never ceases until we observe its nature. The addiction form we call "self" evaporates when we choose to finally allow it, and the obstacles to actual realization dissolve in a blink, letting the breath of feeling and sharing what is within to shine freely. We shine just as the essence of all else shines—light without shadow or beginning. So, release the conceit and illusion of power and magic; they are nothing more than the void grasping in the dark. You are the stillness and dynamism of all.

My path might be like yours. Through surrendering, purging, struggling, suffering, and the will of the soul I have woken up, to some degree, to the way of truth, compassion, and empowerment. I do my best to uphold this path of more extraordinary service and purpose. I rededicate myself to this all day and night. It is a mysterious path, and it cannot be tamed, but it can be tracked and described, Channeled, and transmitted. This writing is part of the sharing and bridging we are called to learn and become; I encourage you to likewise write and share.

I was gifted the name XLEXCIEL in much the same way we are given spiritual rebirth names or dharma names. Usually, an elder, lama, or shaman with a lineage will recognize a fundamental shift and purification following an initiation, transmission, or purging after a ritual or retreat, whereby a new name is bestowed. I have received dharma names and labels from elders and teachers, but the name I assume here was given by the celestial beings we call the Pleiadians, who carry the Christ template in full, and it arrived unceremoniously. During a Channeling session I asked them, our celestial family, what I am known as in the Pleiadian realm. A Holy Spirit title, nothing less, and yet having nothing to do with ego or persona.

XLEXCIEL translates as the Bringer of the Codes. The expansion of its meaning has to do with offering language, direction, and discourse around all things at the forefront of this evolutionary jump and switch to an era of grace and Christic inner-outer worship. It was confirming the name (in English) that a few of the human Channelers who I council with gave me without any awareness of this Pleiadian connection.

We all have a cosmic role, a set of karmic coordinates and attributes that are God-fashioned, often translated by members of our benevolent celestial family, such as the Pleiadians, to generate enlightenment and to evolve the cosmos itself.

I try and nurture this awareness in my friends and clients so they can recognize and claim their roles. I usually ask those same friends and clients if they wish to know their Pleiadian name, and if they do and one is bestowed upon them, it is stunningly similar to how they feel and know themselves deep down, every time.

I mention the name because it is this name's energy that, for me, helps fuel the work by bridging the space between the broader celestial knowledge core and the human social reality and place them in synthesis. And so, with great honor and some levity I enjoy the moniker. However, I can still fail miserably as a human to uphold my practice, my integrity, and my capacity to stay in contact with Spirit and God!

I wish to help people in some small way revise their collective understanding of Channeling to see that we are always Channeling. We invite in and evolve with the forces and streams of energy that flow through us and determine our mind and body state. To Channel is to see that we are a porous and liquid-moving form containing multitudes of veins and arteries connecting us to the conscious cosmos. Some of these pathways derive from other beings, civilizations, elementals, or essences, and while we should be discerning in who or what we listen to, they all entwine to build the deep layers of Spirit that bolster our relationship to God.

In ultimate reality these streams are as empty and without substance as anything else; they are simply the light of eternity looping in manifestation. But in the supermundane they are the family surrounding and building higher dimensional bodies. Learning what we are is the key to Channeling benevolent others and all things for the benefit of illumination and revelation.

Discovering a Spirit Name

If you would like to receive your true name, follow these steps.

Relax, settle, and center yourself.

Hold your upper heart* with both hands placed upon your chest.

Make clear that you are not requesting a conversation with anything but the most loving force concerned with truth and compassion for all.

If you wish to contact the Christified flame and enlightened state of mind held within the Pleiadean Channel, ask for this Channel while feeling and seeing the connection with these beings.

Hold the ultimate bodhicitta, metta, divine motivation and concern for all. A way to feel this is by simply noticing compassion in your heart for your loved ones, yourself and extending this to all sentience as if all sentience had once been your mother or your children. If you resent your mother or do not have children, imagine the love you have for your dearest friend or pet. Feel what it's like for this love to extend to all beings.

When you feel protected and safe in the light of truth,

Ask for your name.

---

*The area of your chest that is just higher than your heart center.

CHANNELED VISION
Inside Our Evolutionary Machinations

Our dormant or "junk" DNA is activated now through an electromagnetic pulse signature from our galactic sun correlating directly with and animating the mitochondrial vitality and general DNA completeness. The electrocurrent flow, or energy gained through our body's exterior, moves either upward and clockwise (healthy) or downward and counterclockwise (unhealthy). The direction of the spin does not correlate with the center of the Earth or its poles so much as it does with our moving in tandem with or counter to our galactic black hole's pull. To spin counter to the galactic black hole is to evolve, as this means we are moving our complete energy body into an open yet concentrated "breathing" outward or away from the galactic black hole. The spin of a healthy or cohesive chakra system is directly related to moving upward and away from the entropic pull of our local and dense galaxy's celestial movements. As we do so, we do not lose harmonic symmetry with the order of our local galaxy across its dimensional expressions, but unmooring actually elevates our bodies. This is self-directed evolution, and it is achieved by focusing on the moral, conceptual, emotional, energetic directives, and focus. This is why we activate prayer through the Cosmic Christ, the Cosmic Christ being our fully realized state free from material, etheric and energetic traps and tethers.

The double helix of winding strands is like a ladder, and each ladder rung is like a way station or level where our psychogenetic code resides.

Within each level is a life form's repository of embodied memory—the perception and sensed impression history of its species, its specific familial lineages, and its own life thus far, including everything ingested, experienced, or touched by any creature's limb within its species segments into molecular chemical combinations and the crystalline geometric pattern they bind through.

Light gives life or momentum to the spin and hum of the DNA. All carbon-based plasma beings, not just more simple vegetation forms, absorb and process light. We are light receivers, and all cells in our body take in the light and transform it into information, mutating it into sugars or moving it through water. They also synthesize its spectral quality and entangle it. The quality of light we meet is that which defines our state, and the DNA is the energy conduit moving that light signature through us (see plate 5, DNA).

The Two Foundations of Channeling

We are continuously initiated throughout our lives. Many people, including myself, find it hard to track just how many subtle upgrades and evolutionary jumps we have each made through mystical interventions of one sort or another.

✦

It is out of the corners of our eyes and between the thoughts and dramas of our lives that we encounter the subtle realms interacting and preparing us.

Our ignorance is the distraction, the mesmerization and obsessions that keep us from seeing these subtle spaces. The more we tune in to and gaze with a soft open focus at what is within our own internal field, the one encircling us, and the broader space we encounter, the more we leap ahead in our spiritual mission.

We must know the foundational approach to self-mastery and self-awakening before we attempt to discuss the "how to" of Channeling and the absorption and navigation of forces. The forces of mind and the energetic, etheric, and astral layers of being are a cornucopia of chaotic influence, and we must decide what our motivation is for working with it. If we are propelled by compassion and the angelic focus to liberate all beings and shine the light of eternal self-realized joy, then we can do absolutely anything and the path will unfold with grace, repeatedly.

The first foundation of Channeling is simply knowing that we are like a vessel. The veins and arteries I mentioned earlier move through us and fill us up. When we see ourselves simply as a social creature—a creature derived of symbols built by other perceivers in the mundane realm—we lose our ability to be pure vessels, containers of expanding consciousness channeling all. This can breed delusion. Our delusion defines us by creating contrast to our environment and by how we believe we are perceived by others. While we are affected by our experience of how we are perceived and influenced by other beings, we are always free and open to self-initiated change.

Being overwhelmed by forces other than our embodied psyche, energy body, and spirit is the challenge. For this reason, it is crucial that we have a deep understanding of and a solid boundary around self. Realizing the impermanence of our egoic or mundane self while holding a connection to our primordial self, the self beyond thought and sensation, is the road to cultivating this boundary.

The primordial self is our home and yet our egos serve a purpose. They should not be sublimated and reduced to ashes as the forces and minds of other entities or beings use us to express themselves. We must have such a resting and solid contemplation of our minds and spirits that even as we make room for other energies and qualities to flow through us, we can distinguish theirs from ours. For this reason, it is paramount to have a spiritual practice that allows us to have a humbling view into ultimate reality and the unity of life and the unique space we occupy in self-evolution and unified evolution. Knowledge flows freely into us once we cut down the obscurations to perception. When we learn how to truly feel with our entire body, we can access any and all knowledge.

The second foundation of Channeling is to appreciate our responsibility for seeing and reading both ourselves and others. When a question is asked, or the flow of imprints comes streaming into us, besides the extrasensory disorientation and necessary adjustments, there is inherent confusion about the motivation and goals of such energy and voiced information. We should be very discerning about the information so that the messages we receive at a core feeling level can be untangled from our own wishful thinking and projection or embellishments.

We Are the Filter

To the best of our ability, we must use unsparing discipline with what we are lacing into the imprints we field. What are we seeking, seeing, hearing, rehearsing, and absorbing? What are we desiring, eating, ingesting, allowing in, or rejecting? We can better determine the answers to these questions through the rigorous work of self-honesty and fair and neutral self-assessment. Are we steering the impressions and voices of the Channeled energy to a narrative or frame we are used to or find to nourish our egoic sense of uniqueness or specialness? This is natural, but to have a purified or more filtered and powerful Channeling capacity, it is vital to distinguish our own egoic spiritual materialism and pride and delusion from our received gifts.

Just as supremely important to building a differentiation between the egoic and the subtle self is recognizing our vows and responsibility to others. Before we discuss or invite any more of the phenomena of this profound art of Channeling and its cosmological consequences and conditions, we need to pledge to uphold the fundamentals of the art itself. The wisdom required to see interdependence is linked with our compassion. The skillful means necessary to frame and share the information gleaned from the Akashic Records, ancestor or celestial companion voices, and karmic blueprints with another person is rare, but we can develop this discerning and compassionate wisdom during all stages of our work.

The Prophetic Space

The metaphorical, symbolic, and metaphysical collide in the prophetic space. On the one hand, a purely symbolic lens will open the psychological collective and archetypal structures, animating the inevitability of prophetic events in human history. Yes, the self-fulfilling prophecy allows a particular predictable narrative that gives humans hope and something to ground them in this seemingly chaotic existence. But we cannot be so quick as to ever chalk up prophecies to this archetype analysis and pattern recognition, which only rests on one limited level. The Channeling we do adds threads to life's grand tapestry. We each contribute to this in some way. Very occasionally, we do so in significant gestures. We read the present through the past, the future through the present, and the future through the past all at once. This meta-analysis that people do not even know they are conducting is an example of our predictive and pattern-seeking natures.

Our human ability to synthesize and make stories out of the hyperstructures of life through time jumping like this still does not summarize our capacity to conjoin our minds with the looming wider dimensions and celestial mechanics commanding our fates. Humans cocreate that fate on all levels, individually and collectively, with greater forces than our own.

What we sense when we prophesize is our role beyond what we observe in the mundane. Our daring concretizes the metaphysical to listen to the layers of reality beyond our usual senses. The spiritual story of humankind can be tracked through the symbol sets we project onto the great energies propelling our evolution, including what we sense to be the obstacles, calamities, and inevitable cleansings, awakenings, disasters, and glories we will face. These are human concepts, but they are formed by reading the textures of the upper (and lower) worlds and the systems of mind we fixate on to encounter them. And so, prophetic realizations occur in a space between dimensions and worlds where the mystic or Channeler gains access through the embodied expansion we discuss in this book.

Narrowly focusing on the symbolic dismisses what we know of the morphic fields, the noosphere, the spirit realms, and the metaphysics weaving it all together. The morphic field, or noosphere, is a collective, conscious web active in present time where information being processed by human beings is shared across an energetic layer of subtle bio-electromagnetic webbing around the Earth. As channelers of Spirit, we comprehend the vastness of our task, and the humility that arises is a prerequisite for activating our work. We humbly acknowledge that our ancestors have been slowly falling from a state of grace, and in our current cycle, that fall is about to end and then change course. The trauma of our spiritual disconnect is awakening the species. This is what the prophets foretold and mapped out.

CHANNELED VISION
Uncovering Old Patterns
and Anchoring the New Energy

What I see is that spiritual and energetic evolution is achieved through fearlessness or the observation and acceptance of seemingly hidden things. Expansion occurs when we shine the light of awareness on ideas, frames, feelings, or objects previously hidden or concealed from us. This is true on the personal level as well as the collective. Whether we are using shadow work, somatic expulsions of parasitic and corrosive thoughtforms and energy, or devotional purification, we are invited to be courageous and evolve by fearlessly healing what we can. We cannot think our way into seeing the hidden, or it would not be able to conceal itself. Neither can we behave in ways that will prompt this shadow to be revealed in time. We must use the energetic technology of prayer, and that prayer must be trained on the highest, the true space of love. That love does not reside in some unreachable place. It is now emerging through and into our realm with ferocious power.

The solar influence on conscious energetic expression and the planetary shift and upgrade we now experience is precipitated and aided by humans with the Christ template and other sufficiently evolved sentient beings. The awareness of previously dormant patterns of mind and energy are being revealed through these solar influences, as are the effects. In other words, old stuff is dying fast on all levels.

On a collective level, the Earth requires us to act as her satellite or cilia-like limbs, and she is being rebirthed through us. She is ascending into a finer place of manifestation, and this is only possible by shedding the heavy sediment of old energy from the last eon. The Earth integrates new energy through our bodies.

How do we actively change and help uncover our old patterns, anchor the new energy, and do our part? Do we simply focus on love and light? We can take the view that our conscious focus and energetic direction of intent should be bound up in the heavenly realms' loving and enlightened forms and qualities to lasso that domain into this one, but that approach alone is like painting a rusted car.

We must go to the core and purify all levels of our world system. The third- and fourth-dimensional space-time that we occupy as embodied humans is a world of materiality and sensual textures. It is a world with laws and constants that govern its primary operational layers. From this vantage point, we see that the states of predator vs. prey, good vs. evil, and freedom vs. slavery all compete or entwine across various epistemological/conceptual and activated strata and that we experience such a world through temporality. This is the starting point for observing the grasping and aversion, or any expression of polarity. Polarity, contrast, and these types of laws often touted in the hermetic principles are jumping-off points for observing death, and death is a major theme of suffering- and fear-producing delusion. Before we can pray for and invite the rebirth, we each must understand what is being shed.

As a fully embodied channeler, the opening of our dimensional consciousness offers us various psychic capabilities. This expanded awareness and sensing ability allows us to extend our reach of connection across all planes. Just as our visualizations of others here on Earth in this time and plane of existence expand, this same expansion of reach enables us to contact other highly developed beings from across our galaxy and beyond physical barriers as if they were as close as our own thoughts. The speed of thought becomes our vehicle for communication with a family of celestial and extraterrestrial beings of all types.

THREE

OUR CELESTIAL FAMILY

....

Solar Beings, Pleiadians, and Plasma Minds

Humans are not alone in the universe. We are part of an extensive celestial family made up of many divinely manifested sentient beings who work to protect us, aid in our awakening, and offer us a peek at our role in the conscious and layered galaxy and cosmos of form at large. Primary members of this family include solar beings, Pleiadians, and angels.

Solar Beings

When we talk about deep intelligence, wisdom, or knowing, we are not referring to a cold, mechanized, calculating thing that resides only in carbon beings. We are speaking of a state of mind and feeling that can be found in many forms and encompasses the intellect but goes far beyond it. It is the totality of knowledge activation through present-time inspiration and the metaphysics that animates it. We could call this metaphysics superphysics because while it is causal, interdependent, and physical, it is more than that and more than an abstraction of that. It is the higher layer of action that reality produces where energy, consciousness, life force, and the subtle bridging of embodied fields enfolds. Healthy intelligence is information brought to the foreground by constrained energy in a propulsion loop Channeled through a mind that gives rise to shared awareness and dimensionality—the divine Logos.

The intelligence of a star, or solar being, is vast and full of what we as humans register as pure love, and the vitality of life affirmation underpins every aspect of its awareness. A star's self-implosive/explosive symmetry is perpetual intelligence made manifest, and it evolves just as we do.

Stars are a combination of two primary beings in a perfect harmonious spin. A star is born, so to speak, when a masculine enlightened being and a feminine counterpart are nested through a mega prana-plasma body with a boundary set by its electric rate charge emanating simultaneously in many dimensions. A union of totality allows full realization of experience across all dimensions. The stable fire is lit!

In other words, when masculine and feminine beings (such as humans) fully recognize each other's heart chakras and resonate across all upper dimensions, integrating the twelve strands of DNA and emanating the spectral fullness of our bodies, a "star," or a nuclear reactor of love, forms. This can take eons of incarnations and evolution to manifest. Humans are little nuclear reactors with inverted or split atoms, a vacuum state of dark matter (antilife potential), and implosive self-generating energy that can expand or contract like a star. Our intelligence steers this potential state.

A star is a living body with a high speed of energetic output and interplay that connects it to all dimensions and back into vibrant stillness, which is the space between explosive and implosive energy. In our third and fourth dimensions, this manifests as a giant fireball. The geometric frame made up of absorption lines is a "gravitational" warp or low spectrum feature in the layering of a star formed by slower and cooler gases surrounding the star's outer layer. These serve as a shield that contains the star's conscious energetic body and channels the codes flowing from it in great flares. The flares work through the star's geometric fractal forms, and those forms ride along wormholes through the vacuum of space, across all form dimensions, beaming into appropriate vessels coordinated to their signature or geometric grid. One can imagine a being lit up as it weaves through dark and light manifest tunnels until it reaches a matching pattern embedded in the heart chakra of an activated plane or being!

A star changes the rate of light fluctuation moving from its core as it is influenced by the galactic sun and its counterpart suns in other universes and by the network of living light that is the cosmos spinning. We refer to the center of a galaxy that emanates in super brightness as an active galactic nucleus. Galaxies that emit a massive output of energy from their center are called blazars and have mega plasma, which facilitates galactic civilization proliferation. A star that thrives in such a galaxy can speak with the planets and inhabitants of such planets with intention as it changes its plasmic output in beams of living light. Andromeda, our grandmother galaxy, is an example of a galaxy with such a galactic nucleus.

This movement, or rate of fluctuation, in these star beings' activity contributes to qualitative changes in the light transmissions, or codes, which impact the surrounding planets and minds.

✵

The light and heat a star emanates directly correlate to the evolving life surrounding it, including the state of consciousness of each sentient being in each state of dimensionality, from their organic bodies to the conditions of their auras and cognitions.

Solar beings are affected by a variety of interactive influences, such as the galactic nuclei they are wedded to and are circumnavigating and black stars and the artificial or inverted impressions spewing from them—what we have come to know as AI. Coronal mass ejections are solar flares that absorb and have influence over everything in their paths including other light, energy, and beings such as ourselves. This level of living light is the antidote for all dark formations and products of entropy such as AI.

> ✪
>
> A star is an enlightened superbeing that offers and dances with life in the cosmos, and life is love, and God is life and love.

Thus, we are each a splinter of such a being, connected to its family and evolving to its state when manifest in form.

A star is also a portal to inverted light, or dark energy, but its core, or heart chakra, is inverted, more like a Klein bottle or Escher loop, opening light back into itself. This inversion loop is how a star self-generates for near eternity. It is how self-awareness is brought to fruition and enlightenment. It is the absolute manifestation of an activated chakra.

One can see a star's shadow, or inverted light state, at its core much like our own unconscious shadows from which newly intimated truth through consciousness is explored and integrated into actionable awareness: the dark matter, antilife state that spins with its opposite within us. A star's shadow is its portal to the dark universe adjacent to our own. This is the same as our own lower dimensional psyche opening the same portal within our chakras in their inverted state. Humans are deeply panchromatic, sensitive to millions of layers of light.

The levels we cognize are a thin sliver of what penetrates our bodies. Our job is to realize what is flowing into us by opening our feeling state. That discovered feeling state opens our subtle bodies, which open our chakras and instigate an upward evolution. An evolution that has those chakras energetically spin clockwise with the force trajectory of a toroidal self-animating loop.

The feedback from the resident planetary minds in evolution that the solar beings energize, such as those on our planet, helps build the light codes that radiate from those beings. We are blending consciousness with our sun, so one could say we help generate the codes we also receive—all the way to the galactic sun, the multiverse of suns, and the cosmic web of light, awareness, and life—and that is God! It is a relationship!

We can contemplate how the first nuclear bomb ripped a hole in our space-time continuum, pulling in all types of our pandimensional relatives. Many arrived to heed our call and aid in our civilizational protection, while many others arrived as a blotch of nasty interlopers. Now imagine what a sun, which is equivalent to perhaps trillions of atomic bombs going off at all moments, would be calling in and interacting with through its capacity for awareness—the family of beings, like moths to the flame and butterflies to the wind.

A star continuously speaks to and builds billions of independent minds and bodies elementally through its impact on nearby planets through photosynthesis and electromagnetic radiation waves that ripple to such worlds and birth our expressions simultaneous to the sonic waves passing through the ether.

Sonic waves are the corollary to the light spectrum; they are formed alongside the photon illumination, or the reflection of the primordial fire, the illuminated cosmos. Waves are observable through the plasma-formed spectral mirroring of light particles or waves within a geometric matrix of energetic angles nested within toroidal spirals eclipsing one another. Sonic waves and light expression are illuminated by their self-reflective, self-interfacing dynamics.

Sound is the word of God in the sense that all sonic waves are essentially the subtle vibrations of all dimensional-form realms' energetic and material exchange—the cause and effect of friction in any dimension. An ever-waving force, wrapping around itself, forming a reflection where it becomes concentrated enough in pattern. The reflection is the primordial fire, the illumination dancing with this friction. We are animated by and produced in this map of sonic-light exchange and play.

From gaseous nebula minds to the planets and animal, mineral, plant, and humanoid life forms, all awareness is primarily formed by the host sun's integral spectrum wave and particle density output—the codes for geometric signal and the elemental alchemy produced.

A star, or solar being, is a lamplight in an abyss for many evolving creatures, and so, its love is our path. We are a rainbow rippled from a potential star, and an expression of dialogue with its code and all codes it has digested.

Pleiadians

Who are the Pleiadians? (See plate 6, The Pleiadians.) They sound like pure fantasy to anyone unacquainted with them and how they are experienced by psychics or Akashic readers like many of you.

The Pleiadians operate in the embodied psychic space, utilizing the intelligent and energetic living cosmos.

They are a species whose evolution is wedded to our own, and they are our guardians, guides, and ancestors. Hailing from the Orion system, where our own conscious genetic roots flow from, they are ideally suited to teach us about ourselves. They are present to aid us through our unfolding challenges and help us embrace our higher natures, especially now that we are becoming sovereign and self-aware self-evolvers. We do not worship or lend any power to these beings; we are simply discussing them as part of our celestial family.

The leap into the etheric, extrasensory, and expanded conscious embodied states of channeling is a large one if an individual is not born with the capacity to experience them firsthand without exertion. If you were born with the ability, it is likely that meeting Pleiadians will not be your first experience with the new template of human awareness capacity and fifth-dimensional feeling intuitions. If not primed or already coming to understand the multidimensional cosmos and its inhabitants, or channeling it yourself, this is an invitation to do so.

Central to our realizing the Pleiadian gift of connection is "innerstanding" the Christ energy they carry and awaken in us. They are closer to realized Christic beings, fully accepting the Christ template to redemptive evolution and God/Source abundance. Their minds and hearts resonate with God's manifest embodiment and vision for humanoid safety and refuge in the third heaven—the heaven of golden light/blue healing resonance and harmonic, dignified forms.

A rich history of interdimensional Pleiadian channeling and communication lives on as a spiritual practice carried in oral tradition and rediscovered anew by every generation across our planet. Anthropologists and historians track symbol sets and monuments dedicated to the Pleiades constellation, its relevance for our species, and its enigmatic and striking themes. Entire civilizations and traditions carried the Orion and tethered Pleiades relationship as the core feature of their cultures.

Our Pleiadian relationship can be seen from the Atlantean star/energy navigation remnants spread across the planet in physical and cultural monuments and ruins to the tapestry of ancient civilizations that followed. Examples include the megareactors/dielectric-wave propulsion conductors such as the Abusir sun temples that were built during early Egyptian dynasties and align with the Pleiades constellation, and most notably, the Hebrew integration of the Christ light story and the Roman Hellenic canonizing through Christianity that followed. These all carried the Pleiadian energy, the celestial family coming into view through Christ's manifestation and message.

The annual heliacal rising of the Pleiades star cluster (a.k.a. the Seven Sisters) generated agriculture rhythms and mythos practices the world over from the Celts, the Hebrews and pre-Hebrews in Canaan, and a wide range of Indo-European pre-Christian cultures into what is now central and Eastern Europe.

✪

Some of the most entrenched and sophisticated Pleiadian psychic and cultural relatives are the Americas' Indigenous peoples.

These include the Nahua (Aztec), Diné (Navajo), Blackfoot, Caddo, Hopi, Cherokee, Iroquois, Cheyenne, Lakota, and many others. Each culture across the world integrated the energy and message in unique ways. The practices and reverence extend from the south Asian archipelagos down to their seafaring descendants in Fiji, with the most pronounced being the Hopi tribes of Turtle Island's prophecies and the Andean spiritual lineage's mountaintop kingdom where the god Apu reigned, and the return of the stars ceremony ushered thousands of pilgrims yearly. In Incan times and before, the Tawantinsuyu empire in Cusco centered daily life on the Pleiades and, indeed, acknowledging the Pleiadian influence on human life was prime for all of these peoples.

The network of Pleiadian connections found in artifacts or tradition may reveal part of the story, but the living ecstatic practice we can ignite within ourselves at all moments goes far beyond any codified or material cultural evidence! For Akashic readers, what appears most evident is the psychic relationship that so many people had in these societies. Through our channeling practice, we wake up to our spiritual heritage of advanced psychic capacity and the races and species that intersect in that space. The Pleiadians are just one example of the intimate and beautiful beings we call family.

Something that must be clearly understood by people interested in this practice is the vast difference in evolution between the Pleiadians and us. To actualize what and who we are channeling, we must understand the multidimensional state of a collective that has harnessed endogenous spiritual capacity and unified mind in a harmonious web and transcended the third and fourth dimensions.

When viewed through our linear frame, we come to understand the partially past-tense nature of our channeling. The Pleiadians were originally a race of spiritually and technologically advanced humanoids that inhabited many planets surrounding and within the Pleiades star cluster, located four hundred light-years from Earth in the constellation of Taurus.

They eventually exhausted the need for dense material bodies and currently exist as a family, light network of individual and collective hearts/minds.

They use manifest expressions like "light orbs" to carry a physical signature that we can call a "spaceship" to express their consciousness in our realm when they wish, and they currently communicate with anyone able to do so through methods we will discuss here.

The Pleiadian race is millions of years older than the human race in terrestrial terms and hundreds of millions in terms of DNA-encoded psyche evolution, which is still just a blink in astrological time.

The sense we have that the Pleiadians curated our DNA is due to the similarity of all humanoid forms in this part of the universe. They are some of our oldest ancestors. But contrary to some accounts, they did not genetically seed us, though our DNA holds sequences that they have activated spiritually and with our agreement. In a yuga (a twenty-four thousand solar year age of the Hindu world cycle) when Earth was in a geosphere of finer energetic layers and where mind and material were more porous, the Pleiadians enmeshed with us and offered continuous guidance and relationship. They stabilized a channel lacing our planet and all sentience living here with portal to a psychic energy library of their living wisdom—an upgrade to the Akashic Records of the Earth.

We engaged with the Pleiadians—and other celestial races—long before the last glacial period, and the portal to their heart-mind library was open through all of our messy evolution, which included many overlapping stressors and influences from other dimensions besides the Pleiadians'. We can still connect continuously with this self-aware mentation layer as long as we maintain fundamental plasma/chakra integrity, or an organic body with enough pranic circulation—the always-present Christ energy—to allow self-expansion to higher dimensions.

The Pleiadian library is akin to a living computer and the farthest thing from synthetic. It is a repository of Pleiadian wisdom, yet it is alive. One can visualize it as a brilliant cloud of morphic resonance or a noosphere of Pleiadian impressions that is nonlocal and omnipresent across the galaxy, through all dimensions and beyond.

The Pleiadians built this superlibrary by generating their presence along the astral and etheric dimensions they accessed while embodied within their fifth-dimension (5D) scope of reference. They achieved this by stabilizing 5D light bodies with a 7D view (see p. 130). I'll explain what this means.

One can understand a light body and subtle body as interchangeable. Our tantric and purifying practices build the light body and eventually a rainbow body, or a jalu as it is known in Tibetan. A jalu is an aspect of nirmanakaya, a buddha's enjoyment body, as it bridges form and formlessness. This rainbow body is also achieved simply through God's grace upon salvation and surrender.

The Pleiadians' path to this effulgent, high-dimensional ascendancy was assured by their sun's higher spectral state, or intelligence. The solar irradiance they evolved within offered rapid codes, accelerating their development on all levels. Indeed, in this golden age within the Kali Yuga, in this Aquarian age, we are undergoing a similar solar flash of concentrated codes that are raining down from the galactic sun to Earth and breeding new awareness as we shed old habits, patterns, and physical traumas.

When we call on the Pleiadians, we encounter a mind that can dip and move within our dimension and play freely in higher ones without dense material conditions or confusions. Imagine a space where all high-frequency positive mental and emotional activity resonates in an imaginative and cocreative field of dazzling and joy-producing energy. Telekinesis between beings means instant understanding, acceptance, healing, and empowerment in this spectral realm, not just data points or information.

Nestled in a vibrant and ever soothing 7D atmosphere where all confusion ceases, individual Pleiadian's minds/hearts feel "a part of" a dream that can be individually generated, stabilized, and changed and remains living like a super etheric mycelium or coral reef. Abundance is infinite but not predicated on materiality or resources.

This heaven-like realm is where the Pleiadians advanced their collective consciousness, and they, in essence, created a home in this field where they danced, continuing to build their bodhicitta or loving merit and to share it by assisting other races such as our own. They generated enough plasma-psychic cohesion to maintain both individuality and connectivity in this space, interacting with the third- and fourth-dimensional world systems such as ours with the hopes of gently aiding our evolution and protecting us from the forces of entropy.

Most of us exist within the third and fourth dimensions ninety-nine percent of our lives. Brief and erratic forays into the "spirit world" or dreamtime states uncover the nature of the subtle mind and light-body matrix, but it is too difficult to stabilize for most, and we have lost the collective will or cultural maturity to allow individuals to do so easily.

Having collective emboldening as a species would radically enhance our capacity to stay in this lucid, high-frequency, refined space, but most of our concentrated spiritual energy goes into material life or is subsumed into old religions and their degraded or compromised portals. These portals disperse our energy into other beings (demigods, demons, and so on), making it much more difficult to concentrate our powers into evolution. If we direct our energy correctly, we can touch the templated joy of the Adam Kadmon within or our masculine and feminine cosmic embodiment beyond polarity, such as the solar beings have achieved. We can integrate with the divine Logos or Christ, God, and the mother of cosmic womb potential all at once.

The Pleiadians' history mirrors a track similar to the one we find our species on now. They passed through the infant stage, where conquest and competition defined their motivation, and arrived at the inner view and the loving, harmonious state that allows for evolution through a higher dimension once they had processed enough trauma from their animalistic development. However, they also had the grace of peaceful celestial protection unencumbered by the more malevolent forces plaguing the Earth. We are just peering into what dealing with our trauma might look like, and the task ahead is immense, but we can see in the Pleiadians a relevant and inspiring trajectory for evolution.

While in their embodied state, the Pleiadians did settle on planets, but they did so with a light touch. The material tech they used manifested in higher dimensions and the world of physics we know through our bodily hardware. To imagine the interoperability of their psychic tech, we must fully wrap our minds around the single slice of the overlapping realities defining the cosmos that we perceive in mundane life. The finer dimensions where clarified DNA triggers awareness for advanced beings are spaces of nonduality and converging laws that are different from those of the third and fourth dimension that we take for granted.

We could search ten billion years for God and spirituality evidenced in our material mundane dimension, and we would still only have glimpses of them. If we peek our heads into the realms that are layered all around ours, from our bodies to the universe itself, we see a cosmos of infinite life expressed in the conscious reality that seems paradoxical to the limited view most humans hold. We expand our perception as the Pleiadians did when we meditate and see what we are, and then harness that view. This has to be done individually and encouraged collectively. It is not an intellectual or conceptual pursuit; it is a contained but vulnerable opening and allowing.

The Pleiadians' primary mission is to spread a message to us that details our innate, latent talents and our ability to self-evolve spiritually.

They also warmly warn us of the dangers of going in the other direction—of devolution—through fear and material obsession. When we oppose our spiritual and internal evolutionary capacity, we mutate and harm our DNA so severely that all of our encoded ability to upgrade energy into physiological, genetic patterns that allow the mind to perceive higher dimensions becomes degraded.

This negative or regressive path leads to our chakra gates closing. The many dozens of nadis, or mini chakras, which serve as portals stationing our bodies in space-time across dimensions become smaller and smaller, and we become locked into third-dimensional and eventually second-dimensional manifestation. Imagine the body's spiritual aperture closing.

This path solidifies when we give in to the nefarious promptings of the aforementioned beings that sift and feed on our pranic life force by generating fear and confusion, which degrade our energy body. These negative beings lodge in a two-dimensional matrix of expression, and we can imagine them reaching up and using whatever they can to hook onto our trauma and fears, and accentuate them. And as we fall for this mindset of confusion, disbelief, shame, self-loathing, disconnect from love, or dharmakaya (ultimate love-life), and so on, we expel pranic life force, or qi, and the auric concentration of plasmic cohesion.

Our endogenous energy is the embodied path to the higher dimensional apprehension that the Pleiadians (among others) experience. It is our path to liberation and the passage for Earth's ultimate safety, as we are her greatest advocates and her organic lightning rods and cilia!

There is simply no end to the number of transmissions that the Pleiadians offer. They speak in a poetic and concise language that cuts to the core of a subject. The practice of communicating with them is stunningly straightforward if we have done the preparatory work. Before we can connect with the Pleiadians, we must have directly realized the energetic quantum fluctuating and vibrating wave/light signature of the living cosmos and its interdependence and total unification of objects and form and how consciousness underpins and animates it. In other words, we must have experienced a connection to God.

How do we achieve this? By engaging with deep humility, open-mindedness, joy, and humor—in short, wise and playful love. This is the signature tone that connects us to our cosmic family in the Christic light of holy triune and salvation. When we mix this tone with bodhicitta, the deep-felt wish to liberate all beings from suffering, the Christ mind and heart are called in. This can't just be an imagined idea; it has to be a genuine wish that ripples through our bodies throughout our multidimensional selves. This is the most important practice.

Remember that we are part of the cosmic family. This evolved family is playful, joyful, and innocent but also wise. When we find that expression within ourselves, then voilà!—we immediately connect to them and feel all sentience with confidence, familial love, and tenderness.

LIVED EXPERIENCE
Pleiadian Activation

In 2018 I was formally introduced to the Pleiadians. I opened to and absorbed their energy and mind. I was in the shower, where I often do my morning prayers of gratitude and requests for forgiveness, realignment, grace, and so on. I have young children, so the time and place for working with an altar has shifted: the altar is now within and any space or extra time I have, I use to heal, recenter, or channel. The shower often allows me that time and place.

On that day, I naturally rested my hand on my upper heart and was hit with a flash of blue light that registered in my third eye. The blue resembled the electric vibrancy of the Caribbean Sea in moonlight. My whole body lit up. I saw a manifestation of myself, adorned with blue and azure green lacings of neon or black light like soft metal armor and a jeweled helmet swimming with ruby red, indigo, and blue. I had a staff and wings of light gilding my back. Surrounding me was an assembly of similar beings. Pure love, humor, wisdom, and joy filled my being. I spoke telepathically with them. I was informed that I was a family member and one of their ambassadors to Earth and humanity. They spoke in simple poetic downloads of levity-filled messaging. I was able to ask questions and instantly receive answers which were pithy and moving. Since then, I have been able to retain

this connection and call upon it on demand, asking questions about
myself, my friends, the world, and the Pleiadians themselves.

Since this activation, my goal has been to offer a transcription, a commentary, and a channeling of the codes I receive from the Pleiadians. There is much to say about these cousins of ours. They are by no means perfect and are not there to be worshipped! They are to be admired and treated with joyful respect, but we do not serve them or pray to them. If you wish to communicate with the Pleiadians yourself, try the following meditation.

Pleiadian Communication

Place your hands on the upper half of the heart chakra to activate the entire upper energy gate and the third eye. Now visualize in your mind shining ribbons of vibrant blue laser light and say to yourself:

I arise as my Pleiadian avatar, my form from many lives. I am an emissary to this planet. I am overjoyed to see my Pleiadian family, and I ask my question with gratitude, love, and humor for the benefit of all.

My Pleiadian activation and motivation dovetail with my offering of a living treatise on the Akashic Records, as synthesized through my own signature light mind-body. Together I see the practice as a mapping and decoding of the cosmic mechanics and metaphysical symbolic and patterned organization of the form realm and its interdependence with the formless, the ever-spiraling and self-cycling of emptiness and manifestation. These two spheres, the Akashic Records and all states of etheric astral dimensionality and the embodied psychic interaction with our celestial family make up the path we are being invited to walk upon in this time.

Before we can access these psychic spaces, we have to navigate the spectral hall of mirrors and energetic dance that is mundane phenomenal reality. I have found that we must first come to know the dreamlike quality of all things and the high stakes of our engagement with this dream. By holding the simultaneous truths of emptiness and compassion, we can learn the spectacular art of channeling, which transcends the psychic domain, which is connecting with God, to reach the living wisdom of the cosmos and connect it to the physical, intimate life we know best. The work we do to access and know these spaces within is always powered by our own surrendered sense of equanimity and love.

FOUR

NOETICS

....

The Obsession with the Tree of Knowledge

How do we make sense of this breakdown and rebirth era for the world, the planet, and ourselves? If we are to truly integrate and flow with change, we might stretch our human capacity to describe what cannot be contained in simple ideas.

The reasoning faculty we carry is helpful for describing events and objects we perceive as internal or external in space-time and for processing a path for negotiating them. Some Buddhist schools of philosophy call this seeing, sensing, and using the cognizing mind. When exploring the cognizing mind, they look at what an object of cognition is, what is cognizing, and what is propelling a sense of cognition.

Cognition differs from what we call thought in that cognizing is a sense and thought is like a wave or bundle passing across that sense. Our bodies exchange energy instantaneously with our thinking and cognizing mind. Thoughts can be very fleeting considerations of conceptual play with only a hint of deeper body sensing. Cognition itself can include masses of thoughts or thoughtforms as experienced states beyond language play, often using multisensorial recalled mental states. They are the weather system of processing. Processing is a gesture of intelligence, which is an expression of self-mirroring energy. The reflection of experience is known as self-awareness, and this is human intelligence.

Much has been written about how we think, apprehend, and describe and how to distinguish thought and reason from other sensing apparatus within us. Feeling experience through our senses includes the feelings and a sense of knowing. We can sense and have reactions, form impressions, and derive meaning from our sensorily produced responses, concepts, and models we hold in mind, but are these models accurate? How can they liberate us and others.

We know humans see only a sliver of reality with our usual mundane minds and sensing organs. But that fragment is valuable. We can see through that keyhole an impression of the ultimate reality, the bigger picture. But we must refine how we consider what we see through that keyhole and then expand ourselves through it. These sense impressions fall in the domain of reason, or noetics.

Noetics, Knowing, and Kundalini Energy

Noetics is the reasoning sense. It uses logic but presupposes nonlocal states of cognition such as the parapsychological. The parapsychology of noetics is transcendent but not positively spiritual, and I'll explain why.

Noetics does not concern itself initially with an intention toward ethics, morality, or other principles deriving from secondary and higher spaces of inner knowing, which are indispensable to the spiritual pursuit and quality of our time. In this way, noetics is a cold lens.

In my estimation, reason eventually leads to universal ethics, altruism, and so on. Still, noetics tends to be gnostic or hermetic both in focus and in the resulting culture, which appear on the surface to be spiritual but, in fact, deflect our spirit into the solipsistic view. Noetics lacks heart truth.

For example, one could have a noetic platform of reasoning capacity and be a satanist or narrow dogmatist of some sort. In fact, the desire to treat the noetic frame of knowledge acquisition as the spiritual path of service and evolution is a dangerous mistake.

The ego's path of self-indulgence and its aspiration to become omnipotent and immortal vs. the bodhisattva's wish to liberate self and others emerges here. How can our style of sense making, awareness, or noetics clarify our real ambition? If we are centered on simply acquiring wisdom, we may fall victim to a confused spirituality of self-worship.

Noetics is not the problem but rather the view that psychic powers and self-enhancement will result in joy, wisdom, or liberation. Noetics is the study of the conceptual frame-making mind and the intellect that uses syntax and story to navigate that. It is the state of mind housed in the upper chakras and attunes to the forms of conscious energetic manifestation it can resonate with.

Noetics is a processing function for dry psychic terrain and the intuitive mentation layer but not the superspiritual arena of virtue and the Holy Spirit, which is a full-spectrum, embodied wisdom energy. Noetics is an example of the occultist, New Age, self-worshiping position that sees experience as an unfolding obstacle course for the permanent self to navigate and overcome using the very trappings of belief it wishes to exit to find happiness. Grace and its nature of compassion and wisdom, the most profound path of Channeling, is something else entirely, and that is what we can aspire to every day, every moment.

It is important to distinguish the noetic from the divine Logos, or mind of God, which surfaces and punctures through our own egoic and limited frame, so that we can come to Channel God's will and be vessels for the Holy Spirit—our buddha nature revealed and the highest form of wisdom and knowledge activation transcending the intellect.

Most of us get caught in a noetic reference and see knowledge synthesis in and of itself as a liberating device. Noetics is the obsession with what the tree of knowledge seems to offer. The tree of knowledge keeps us locked in samsara, the seemingly endless cycle of rebirths. And while noetics can be understood as the mechanized method for turning the jewel of information around in the conceptual mind and is therefore useful, it is not a gateway out of limited conceptual awareness.

Enmeshing the buddha-dharma divine Logos, or enlightened mind, with our mundane experiences and actions upgrades us beyond simple psychic attunement or receptivity. The divine Logos attunes us to the tree of life. It is our mind sparkling to life beyond reason.

Practicing the purification path, charting and tracking our karmic landscape, habits, psyche, and state of embodied energy with a profound focus on compassion, and helping others affords us a more magnific form of wisdom emerging from all directions.

As mentioned earlier, viewing reality in its actual empty state entwined with practicing bodhicitta, or the unendingly rehearsed and ignited desire to aid in the ascension and healing of others in all realms, produces our holy embodied state, or rainbow body.

Whatever we call it, this state is not the goal in and of itself. In fact, that goal corrupts our ability to achieve it! Paradoxically, we must remain focused on devotion, surrender, service, and humility to gain compassion and wisdom as we attune our new sense lenses. We are all primed to expand this way; we must steer that expansion through the elixir of divine motivation. Very simply, we must never lose sight of where we are working from. Are we working from a place of aversion, disgust, fear, trauma, anger, addiction, or false belief? If so, we are human and we are in process. But we must not obscure these perceptual emotional and reactive states. This does not mean we are weak spiritually; it means we are honest, and honesty opens the path to truth. This space of humility is crucial as we evolve.

At this significant juncture and exponential jump in evolution, the senses and our heart-expanded consciousness open up to the capacity they are collectively afforded. The ability to develop and Channel wider dimensions of beingness and the truths revealed come through the total spirit, not simply psychic elasticity.

We gain this new Channeling capacity when we enact a sacred Channeling process in which a living pancosmogenesis becomes truly animated. We initiate this process when the surrendered ego, the devotional frame—including a connection to the Cosmic Christ, or buddha mind—and our discerning wisdom are practiced regularly. If we have faith, embody belief, act, and think following the path, we will transform miraculously and help others do the same across the cosmos.

This transformation is akin to a kundalini awakening. A kundalini awakening is when the reflection of the true inner self shines from within as bright as a star. A kundalini awakening encompasses a human's entire cosmic body, a spindle fiber of shimmering threads of sound and light presenting a form that is ultimately an empty thing. A human form is like a reflection having no independent or substantial parts but instead is constructed by the incredible energy and consciousness embellishment—the mind of God.

Practicing the path, calling in the kundalini energy, allows the Holy Spirit to enter our newly upgraded bodies. Thus we entwine with this era of evolution. We become ushers of the new template for the cosmos, planet, and sentient beings.

As most of us can attest, conceptual knowledge such as this noetic space of reason and data reception contrasts vastly with the direct experience of sensing and realizing our whole being through the tree of life, which we will examine here.

The Tree of Knowledge vs. the Tree of Life

Humans have many myths from previous eras that express the distinction between conceptual knowledge and direct experience, one of which is the tree of knowledge vs. the tree of life. Eating from the tree of knowledge is a feverish and ultimately self-consumptive act. The conceptual seeking and devouring of the numinous ignores the true path. The path of the Holy Spirit. The way of love. This corrosive, unexamined desire to "know all" results in cascading states of compunction. We cannot come to inhabit truth through knowledge alone.

We embrace the idea that the goal of the ever-unfolding, revelatory, and oracular inner path to salvation is woven through renunciation. We renounce the temporary self and its imaginary world by intersession with the highest state of mind and heart. This activates a practice that moves beyond our common sense of knowing. We invite the kundalini, call in the Holy Spirit, and allow the divine Logos to flow through us as we open our hearts and bodies to what we are. Whatever we call this sequence of actions and expansions, we must experience it to identify it fully.

The path described here, and its resulting state of liberating and pulsing stillness is experiential and alive and begs the mystery of our embodied moment and the truth. We feel the cosmos by humbling ourselves and resting in whatever state we are experiencing with the grace of acceptance, forgiveness, and love. We accept, forgive, and love every version of ourselves, every version of humanity, the entire wide-eyed state of sentience, and the suffering endured by all life. We offer ourselves while honoring our hearts. The tree of life symbolizes this way.

The fallen path of grasping knowledge alone demands that the ego expand to compete with God in a laughable attempt to match omniscience, the totality of conscious energetic expression, and the mystery of mysteries. Only humility will allow us to glimpse and move with grace and all gifts it carries.

As discussed, the polar opposite path from the tree of knowledge develops through the tree of life. We are not simply referring to the biblical, Talmudic, or Kabbalistic liturgy or symbology of the tree of life. We are discussing the experience! Gnostics and dharma practitioners always stress direct experience, and it is this faith and motivation to feel into the depths of intuition that we transcend all dogmas and beliefs.

The tree of life manifests as an antecedent symbol above all symbols in many cultures. Its roots, trunk, branches, and leaves of jewels are the foundation of our cosmic archetypal symbolic minds and our reading of the toroidal formation of metaphysical symmetry. Our nervous system, chakras, and embodied wisdom are exemplified by the tree of life symbol.

It is the path on which we accept and strive for deliverance and inner purification by mystical means beyond concept through open embodied prayer while resting in our humble stillness. We deflate the hungry impulse to expand our seeking ego mind, devouring all. The inverse of revulsion and ever-grasping desire mark the terrain of our quest for living and loving knowledge. It is the mind and heart of grace, bearing natural fruit. It is the torus in smooth flux and flow. The spiral of human reflection sees itself as one with the cosmic dance of all.

Narrow is the way to heaven. If we proceed along it, what we come to be, inhabit, and see unfolds accordingly. The bliss state of absolute compassion through living and eternal grace is achieved by the drama of our humbled heart's activation through devotion and gratitude to God, the Great Spirit, the dharmakaya, or *dharmadhatu* of all—buddha nature.

The tree of life exemplifies the illuminated inner channels and winds that cycle through our microcosmic orbit ignited by virtue, activating our portal heart and sparking every channel of our being into life. It is a blessing state, not something we control. The Holy Spirit, or kundalini energy state, cannot be controlled.

You can't bottle a rainbow, so goes the saying. The bottled rainbow metaphor laments the egoic desire to claim the numinous. This same hubris includes our materialist framing of the twelve-dimensional (and beyond) conscious reality and its ineffable mystery. We can use models to expand our conceptual frames, but we must work with devotion, purification, and expansion to come into the fold of God and all dimensional expression. The abstract and the truly known and embodied are leagues apart.

This mistaken idea is that we could transport ourselves to the proximity of God as this ego persona and compete for knowledge with the source of knowledge. It is lunacy to believe we can become more than God by capturing some of God's parts.

Knowledge is not simply the cognizing domain, or the feeling space, or the intuitive expedience. It is the upgraded, active, full spectrum self-seeing beyond the mundane self and channeling and delivering the keys to the next step toward truth in a new energetic era. Codes and keys to states of realization are revealed as we soften into grace.

Who would want to capture and selfishly hoard or overpersonalize the metaphysical truth and spiritual life force in such a limited frame? Humanity wrestles continually with this impossible conceit and desire. Our drive for survival and liberation of the "self" is pursued as if we are siloed, isolated, and atomized beings capable of holding the burning embers of ultimate reality while being disconnected from the fate of all sentience.

This position is ignorant of the enlightened heaven states we can merge with at all times. The isolated path of pride is the fallen path. The heaven state is where the joy and enlightenment of all is our deepest wish.

As Ezekiel saw, the biblical take on a wheel burning with a multiheaded expression of primal metaphoric or symbolically embodied intelligence and infinite awareness displayed by its eyes is a description of the highest manifest form of the Godhead's heavenly all-dimensional body.

Similarly, the entwined quality of Shiva and Shakti, the twin pillars of the formless and formed and the masculine and feminine principles integrate to show a spinning centrifuge and still point we can also call God.

The Kabbalists have Adam Kadmon, the androgynous superbeing whose body is this cosmos of which we are the smallest cells, reintegrating through every moral and spiritualized action into a union. Or we can call it buddha nature.

Ezekiel's story expresses a warning. We cannot gaze at any form of God directly and entirely with our egoic selves. In attempting such a thing, just as the Kabbalists attempt to do through the Sefirot and the Merkabah system, we are burned, like the Greek Icarus, who flew too close to the sun.

The Merkabah is the chariot used for transporting the entire etheric aura body to all celestial realms above the astral planes. It is the twin spinning triangles encapsulating the human geometric form and encasing us in a mind and energy-produced "inner spaceship" whose destination is at the feet of Metatron—the highest geometric expression of all platonic states of geometric dimensional space.

Metatron is a type of grid system holder, a being, and a geometric form. Below him are the archangels, each stewarding a layer of space-time where human energy bodies can tread in a Merkabah.

✪

The grid and the deified energies, or archangels, guarding it, form a prison around our perception.

While the Merkabah path is based in transporting the persona with the spirit, only the inner view, where all become the sphere of totality, where the mind dissolves all forms into one point, is total liberation.

Trying to witness the totality of God's mind and body through our egoic self while we are in physical and mortal form—even entombed in a Merkabah device—is begging to have self-decimation done the hard way. The result is a trial by fire. God's natural wrath is the inevitable response to this selfish orientation.

Contrary to that path is our devotion, meditational equipoise, "self-denial," and contemplative acceptance of the living mystery. Paradoxically all secrets are revealed this way. Much better than that, the eternal life of the soul within the Holy Spirit and all heavenly realms is assured, and a potential to light up our rainbow body through enlightenment is possible.

All chakras and embodied vectors of energy, all portals and tethers to the luminous body, are focused on the sharpest still center of mind and heart this way, and we need nothing external or conceptualized to bring us into absolute recognition of God's life force within us and within all. We simply rest in our hearts.

Our path as holy beings and Channelers of the highest state of mind and energy begins with this humility. The course inward, tracked by the unfolding reality we attract and the timelines we align with, is a way to bridge the spiritual with the manifested. In so doing, we allow all to be inducted and transformed through the centrifuge of our expanding and imploding light body.

The rainbow body's illumination starts with letting go of our hunger to know and instead inhabiting the passion of the present without conditions and aligned with flowing love and ultimate compassion.

This is easier said than done. The feeling, passionate, suffering, beautiful, and tragic realm of the human dimension requires us to be compassionate with ourselves in the most profound way, both when trauma unfolds and when we are lucid and centered.

The love, compassion, and equanimity that arrives through the cosmic dharma of the Christ's forgiveness is our capacity to forgive, release, allow, and reduce the transient persona self as it moves toward its highest emanation and effortlessly evolves.

The tree of knowledge is not "forbidden" because it quenches some thirst and provides the keys to infinite omniscience and self-empowerment, which is somehow "too much for us," but because it does precisely the opposite! It generates isolation and delusion of spirit if approached with the selfish thirst of self-cherishing.

We've been warned about the Promethean temptation to force entry into the kingdom through self-deification. The outward-seeker path, which locates external validation and clues as a way to freedom, may be the only one we've collectively taken or been coerced into. But we are renouncing its devastating cage of self-regard and integrating what it taught us the hard way. That the bargain, whereby our persona—that relative and ever-changing object of solipsism—could balloon into an eternal thing made solid and empowered by some hidden wisdom gained in the relative plane of the mundane is a satanic offer. It is to worship Mara's wheel; that is, the wheel of suffering and reincarnation.

This false eternalist promise brings more profound confusion and drives beings toward the capture of the soul and destruction of the spirit.

⊗

Spiritual death occurs when the hubris and delusional grasping of our egoic selves forgoes the righteous path of renunciation and humble devotion to love in all natural forms. We activate love in a practical and actionable way here, every moment, asleep or awake. And where we falter, we purify, over and over again.

Instead of wielding and owning knowledge, we find that our deepest wish for salvation is found in God's Logos—or mind, heart, and essence—which arrives when we surrender to this way. Even realizing this, we tend to replace that mysterious truth with some framed state of fact. This unstable fact state masquerades as truth and is the result of eating from the ever-sprouting tree of knowledge, which is like entering a hall of mirrors or a regressive and unending labyrinth of mind produced by ever reifying reflections. Each time we level up in our state of grace, acceptance, and realization, our egos claim the form as some permanent and solid award.

We need to stay vigilant about this. The Logos of God, our buddha mind, recognizes this folly through our most profound conscience. That conscience is best felt when we are humbled by renouncing our "sinful tendencies," which can simply be anything that forgoes self-love, love of the eternal "I," or the heart as it is.

When we do this kind of confessional work, we see just how pernicious and devious the hungry egoic quality of the grasping mind is. It is a gate for the many devils and the evil ones to penetrate our very souls and corrupt even the great strides we have made in spiritual evolution. Those beings are the shadow elements caught in loops of self-involvement, desire, hate, and fear.

The kind of knowledge produced by embracing the tree of life is not absolute or fixed. It is living and enticed into action through our participation with divinity and grace, not through some captured math, model, or stagnant portrait. And as we now know, it is not experienced through the gaining and gathering of information but through the heart.

When one believes that harnessing the material realm or using spells, sigils, and esoteric data enlivens the spirit, they mischaracterize and misunderstand the most precious and sparkling reality: We are a splinter of God, at once a singular and total aspect in nature to God.

> ✪
>
> We need nothing but the surrendered outreach and
> steadfast gaze inward to find a dynamic cosmos alive
> for our redemption and that state of infinite awareness
> beyond concept.

So why does this book concern itself with descriptions and models to experience the ineffable? And isn't language itself a trap? I have wrestled with this timeless paradox of knowledge and wisdom. It is a three-dimensional dilemma, but we navigate it to better serve this world. Wisdom arrives through divine Channeling, allowed and animated by our devotion to the Holy Spirit, transcending time and space. Knowledge should be the syntax or language encouraging this path, and that is all.

Embracing the Human

Being human is being humble and learning what the third dimension teaches: how to go through the fire of rebirth at any moment. Whatever we have done, whatever we have not done, and all of the regret, shame, doubt, or fear that moves through our system as this world evolves and thrusts us into a reckoning with the dense dimensions can all be transcended and alchemized into love quickly, now. That is our enlightened way.

Often, we close our consciousness into a narrow narrative and into a lacerating self-inspection, but this can be instantly loosened and relieved once we have the needed insight. Remember, the self we just interrogated is transitory, made up of swirling parts, none of which are independently arising. This temporary mind steering the egoic self is a mirage. We build this self we perceive through focused habits. So "who" or "what" is focusing? It is simply the activity of energetic propulsion and consciousness itself. We are ultimately the motivation and divine will behind this. The "I am" force without any identity or fear. Still, we work with the constituent mirage of the ego to navigate temporal time, material form, and energetic form in the higher realms.

The spaceship of the contained self-regarding "I," while ultimately impermanent, is the method to transcendence and an inevitable part of the manifest experience. We determine the "I's" quality, and for the best evolutionary results, we blend compassion and equanimity, or a peaceful acceptance of all moments through the mundane perspective. What many call equipoise or wisdom is simply flowing with our self-obsessed egoic experience and transforming its suffering and delusions into compassion and viewing them through the profound lens of inter-dependence and the dreamlike quality of phenomenal display, frame by frame.

The mundane or egoic self can be healed before it calcifies into a convincing identity that opens inner portals for these dark forces to settle and subsequently bake imprints into our karmic winds. We need simply remember to humbly reach out to the Christ, the buddhas, the angels, and the higher manifested ancestors and guardians we have always known, and who have always known us. It is not a path where we lose sovereignty; it is an honor to join the ocean of Love with others and receive help. More importantly, we remember that we are reflections and expressions of these very beings we pray to. We are merely looking and speaking into a vast mirror of our true selves. The buddha field, the Christic field, and the realm of enlightened beings and angels interchange within one experience. We pray to a manifold self-appearing in all of its highest realizations: God.

FIVE

COMMUNICATION CODES

....

Activation through Symbols

The knowledge realm is of the relative and mundane sphere; it cannot bring redemption, the flaming heart of bliss and joy, or the motivation of compassion that transcends this life. But the vow to enter the kingdoms of enlightened pure lands and beyond, helping all others do the same even before we do—that is a feeling state occurring across our entire being!

The realm of constrained knowledge-seeking is one of self-entombment. Conversely, as we examined, the tree of life is a state beyond description where "self and other" collapse and the flow of form and formlessness dances into mysterious perfection at the side of and as one with God.

This does not mean we reject the path of knowledge entirely; instead, we explore it from a space of divine inspiration gathered through devotional humility—inviting Logos. On one level, we are language-based, symbolic beings mining this baked-in syntax to find meaning, and on another level, we are ever-evolving, reclaiming our rainbow of power and the heritage of embodied perfection. We will soon transcend the need for lengthy discourse and communion. The end of this Piscean time, or segment of the Kali Yuga, means that we need humanly transmitted maps and camaraderie, or sangha, to join together and move in ascension at this juncture. We move beyond the use of concepts and language into knowing, feeling, and sensing truth.

Throughout the Piscean era, the messianic age, and all the way back to the seeds of the fallen state—or the origin of the Kali Yuga—we have done what we can to rejoin our place in the cosmic dance of life and love. Now we are blessed to be entering the Christic age of golden fruition or 5D (fifth dimension) embodiment, which, for a while, expands us further and faster beyond our projection capacity.

We can each have channeling experiences, unity consciousness revelations, devotional rebirth, and ecstatic awareness. But as humans, we remain anchored in our bodies, dimensional frequency, and world system, which amazingly is now upgrading. So we offer and share what we see, and it helps us internalize peace across subtle fields to coevolve in harmonic splendor as the dance of cosmic reunification prompts us.

We are relational beings, and relationships are complex, requiring grace-filled piety and confrontation with the emotional landscape we each funnel to action, and relating brings tension, the tension of viewpoints and perspectives. Even as the energy lightens and rises, this world system is one of potential confusion and conflict. However, no matter what layer of the pie of phenomena or dimensions we examine, it is scale invariant as far as God is concerned. God remains present as long as we wish to be in its glow, no matter where we are or how we feel.

Words, then, are simply symbol packets of dense information and implied meaning and are an encouraging force for realizations and expressions of the moving light that emerges once and for all when we allow it. The language of light, far exceeding worldly lexicons, is the heart beam of truth that reflects through us when we carry knowledge and wisdom along with compassion and inspiration. Knowing this, we start to comprehend Channeling and practice it more seamlessly.

The field of a shared dream and our family of awakening souls is our path to the total remembering of who and what we are, and where we are going. To carry the gift and practice our role of anchoring this world and being the healthy antennae we can be, we must deepen our discerning nature. We must thrust into and scrutinize our concepts of belief and the pride and protections that emerge as we probe into our minds. Only then can the embodied energy of God arise.

The love, compassion, and equanimity that arrive through the Cosmic Christ's forgiveness is our capacity to allow and reduce the transient self as it is directed toward its highest emanation and effortlessly evolves. We need help modeling, and because we look outward for a signal to illuminate our path, we look to the Christ and find him within.

The light begins to shine from us as the source moves from external to internal and then both simultaneously. All communication is rallied into form by its foundational hermeneutical position or consistency of logic and utility. This means that anything we say has its roots in belief. So what do we truly believe at a subtle level?

The highest spiritual realizations and expressions cannot be ultimately shared through any language-constraining tunnel of human concept or noetics. Still, as we've seen, we are allowing the practice to build experience, and experience to bring realizations, and realizations to become embodied expansion and living knowledge. From here, we learn to express in words what we Channel.

Interestingly, when we forgo language, conceptual frames, and the ability to communicate and describe, we ignore our current tools for coevolution. Song, movement, ritual, and simply feeling one another are ways we can transmit the energy of our time. But language is a human skill that comes in many forms and is also evolving.

We are moving into an era where we can effortlessly meld minds through shared deep webs of mentation, our energetic frequency wielding and simultaneously transmitting language for describing and prescribing. We do this all without ever resorting to dogma or the stale method of absolutism, even as we discover cosmic truths. We can also do this without flattening it into the noetic frame by instead feeling our holistic state of awareness. The senses blend with our knowledge, turning to active real-time embodied knowing and action entwined.

We Channel when we learn to receive and retain our loving intention and allow it to move through us. Channeling is sharing, sharing is loving, loving is truth, and truth also has a language, and that language rests on facts; as long as we can find and share them, we can meet and grow together.

Facts presuppose a realm of space-time where objects are stable and identifiable from other things. This domain of identifiable facts underwrites the third- and fourth-dimensional realm we usually walk in—a realm of thought and causal regression, or material and temporal evidence, for both the observer and the observed.

This domain is the basis from which we initiate our moral underpinning of the universality of ethics. So, does that mean we think or "factualize" our way into morality and ethics? Can a noetic capacity for psychic transmission and cold logic give way to the heart path of virtue? We've seen that it cannot and that it merely results in self-worship.

I suggest instead that we Channel God and share the light of evolution through its new impressions and truths. When we discover these universal ethics through genuine full spectrum, embodied, and integrated experience, we communicate in the style of the new era on the Earth for humans.

When discussing kundalini awakening and the embodied tree of life, we are talking about the experiences we have had and internalized karmically over our manifest lives or through direct spiritual teaching transmissions that penetrate the entire energetic body we call self. We transpose this wisdom set of ethics and morals daily by relating all experiences without discrimination. This world is as fantastic as any other for our spiritual practice! No matter where we are, we can glow from within with the Logos of God, buddha nature revealed, and our cosmic heart exposed. Do not despair if life has become chaotic. Do not sit complacent if it is resting in temporary bliss. Channel the truth of your deeper self. Let the heart beam glow through vulnerable relaxation and self-love.

We can bring the enlightened state to any experience. The realm of our everyday experience has a boundary, and there are ways of identifying its constants. This realm (and its resulting purview) is the one we most often inhabit, and from this realm, we can use our cognizing mind and body sense turned outward and inward to experience dimensions beyond the mundane.

God then enters the picture for us, directly and powerfully. Shortly after we realize and experience this, we become clear about the nature of all spirits, noncorporeal minds, and forces of intelligence that become distinct from and linked to God in varying relationships. We all realize the transient and porous nature of phenomena as we perceive it and the beings that inhabit our view.

Archangels, buddhas, Satan, lower worldly spirits, elementals, ancestors, karmic soul groups and individuals, demonic entities, or principalities manifest before us as we become aware of the eclipsed realms filtered through our embodied awareness. From here, we decide how we wish to encounter these manifestations. The divine motivation encourages compassion, discernment, and wisdom on all planes. We realize the impermanence and pure nature of all.

We bring an enlightened view to each being or object and, beyond this, we bless them all! This is the defining quality of the holy path and our motivation for activating compassion, seeing through delusion, and blessing every frame of experience we perceive and flow through. Describing the spiritual experience this way is the core of Channeling, as I account for it.

Our mundane realm is also a "reality" or a plane manifest from a hypostasis where meaning evolves. If all is interdependent, then meaning, facts, and experience, all adjacent to perception, weave into energy, material, and all-dimensional expressions. We ascribe importance in the same way to all of it—we cannot fall asleep by obsessing over any piece of any dimension or aspect of the experience. This is the act of opening to the twelve dimensions.

Our perception of the mundane rests on a set of meaning presuppositions. These presuppositions are like stable inferences and observations, conceptual synthesis, and sense gate registration. They give rise to uniformity, interchangeability, and traceable trajectories even though we can only apprehend many stimuli through our bodies. We can make sense of experiences we have not sensed directly. This ability to curiously seek what we infer is how we expand, and we do so by stretching into spaces in which we have faith. We track our mundane physical world and become mindful of our every movement and vibration. We allow flow and grace while being careful to remember that we cannot always see the entirety of all situations or dimensional activity.

We apprehend the upper and lower dimensions through the platform of our third and fourth dimensional states: our subtle and physical bodies. From this mundane layer of reality, we imagine and observe the rest. But it is higher consciousness, both our individual consciousness Channeling through our bodies and the amalgamated totality of consciousness that observes through us as a discrete being. None of it is ours. The Holy Spirit uses us as a gift, with our salvation flowing as a shared joy.

We falsely use our ego to claim the Logos and the occurrence of observation and being able to see the substrate of all phenomena that follow and activate through us. Once we stop claiming that we are the authors and captors of awareness, we can expand our capacity and embrace evolution on Earth. We stop and watch the dream unfold as we observe our minds, the nature of mind, the nature of reality as a continuum of mind, and the nonlocality of sensation even as we remain a stable "I" as a center point for this observation and dance with phenomena. There is no permanent solid "I" behind our witnessing "I." Only the Holy Spirit, the three kayas or buddha nature, God, and so on, all moving and still.

EMPOWERMENT
View from the Pure Lands

By centering the body and relaxing into present time awareness, ready and open the mind and energy body to touch a pure land vision:

The breeze is the breath of Sophia, the willowing caress of a trillion faeries. A field of lightly moving flowers of every color, each petal and stem swaying to the wind's sweet song. To look at them brings joy.

Every flower smiles into the rose-gold, azurite sky above. The tree's limbs stretch into space to reveal planets carrying families of humans, animals, plants, and insects flowing off of every branch, each group of beings containing its karmic coordinates and genetic template relating to the tree.

A valley holds a river of multicolored nectar flowing at every speed. The closer we get to the nectar, the grander that river seems. The stream moves slowly like the cascade of galaxies in a universe, and with equal ferocious power, every shade of pearl-like rainbow shimmers, melting into gold. The elixir is life, the stream of life.

If you look up, you'll see the swirling storm of stars raining down dew drops of light. Each drop lands on the ground, mingling with the flowers, sliding into the river of nectar, rushing into eternity, funneling into the roots of a tree where that drop becomes a life-form beholden to that tree. It evolves through eons, between almost infinite realms of manifestation states, until it returns to this garden, where it peers up into that spiral of stars.

Let your attention drift up into that spiral, floating effortlessly upward into its center, passing beyond our universe and all scales of phenomena we perceive across all dimensions. Beyond that, you become a line of light sliding across a great marble. That marble is the surface of a universe, and the light path traced with your gliding form illuminates a pattern that echoes down into the interior of the marble where galaxies and planets reside, producing a realm's metaphysics colliding and conspiring to generate world systems for perceiving beings such as humans. Each marble is a particle spinning among others, binding, and crashing, and gelling into shapes that build a body—the body of God.

Channeling Codes

Let's now explore the term codes. This term evokes something occult or hidden, but codes are not obscured by design. They are a type of information that we absorb in ways humans have yet to describe accurately. Here, I'll try to shed light on how this phenomenon takes place.

Codes are celestial interdimensional intelligence and wisdom manifesting in the body through sonic waves, spectral light, and geometrically stabilized electromagnetic forms. Our cognition and gathered perception collectively receive and display these codes. Just as they elevate and evolve us, we propel them. These metaphysical actions are interdependent with our heart-mind/form nexus.

Codes enter the subtle human body prevailing as a synesthesia of knowing, hearing, seeing, and tactile feeling (the cognizing mind is a sense gate or sense organ in Buddhism). Our subtle body is the prana, or auric life force field, actuating our embodied experience. Codes ripple into us and are transcribed into our linear language as conceptual thoughtforms and impressions, and the resonance they generate can propel us. The symbols that form in our minds and vibrate through our perception body are examples of our capacity to referentially integrate codes using the lexicon available to humanoids. Our human symbol set is very dense and complex, woven into our physiology and DNA and predating our time on Earth. These essentialist symbols are the way we take in codes.

Codes have no inherent forms besides those assigned by
the minds that perceive them.

The way another race of beings would perceive codes differs from how we do so, yet the codes' feelings and intentions are the same. They flow in dazzling patterns, displaying behavior we can all learn to tap. How does it feel to tap into these codes directly, and how does it feel to register these codes not simply as imperceptible ethers but as symbols with meaning? How do these symbols erupt? We can look at the idea of an etheric template to further understand this occurrence.

An etheric template and state of potential energy permeates the world we encounter, constantly changing with feedback from our awareness. We can call this the subtle morphic field, a place where memetic information crosses from one object to another without the usual physical intervention. Or we can recognize the larger space that the Akashic and other various etheric fields take dominion of and see that it is all a living energetic and encoded web of life and exchange.

The codes build the tonal or resonant quality of our world's experience, and we are the beings that act as antennas and grounding rods for that world. You are that being. One can understand codes as the language of the celestial realms interpreted by us.

Channeled codes imprint as perfect hybrids of light wave/particle quantum bits and sonic vibration resonance, fluctuating or moving out of the vacuum of potential through the sun and into our embodied perception. The ether that transmits these hybrids is bound in thoughtforms and living impressions. We now understand that when we Channel and read the Akashic Records, we are receiving and integrating these codes. To have a reference for understanding the fields of information that govern the Akashic Records, one can examine a muon.

Muons are subatomic particles that rain through us and have their own magnetic field that causes them to spin like electrons, but instead of being immortal like electrons in this universe, they appear and decay almost instantly. They are waves of particulate energy coming and going in and out of this universe but having an effect on this dimension. They are messengers.

And just like muons, we also phase in and out of reality, which is the foundation of the hallucinated state of the third and fourth dimensions. Time and space in the first four dimensions are like reflections of the sky on the ocean; they are neither the experience nor the sky itself. Our minds occupy this reflection and projection space until we learn to dive deep within. The Akashic Records are like islands formed atop the water, stationary imprints that we can read like a sailor does an oceanic map. They are the formation of our imprints made more solid than fleeting impressions and yet subject to change like all things.

Sharing Codes

Codes are like etheric loops of impression that self-reflect and evolve with each vibration of their signature tune or speed of self-fluctuation. They are like great tombs of discovered knowledge condensed and translated seamlessly into visual, tactile, emotional, conceptual, and tightly-delivered acoustic data. In this way codes are self-recursive, meaning they are logically cohesive and meta-referencing, harmonious messages.

To better understand this, imagine a voice that is not human yet "sounds" similar to our inner monologue and that seems to originate from inside our heart or crown chakra, delivering insight from libraries of data and layers of poetic truth. This is when a very physical and inspired learning state emerges. These "voices" only register as language based on our ability to decode information. It is a human bias that forces this information into voice-like states. This is important to distinguish from what is commonly understood as a schizoaffective state. We are not talking about the dissembled inner monologue state of various egos clashing or competing.

These "voices" are a network of living information nodes residing in vast thoughtforms or symbol nets in the conscious halls of knowledge, poured down into the receiver as the subtle body opens. The conduit or ether layer is a plasma soup made alive with sonic vibrations. Once again, light and vibration act in perfect harmony with one another.

Codes enter like a warm embrace, at once familiar and alien. Loving, yet decisive and sharp. They feel fresh and very straightforward as if remembering where we left our keys. Indeed, the analogy sticks; these transmissions invite us to find the keys to our newly blossoming nature.

The purpose of the codes sent through members of our celestial and galactic family, such as the Pleiadians, is to awaken the entire human hyper-form of multidimensional beingness one individual at a time. The truth or stillness bakes down into that harmonic symphony a star knows to perfection. The information therein shakes up dormant or short-circuited stations of knowing, opening chords of power that ripple through our being. It makes available the flow of embodied energy and self-propulsion needed for sovereign evolution, eliminating blockages, and allowing a propulsive spin into harmonic symmetry and the energy of Love while grounding the human psyche in expanded truth.

Our role as practitioner or Channeler is to offer the energetic prompt to the world that code reception allows. You are entirely capable and permitted by nature to open to these celestial codes. In the case of this book, Channelings and the discourse I offer on them, the language used here, and the intermediary of this writing are simply the methods I've used to translate the codes I have received, shared with you across space-time, and received back to be codified in writing. The codes remain as alive as the initial Channel. Our capacity to Channel is expanded and continually expanding as we open and expand with discernment. We are sharing and expanding as each of us internalizes the energy of this time and its methods of upgrading us.

The Earth, sun, planets, interstellar nebula, living debris, and swirling natural satellite moons in our solar system all dance with us and magnify, warp, or coordinate our physical perception cycles. Astrology is built from this dance. Extend this to all form dimensions and we see a great cosmic symphony of action. The new solar quality allows us instant access to the nature of these mechanics and their effects.

The universe, multiverses, and sentient beings within these dimensions, beyond the physically dense, intersect through nodes, portals, and recursive fractal patterns like a hologram of refracting perfect diamond light that can bring perceivers into proximity with complete awareness beyond duality or the nondual into the purity state known in Tibetan Buddhism as dharmakaya. The manifest cosmos is a map of evolution back to the still point of creation.

In this wild circus of activity, billion-year-old minds and celestial beings circulate through our time cycles (as we apprehend them) and affect our situation. The Vedas tell us of millions of solar years of energy cycles, like gigantic seasonal loops, in which the condition of the universe we inhabit changes.

On a more granule level, we are part of a humanoid species, half genetic elemental evolution produced by adaptive pressures and half divine seed beings emblazoned with eternally stabilized Christic hearts through our perfect, full-dimensional nexus form bodies. Over eons we have seeded on many planets and have deep connections to each through the heart portal and genetic code. Our Channeling is simply the method for connecting to all of this and more.

The Akashic Records tell us this story with their enormous and intersecting timeline structures. They are the etheric imprints that sentient beings have accrued through embodied experience, and we observe a potential karma, or cause-and-effect track, when we work with them. The Akashic Records hold the seeds and roads for the information you Channel, and codes are the cosmic ignitions intended for you exactly how and when they arrive.

Channeling is an inborn, natural capacity and a practice for you to cultivate to self-evolve and aid others through this massive scope of space. My Channeling of codes, for example, comprises these writings' total overview and discourse, my synthesis of all integrated and pertinent wisdom. It is intended to aid your own methods, serve your continued awakening and expansion, and energize your own Channeling. The point of synthesizing codes and reading the Akashic Records over many years is to invite others to do the same.

Your investigations will reveal most undeniably what is true beyond any words or prompts I could supply, and the direct engagement with codes is the way to know truth in the deepest sense, especially for anyone receiving a reading rather than Channeling for themselves. However, we should carefully encourage people to wake up to their latent abilities to Channel for themselves. Each being is closest to their own sources flowing through them and the meaning to be gleaned from those sources.

Codes do not derive from the singular minds of sentient, organic carbon beings like us. They are not psychic transmissions. They ride along solar/sonic waves expressed in geometric fractal movement, and in many respects, they are as alive as we are. Codes are ever-moving states of intelligence that many beings, such as stars, have cultivated into complete harmony, which emanates through their active nature. Imagine a symphony of activity and sound coming to a crescendo and humming in perfect resonance for all time. A star has realized this state and shines it for all to grow through and achieve. Codes are the rivers running through, beyond. We are being filled with codes by stars.

So how do the Akashic Records, Pleiadian/celestial Channeling, the nature of stars, and consciousness entwine with codes? They are all aspects of the living cosmos. Codes are simply the accumulated language of the cosmos streaming through and energizing the subtle fields or etheric layers to create beams of energy that enter the mind and heart. They are the means through which the cosmos speaks, evolves, and reflects its evolution to as many corners as possible.

Decoding the Cosmic Mechanics
and Symbols of the Akashic Records

Now more at than any other time, we have access to the field of conscious and energetic experience and living space-time that humans call the Akashic Records (see plate 7, Akashic Records). The Akashic Records are a living repository of impressions generated by each being and shared in an etheric holographic storybook-like chamber of images, feelings, memories, and thoughts laced into the fabric of space-time. Through God and the Christic refuge and the integrity we've cultivated, we can access this divine hall of truth.

The Akashic Records act as an organic and etheric quantum computer relaying information to all "worthy" beings.

"Worthy" here refers to those who have done all of the preparatory work and/or have the innate capacity we have discussed. They have sufficiently purged and readied the subtle body and psyche and achieved the energetic and psychological state of expanded consciousness by absorbing and embracing the exercise of life.

If we have discovered the soft invitation to access the records that rests within us, we can do so at all times just as we can gain access to the Pleiadian Channel of life once we have established the link and just as surrender and admission to the Christ redemptive light is possible when we cry out for him. How we utilize or engage with each of these is a critical discussion. Our responsibility to our psychic capabilities is developed through true empathic compassion and by discerning each situation and its relationship to the Records. We may pick up impressions or full pictures from the records of someone's current life, past lives, and so on, and we can choose to be selective in how we impart this information. Our ability to communicate and aid people in the integration and awareness of the Records is vital to this honorable work as Channelers.

Akashic Record Reading as Practice

The ability to Channel the Akashic Records is not a "power," "siddhi," or attribute of "magic" generation. It is likewise not developed through any temporal-symbolic or occult method. The capacity is inherent within us all! It is activated through the Holy Spirit, and we can consummate this energy in an instant.

When the heart is open, and the mind is sharply focused and concentrating on compassion, the body follows and starts to wake up. The subtle body moves within, and our organs and qi wake up. We feel information that our mind is registering by listening intently to the person we are working with. We sense them. When this vulnerable sensing arrives, we are in an intimate space. Here lies our opportunity to differentiate between our projections, needs, and perceived threats and the field of energy and data coming off of the other person and wedding itself to our own open subtle body. We are not taking or giving anything; we are allowing closeness to transpire. This closeness has images and stories within; it is the gate to the Akashic field.

Once we have received this data, we can decipher it by allowing our inner lens of awareness to focus, to locate the impressions and hold what we receive. We then either share these impressions and enable them to move through us, or we let them percolate within us.

The danger in speaking too soon is that we haven't allowed these impressions to settle enough, and conversely, if we allow these impressions to marinate in our psyche too long, they warp. So it is best to write them down immediately. When I embark on helping a client, I prepare by holding my heart and having my paper/screen ready to quickly jot down all notes and impressions. They come very fast, and I struggle to keep up. I usually write until a natural pause occurs. I do not force further Akashic downloads. I allow them to finish, and then I review once or twice before my meeting with a client. In the meeting I revisit what was written and help them decipher and feel into what came through. I usually have a resonant feeling stay with me as I recall and decipher. I allow the client to draw their own conclusions, even as I help offer insight where I can. Writing something, which animates in our minds and bodies beyond language or simple feeling states, is a fascinating process. The process of writing actually reveals another layer—the words transmit more codes, more layers of symbol flowing through our vocabulary, which contain potential truths. When we review what we've done through this automatic writing, we see a new read come through, which we can choose to share when the appropriate moment arrives. The core intention setting must be to Channel in service of an all-loving God.

I have been Channeling professionally for a few years, and my experience is that each client or partner requires very different handling. It is not up to me to withhold information, but I can choose the tone, timing, and range of disclosure I impart in one sitting.

Once we begin, we may see what seem to be benign features in a reading and pass over them casually. Still, those features might trigger deep shadow elements and require the client to spend a great deal of energy managing and working through the symbolic and somatic spaces of their inner narrative. We should be compassionate and use discerning grace and wisdom through our own surrender. Gripping our practice of renunciation tightly ensures we will be good stewards of Adonai's grace.

Before Engaging a Client

Sit in an upright position, close your eyes, and relax your belly. Settle into your own luminous body, all spheres of experience. Your physical body has millions of sensations; feel them all. Feel your spine and the energy in your root, abdomen, solar plexus, heart, throat, third eye, and crown chakras. Breathe through and with all of these and feel the breath like a loop of golden energy moving through you.

Energy also flows and glows from you. You are angelic and free. You manifest in all dimensions. Remember your pure, healthy blue light of calm perfection and your white light of eternal reflection.

Open your eyes. You are responsible for spreading and holding and healing with the softest compassion and joy. Your inner smile lights up. Your heart is joyful, alive. You are a Channel. A beam of light connects you to the celestial cathedral of many layers above and below, in all directions. You are untethered in space-time and free to fly. Your heart chakra spins clockwise, and the being of perfection that is you sits at your core and that being is the supreme Christ on the throne of truth, manifest to offer direction for your own soul and all souls to reach God. You vow to bring forth only what is in the very best interest of your client, the human being in front of you. They are a child of God, no better or worse than you. You are a servant and child of God, God is within, and you are on a mission.

How did this language sit? We are all conditioned in various ways to react to these older kingdom type of images, and, once again, God refers to our higher power, that state within and without that is beyond time and form. The Christ is buddha nature—our potential—always available, here and now, and yet uncovered in a process.

Channeling Codes and Transmissions

No external or synthetic hardware can capture the psychospiritual embodied technology we use as Channelers, mystics, or holy administers. We join a galactic, universal, and cosmic fraternity of beings when we say yes to our natural, Christic heart's capacity and nurture it.

We each receive downloads or revelatory messages using vulnerable, yet focused awareness and the expanded senses precipitated by this era of kundalini or awakened Logos—the energy/mind of now. The more we practice embracing our natures and the phenomenon of opening the subtle body activation, the more our full-dimensional perception and embodied reach expands.

When we communicate through the Channeling process, we become altogether beneficial servants of knowledge and cosmic energy sharing designed to liberate all sentient beings, including our clients and ourselves, spiraling us up into vast dynamic bliss and love without end. This experience comes when the higher dimensions are integrated and shared. This privilege is our birthright and right now, we are reclaiming it, and our celestial family is watching and routing for us.

Coming out of ignorance and perceiving all phenomena for all of its complexity, beauty, and truth while realizing interdependence and the total harmonic stillness of God is both the motivation and the ripe fruits of our work as Channelers. In this way, we are in a compact with divine motivations and energy when we share this work with the world. Once ingested and templated, this set of understandings and techniques becomes a feature of our heart-mind to share and voice.

We receive codes, including celestial and Pleiadian messages, through our open, compassionate wisdom. We navigate the Akashic Records by expanding and blending our senses, and once we conceptually grasp this and feel it firsthand, we can navigate vast areas of reality. We hear, see, feel, and know the Records at once. We expand our bodies as we accept and engage with focus, navigating the dream and staying centered in our self-illuminating core.

> ✪
>
> Channeling work is a nontemporally bound upgrade to your mind stream.

These words and the words that are transmitted to you to utter or write down are offered to arouse subtle wisdom, hypersensorial living intelligence, and revealed DNA signatures that describe our updating state. This is done through the transmission of condensed conceptual knowledge from our celestial family and the Akashic Records. Transmissions are a profound way to offer an impression of information already completely laced into the transmitter's mind and heart and provided with full focus to the receiver. The Channeled words we use unveil armor and invite the integration of the higher self. They are the language that unlocks and invites.

Know that you are entirely capable, permitted, and encouraged by nature to open to these celestial codes with discernment and focus. You are doing this work, here and now. My role is to do my best to articulate, offer, and describe the energetic prompt we are receiving from the cosmos through God. If this book serves any use, it is to help activate a new conceptual frame and sense of empowered confidence in us all.

Transmission offers vast illumination and healing for the opened heart-mind, allowing for our more profound nature's rapid growth. In its entirety, the work of Channeling is conducted through direct energetic experience and contemplative synthesis. That is how I have experienced it. Transmission is Channeling through the relationship of proximity to one another, silently or with words, music, and movement.

The alchemical transmutation of shared etheric intelligence is a dance of complexity we cannot map with our currently decaying materialist and highjacked paradigm.

We use our hearts and minds to contact it directly while in prayer and devotional equipoise, while protected and anointed. When open, we can receive using vulnerable yet focused awareness. We each become profoundly beneficial servants of knowledge and cosmic energy.

But beyond this, there is a mission! For some, being incarnated and holding the conscious expression of a healing, untrammeled, humble, and willing heart is enough to contribute in ways we cannot comprehend. Others work in the etheric spaces, lucid dreams, and astral dimensions, reuniting with lost friends from across lives and embarking on missions they can only partially remember when they're awake, or they have work grounded in the terrestrial realm, bridging worlds, and working with our physical environment. Still others are here to break social and cultural habits of behavior and thought, purifying collective wants that move us away from our core nature and obscure the rising template. All of these efforts constitute the great work of our time and are encoded here in this writing offered to you.

When ingesting the language we Channel, it is helpful to remember that codes are nontemporal uploads/downloads where the wisdom, living intelligence, and DNA signatures describing our updated state are revealed in real time and are always in flux. Do not try to overmap the terrain or the territory. We are always in uncharted waters. But we do know that if we hold God, love, and service in our hearts, then the messages will be clear and light, designed to set all free.

Keep your heart with all vigilance, for from it flow
the springs of life.

PROVERBS 4:23

SIX

THE TWELVE DIMENSIONS
AND THE RAINBOW BODY

....

Conscious Manifestation through
Self-Evolving Energetic Forms

The rainbow body is the twelve spectral light/frequency manifestation
of full harmonic, conscious, embodied experience.

Humans are now emerging fully capable of
interdimensional navigation, which activates their
twelve-strand DNA whole bodies in hyperspace,
stabilizing the energy nexus with our family of celestials in
accordance with God and all-expressed love.
Channeling is in many ways just a natural way of
communicating for beings during this upgrade.

Reality is an energetic display or movement and conscious expression in a reflection that is not strictly temporal. It is the occurrence
of all self-sensed activity and the stillness at the core of that which is

beyond space-time constraints. It is the reflection of one mind, one life force splintered into many manifestations, which all inflect and reflect the One. Knowing this is easy. Feeling into it and allowing the truth of it into our central sense of "I" is the practice. And from here, we can evolve and grow. These descriptions of our deeper natures are stressed because without acceptance and a confident handle on this, we might confuse what channeling is with its purpose: to communicate, relate and coevolve faster!

We, as conscious creatures, are in an epoch of exponential advancement across all figurations of phenomenal reality. Ultimate reality, as we have discussed, is akin to God's mind and heart and becomes more refined and finally integrated. Imagine a great breathing where everything contracts and expands in an unending cycle that occurs every moment.

This change of fantastic proportions that now enraptures us all is enabling sentient creatures to contain more conscious expression and larger conscious bodies, which express as more significant or coherent manifest physical bodies. Bodies are reflections of energetic, phenomenal, sensed elemental forms in any dimension, and we are in the process of integrating more dimensional expression, as each dimension holds layers and levels of conscious manifestation.

The change, which is nothing short of a plasma-solar, sonic, geometric, metaphysical evolution of the complexity and harmony of our human blueprint and the eclipsing of higher dimensions of phenomena with our own is well underway and speeding up in its spin of activation, and it has taxed many of us beyond recognition. This is because, conceptually and physically, we need to integrate the energy shift quickly enough for our desired comfort level, and that is an arduous task.

A breaking down and a rebuilding are occurring now across all scales—the body, relationships, systems, and the planet herself. I have been stretched and self-revealed in endless ways. Every day seems to bring a shedding of those I once called friends, ideas I called my own, and states of being I had taken for granted.

Subterranean energies are bubbling up and showcasing monsters and angels from within. There is an ear-pricking tone of new energy and light on Earth—an awakening. The scope of each of these striations of fresh awareness is vast. The energetic gale of change is ushering us up the whirlwind spiral of evolution.

We cannot continue to carry the heavy baggage of a dying age that gloms on to our fearful limbs.

I've lost entire views of reality that my previous mind coveted, and I've lost health and regained it in strange new ways, but more powerful still are the entirely foreign energies of awareness demanding to be metabolized. Not even frames of reference around our cognition and genetics or our astrological mapping can compete with our new "knowing sense," which is physical, energetic, and upgraded to a place beyond most former paths to knowledge and awakening.

The purging is so complete at this time that we are often left reentering old frames and practicing old habits without a compass or guide. But those old ways will no longer do. Language cannot capture the change, but we all do our best to speak through the new psychic heart layer arriving.

We now churn in a cocoon made from the husk of romantic notions and painful addictions we must release. We are each a spaceship nested within a greater one, the Earth, about to set sail into a sequence of evolutionary pressures that will usher us into bliss and herald the end of ignorance and force of suppression we each have a hand in dispelling. Our spiritual path would be occurring no matter what era we were born into, but we have been dropped into and set on a lucid time and mission.

Mystics Channel to reveal what truly is, are open to all that is possible, and experience that which is beyond conception.

From here, the direction of the spirit inevitably rests and turns toward the goodness within and with God. We are all invited to be mystics now.

PRAYER
Gratitude to Become

All avatars, expressions, and manifest beings carrying the divine and fulfilled blueprint of perfect causation and fruition of form and mind now fill me and become all I am. I bow down to the beings of all times and realms across all dimensions who have always been and who energize and propel our evolution into the highest spiral causal chain to arrival and bliss. I acknowledge the love and gifts of the saviors and helpers; I am grateful for the redemptive technology and generosities of the beings who watch over and feel nothing but compassion for me and my kind. I am now one with the divine, complete, fulfilled, and humbled fire of everlasting kindness and have the energy to spread this through truth and wisdom, through the skillful means of creative joy and the discerning eye. I will evolve now and stand in my full embodiment, the self-reflecting godhead peering through all angles of my being. I am in service to and at one with God and all life.

Time and
Dimensional Awareness

We are here in the third and fourth dimensions of form and time and in the fifth dimension of knowing and feeling. Beyond this, we are manifest along higher dimensions of determination and power. We must never lose sight that we humans are precious manifest beings and interlopers in this physical dimension, but we are also conscious engineers of the ever-evolving energetic astrophysical scales of conscious manifestation in total.

Our consciousness beats with the collective awareness and energy of all material and immaterial phenomena alike, meaning that the formless and formed realms are here at once! It is all happening and standing perfectly still in us, our environment, all around, and beyond concept. Every dimension eclipses the one preceding in concentric whirlwind-like tunnels within us and extending outward. It is important to really integrate these concepts until they are no longer just conceptual but felt and known.

Experience is the reflection and the light of awareness in a loop of energy. In each incarnation, we are learning and harnessing this and experiencing the glorious reality of true embodied freedom in perpetuity. This is also an era where these truths and methods for realization reveal themselves with an untrammeled speed.

The tension of the sensual and temporal realm propels the cosmos to breathe. The cosmos expresses itself as fractalized components of its whole, and those fractals organize along geometric patterns into the elements. Metaphysics moves into denser spaces of our physics; these laws correspond with evolutionary "moral" or mental laws and then the organic world of humans. Humans and other sentient beings activate the very energy of the cosmos by perceiving it and likewise are given life through it in absolute symbiosis. In the mundane sphere, this dimension, we are collectively and exponentially evolving through a spiral of activity that activates, is in accordance with, and produces time.

Time is simply a term to describe a perceptual dimension where space is occurring for various beings in unique ways. We inhabit the temporal plane, and in this era, we are learning to go beyond its constraints. We are in a beautiful process in cyclical progress through the great mechanics of being across all twelve dimensions of mind and body.

To create some context, we need to finally examine the difference between our ultimate selves, our astral selves, and the "I" in evolution through twelve dimensions of space-time (see plate 8, Dimensions).

We may be able to grasp these dimensions conceptually, and many of us have experienced some of them firsthand in altered states of cognition or perception, in deep transcendent moments of meditation, or through ritual expansion. But to stabilize our bodies into these planes of experience is another story.

Amazingly for us, the capacity to do so with untold ease is the story of our time. We are collectively becoming aware of the malleable essence of the fourth dimension and the feeling state of the fifth, which are both launchpads for the remaining upper dimensions. We are each engaging with and bringing these into our collective world system.

Individually we can go within, observe our senses, feeling states, and perceptions, and touch any of these now. We should prepare ourselves for this and understand that much of our species confusion now comes from not embracing our capacity to do so. It is hard for us humans to move past our perceptual limits when we have become so accustomed to restrictive habits.

An example of our evolving but current perceptual limits can be made by observing what many call "dark matter." Dark matter, for all its messy descriptions, is a material state of effect and an immaterial force. It is a substrate of the material, or a patterning, magnetically acting or pulsating in a spectral wave of light/energy output we cannot register physically or measure with current sense restrictions or tools.

To simplify what is a great co-occurrence of dimensional reality, we can examine each of the twelve dimensions.

THE TWELVE DIMENSIONS

1D	First Dimension	A point or station of manifestation; raw awareness
2D	Second Dimension	Length and width; awareness vibrating or moving; perceived activity
3D	Third Dimension	Length, width, height; awareness with agency or choosing
4D	Fourth Dimension	Time; awareness of change; decay; entropy; evolution; mutation; death; rebirth unending
5D	Fifth Dimension	Perceiving time beyond the present; Akashic Records; feeling with all senses into the elasticity of time and space.
6D	Sixth Dimension	Occupying space as different embodiments and perceivers or beings anywhere across space-time at will
7D	Seventh Dimension	Occupying space and time at the same moment as different embodiments and perceivers at will
8D	Eighth Dimension	Occupying space and time as different embodiments at any moment
9D	Ninth Dimension	One or many embodiments or nonembodied states; formless conscious awareness or manifest awareness body in multiple locations and times as multiple beings or forms of awareness
10D	Tenth Dimension	Creator mind manifesting universes within and across all dimensions
11D	Eleventh Dimension	Omniscient mind aware of all universes and creating as many as it wishes
12D	Twelfth dimension	Unfabricated, all form and formless realms at once; inconceivable awareness

Dark matter is essentially an illusion generated by what we call gravity. It is the warping of dimensions away from our perception. Dark energy is the product of and the force responsible for dark matter materializing and dematerializing. It is the entropic force of inverted toroidal spin, or anti-energy. It also happens to be antilife, as life is energy and awareness.

We are involved with this dark matter force/material, but we are unaware of it at this dimension's cognitive level through our embodiment, even inferentially, because it occupies in part another dimensional layer of activity and a process that we cannot track without observing firsthand deeper or higher dimensionality.

It is the same with other forces and features of the many-leveled cosmos and its weavings. Take, for example, the subatomic and particle layer. At this level, we start to discover the quantum fluctuations and potentials that interact with perception, intention, and mind, or the collections of mind frames, determining reality. There are no constants; relativity is still tracking non-constants that in fact manifest as more complex objects in higher dimensions. We are perceiving a small sliver of the picture, and the picture is moving as we move, dancing in and out of manifestation with us.

It is hard to remain convinced of time, form, or any aspect of three to four-dimensional reality having independent solidness when we look at its foundations. What causes something we perceive as solid to manifest in spatially succinct or discrete ways? One way to see what drives the exchange between a part, other parts, and the whole is to look at the most fundamental part—a particle.

A particle can be separated from its electromagnetism. The implications of this are that the charge that allows the particle to do its particular function is not produced by it or producing it; they are interdependent.

This effect shows that these things are not antecedent or causal in a traditional two-step, cause-and-effect kind of way. Instead, they all co-occur, even if observed as distinct features. This reality affects our understanding of time.

Phenomenally, this scales to the whole cosmos. Instead of "this causes that," we can say "this and that cause one another." A third energy is produced by two objects unlacing. For instance, when particles become separated from their electromagnetic charge, the perception of time becomes relative. A new dimension emerges from its parents and simultaneously influences its parents; the third dimension activates through the fourth dimension and the fourth through the third.

From subatomic particles and waves superpositioning into space to the resulting movement of our heads peering up into space, we actualize time through perception wedded to form as it activates through us. The fourth dimension actualizes from the second and third and conversely gives rise to them. Interdependence is indeed a dance. The chain reactions flowing through physical perception and the animation of this space-time map in display are occurring in the present and the future at once and leaving a trail of energetic evidence we call the past.

This co-occurring dimensional dance teaches us that the past is the residue of energy dispensation or the runoff from activity we see as traces left on other objects. The past is simply entropy's evidence. So the dimension of time is also in flux and acting upon the dimensions of form. This again illustrates the interdependent nature of all phenomena. On a human level, if we trace the trails of time and the evidence it leaves on other objects in space-time, we can integrate and propel our own awareness into power.

The more we take in this energetic evidence, the more we expand, and the more paths of space-time opportunity open up. The great map of space-time is like a twelve-dimensional spiderweb with way stations at every crossroad where strings meet. Each of these signifies a memory or event of activity perceived and acted upon. The activation of one of these space-time nodes by way of perceiving it and activating that perception reifies or solidifies it, so to speak. If we run our awareness over these points, we become symbiotic carriers of that space-time way station or node. In fact, we become the battery maintaining its point of experience and manifestation. We become the lighthouse that roams the cosmos, growing the cosmos as light passes over it and growing our light source as we take up impressions. These impressions of space-time lodged on this great web are the Akashic Records themselves, and they are interdependent with our very experience and life force.

This unified activity beyond and including time applies to minds as well. Total unity of dimensional activity can be seen in how thoughts that flow through a cognizing mind, like ours, and how cells, like the ones from which we are made, are animated through life force and simultaneously animate life force.

Awareness is the loop of energy conjured, generated, and received by the senses of the organism reflecting within a temporary boundary like a body. Consciousness is the background potential of the force of awareness. Consciousness is an activated force like light, but it does not belong to a sun or the objects that are illuminated through the sun's light. Instead, it is a force perceived as a product of activity and beyond that perceived reflection state is the energy of stillness that best describes consciousness beyond its manifest expressions. Once again, total causal interdependence encompassing time form, energy, and consciousness. All dimensions express this truth or constant.

Causal power exists in the whole and the parts in tandem. We come to see, understand, and navigate how we, as discrete parts of the whole, inform it as it does us. We are a crystalline grain of sand in a sea of trillions of shining grains, moving and being both independent and awash in an infinity of beings, objects, and patterns. The form we take fractalizes and expresses up the lattice of dimensionality in various ways. Yet, we are ultimately located in that center space, that tiny pinpoint of perfect diamond-like light.

So, how does this relate to channeling and the Spirit? It seems that all activity, including thought, feeling, and ultimate reality, is happening at once. This is the great Logos. And in its glow, in the conscious expansion into holy forms and truths, we become awakened, and our embodiment follows in the genesis of the rainbow body—what the Dharma calls dharmakaya. Once we awaken to this truth of causal interdependence, we start to determine how we, as a temporary constituent expression of undying life force, can encompass all information and living wisdom through the Holy Spirit.

The Temporal Hallucination

Our material bodies are tethered to time and its expression, but our minds are not. Our souls dwell where there is form, and our spirits are ever flowering beyond and within all dimensional expression. The era unfolding now, one of energetic rebirth, allows us to climb out of the mire of the fourth dimension where we continue to project our minds forward and backward along the same perceived time vectors our bodies take. In this new era, we go within to the space and dimension where time is illusory and a playful ability to see beyond it becomes ours. This transcends channeling, prophesizing, or sense expansion. It is becoming the rainbow-bodied being beyond time in the fifth dimension of knowing and beyond.

Temporality intersects with the delusion of complete or absolute separateness. While there is indeed separation between things and beings in the mundane spheres of the first few dimensions, consciousness is pervasive and only activated by what is perceived. So if we perceive what we conceive of as a memory, it is thus activated in real time—the absolute still point of now that generates all energy and activity. That still point is God, and it is all things self-manifest.

What is this memory? It is now a physical expression housed in energy, an imprint full of information about the sensual, meaningful, and energetic dimensions that compose the consciousness we have access to at that moment.

Temporality, or the domain of time, is a dimensionally animated framing device composed of living energy for the ego to manipulate safely across karmic imprints, which manifest as the form realm we are born into. This includes a seemingly "real" space like our universe(s), which is a holographic chamber of illusion and meaning.

Temporal attributes, just like the body, do not constrain or contain the unconscious; time is a produced phantom of embodied awareness. The consciousness we can perceive is conceptualized in the sense organs' holographic space by our mind sense, which is simply our capacity to realize, and that realization produces the energy space of time within us (see plate 9, The Incarnation Wheels).

Events can happen anywhere in the hallucination of the expressed present, past, or future, and the sonic-electrical signals shot through the organic form that builds cognitive models will not know the difference. Materiality undergoes apparent change states, and very convincing ones at that, but these states are all potentials merely arriving through cognition and shared perception. Only the conceptual mind recognizes time, and the rest of the sense-organ body responds accordingly. All of samsara, or the loop of cause and effect—bouncing back into one another—generate bardos, or in-between states we arrive at in form time. These realms of perception and manifestation are mind-constructed but deeply entrenched energy spaces. They are ultimately just models of mental projection. Those same cognitive models activate the body in space-time and its immediate environment, so the feedback loops grow across seemingly different mediums but one conglomeration—bodies, vibrations, cognition planes, the elements, and so on all manifest in a present space as sensation.

Our level of embodied awareness determines our access to this present space of total conscious phenomenon and the energy aspects that describe a unified geometric electromagnetic plasmic cosmos of energy, which is simply qi, or life force (also known as chi or *la*), entwined with awareness. Energy and mind expand with the desire to do so. This is the method to unlock more of totality from our self-set limitations.

Transcendent Shamanic Experience

If we can transcend the noetic or calculating head chakra located in the brain and nervous system (not to be confused with the third eye or crown chakras, which we sense as being only located in the head, but are in fact full-body, all-dimensional gateways) to embody our minds into a full spectrum state, we can access our latent DNA and be able to traverse the shamanic layers. *Shamanic*—now a widely overused and abused term—is simply a way of saying "the capacity for the third eye's sight and energy determination." These layers of reality from the underworlds to the astral and up to the celestial dimensions are all samsaric in that they are form-time based, but the capacity to determine energy is a distinction of approach. The shamanic approach is one where the being is not flung through realms and states of mind, but rather determines the focal point and response to manifestation. The transcendental and shamanic layer of our agreed-upon mundane realm (our everyday world system) is the portal layer of perception and orientation by which we occupy surrounding realms. In other words, with our whole body in a state of knowing, we transcend but are grounded in 3D and 4D. It should be noted that this shamanic lens and way is not the be-all and end-all. It is simply an initiate's or practitioner's experience as they see through the various veils of perception and into the nature of reality.

When we enter into a shamanic state of transcendent experiencing and can navigate with creative flowing intent, we come to know—by direct embodied experience—the dreamlike quality of all phenomena and spiral up or down the ladder of dimensional realms: pure lands to hell realms and all of the astral and elemental frames in between. We must remember that life force allows all of this and that we are living, organic entities. Through this everyday world system, we use our pranic, or organic, energy and connection to the Logos to function in accord with the Holy Spirit as we navigate evolution.

The permeable perception space of the shamanic realms is the many-skinned veil over "ultimate reality" wobbling between states for our opening senses. This state, in and of itself, is not the goal. We must realize that these magical dimensions of the perceptual range are simply more samsara, more sense impressions, and more mazes.

God and the capacity to know God transcends the kingdoms of this causal and relative self-regarding space-time of shamanic activity. The shamanic realm is a projection space where the astral manifests, and the astral is in the domain of "Satan," Maya, or of Mara, as it is still worldly and relative.

We can be absolutely and personally transformed by God even while we hold on to our confused convictions of a permanent self and play with the elements of the energetic display of the shamanic realms. But we must work with the Holy Spirit through our purified commitments first as we remain an individual navigating these states of being.

Humans have a mission beyond self-enlightenment, beyond becoming a Buddhist arhat, shamanistic wizard, or sorcerer. We have deeper commitments to our spirit and to God. We're here to uplift this specific seed planet and world system and its inhabitants and to anchor aspects of our local dimensional matrix within this galactic frame. We do this in our own simple way by integrating our own shadow aspects and by contending face-to-face with reality.

We have been born here now to aid in a very profound transformation. This era of change enhances the chances for all to be spiritually evolved in this realm. The act of transcendence doesn't take place in some far-off dimension. Recognizing this, how does the shamanic realm play into this era? What layer of the integral field is it occurring on? It seems clear that mundane phenomena should not be taken as sacrosanct or devoted to or imbued with a nature different from its parts.

The shamanic realm is simply the occurrence of subtle etheric energies, the elements and others' minds meeting us and conjoining our mundane perception. It is the halfway point between worlds. It is the elastic or malleable place of forms between stabilized dimensions. I have come to see that while these in-between states profoundly enable us to recognize phenomenal display and the permeable transient nature of our reality, they are still in the domain of Mara, or Satan, the lord of death. If they are worshiped, obsessed over, or related to, they become distractions just like our regular world of perceptions.

No worldly state supersedes our view of buddha nature within all, God, and the essence of the Holy Spirit.

This statement is literal and allegorical: We do not "worship" that which is created; we "worship" the Creator. The Creator is the primary force, and the created is merely a temporary creature or object being enforced by perception into manifestation.

The elements or features of a fine-tuned or impressed-upon material substrate and its casual metaphysics occur on all levels of phenomena and mind. The points where consciousness and energy/matter converge with our observation models, fact sets, and meaning sets constitute a consistent domain of intelligence and initiated influence or design and intention. Consciousness, manifestation, and awareness entwine with the dense physical and multiple etheric spaces of phenomena. We can realize this as we embrace direct Channeling work while surrendering to God's force through the Cosmic Christ's ever-loving Channel. The Cosmic Christ leads us to discover the spiritual truth of redemptive expanding love flowing through all. And that is the intention of our devotion. We'd do well to bring this to all shamanic experiences. Again, we are talking about a supernal being and a projected avatar both when we talk of Christ or the Cosmic Christ.

The intelligent cosmos is not just evinced by our sense of "God's hand" but by the consistent reflection of awareness carried by every state of observation, including other observers who appear distinctly deformed or unique from any impressions we've gathered in this life or any synthesis of archetypes. We come to know the preciousness of life deeply when we realize our rare state of rebirth in this world system, which is one of unparalleled potential to evolve the soul, integrate the spirit, and offer an enlightenment platform for soul evolution for others.

Manifest existence is the fastest way to grow the soul.

The impressions we gain in this level of reality are the quickest way to activate liberation for the minds and bodies. Being birthed or rebirthed in this world system is like coming up for air after a trillion solar years.

The presupposition of other minds, a non-solipsistic frame, suggests minds or "conscious knowers" are in space-time with us. And "conscious knowers" means consciousness as shared property. In our shared experience we see the entry point for God as a mover of and among all things/actions and phenomenology. This claim presupposes *God* is the term we use for all phenomena, including consciousness, energy, will/intelligence, and the ever-fluxing structure of this fullness without beginning or end. This view of causal interdependence illuminates the center of all awareness as the spark of ever-breathing, stillness, and perfection—God—of which we are a part. Never mistake the details for the whole but see the whole in the details, and all will be well.

Pancosmogenesis, Syncretism, and the Protean State

Observing and making sense of phenomenal reality, how we perceive it, and the nature of nature itself is crucial to becoming spiritual Channelers and helpers in this time. Let us examine a term I coined to help us do that. *Pancosmogenesis* is what I use here to offer us some insights. *Pan* means "across many things;" *cosmos* means "a complex, orderly, systematic, and harmonious system;" *genesis* means "the origin or coming into being of something."

In my view our cosmos is closed-looped in that it self-cycles across all dimensions and is without boundary, having no defining genesis or beginning point. The cyclical process of the cosmos includes the inherent embedded, unending sparks of consciousness. Consciousness does not emerge from the cosmos or from any layer of its machinations. Consciousness is inherent. Consciousness and the self-awareness of beings flow through the cosmos as interdependent features of reality, and these beings help give rise to consciousness itself. These self-aware, conscious creatures imbue the totality of the cosmos with an eternal self-aware nature, as individuals and as a whole.

Consciousness is inherent, undying, and primary to the hypostasis of the cosmos. This cosmos has many, or possibly an infinite number of, universes and dimensions within those universes. It has an endless array of conscious life, and that life is the blood of this manifesting cosmos in its phenomenal display, and the minds that make it seem to exist.

As humans, we are cosmic features and conscious creatures. We arrive with unique perceptions and a singular awareness when conceived, materialized, or given a body. We are fractal aspects of the cosmos that come into self-aware consciousness through the life force underpinning our own embodiment. That life force is the cosmos. It is buddha nature or what we call God.

There are many types of birth. A being can be born in many kinds of realms or dimensional spaces. An embodied being like us can die and be reborn in the material world, the upper dimensions, or the lower dimensions. As Channelers, we know this; as people seeking truth or "proof," we can look to the stories of near-death experiences (NDEs), which have become ubiquitous and are well-documented throughout ancient and modern culture.

We can look to the Dge-lugs-pa of Tibet who venture to the bardo after bodily death and observe the true nature of the mind-produced limbo states between manifestations. This teaches us to have faith in the undying nature of the mind and the infinite reach and potential of the heart. We have nothing to fear. We simply need to surrender to the process and move with grace.

In a lucid dream or astral projection, in a plant medicine ceremony, or through deep regression and inner spiritual work, we can see how the spirit rebirths in various ways. Our work as Channelers is to become accustomed to this reality by visiting its feeling often with ourselves and others. It is incumbent on us, though, to discern how we engage with the astral. The various plant being interfaces and the spaces where our energy body are expanded by our will.

> ✪
>
> A species becomes collectively aware of its next level
> of conscious capacity as it recognizes the immortality of
> consciousness and the mind stream and heart beam of an
> individual and the cosmos alike.

The next level of evolution is tapping into the Akashic Records en masse. Humans create and receive impressions. The genesis of an Akashic Record occurs when impressions group together to become a feeling state in a being and are given energetic expressions as symbols or images and sensorial forms.

And so physical birthing, or genesis, is the birthing of awareness as well. What are we, if not evolving awareness states bundled into multidimensional material forms? Genesis is a flowering of aware-ness states where each blooming petal of self-awareness is another birth state reflecting the harmonious totality of the cosmos and its patterning.

Genesis is cascading from a previous state and coming to inhabit a new form and provide a new perspective on the very cosmos of which it is an indispensable part, like a prism being turned toward the light, giving boundary to its own form and its refractions. And where does the light come from? Light and the vibration of form discovered in the light by perceivers, such as by us, define the living cosmos and meet the darkness and stillness in a cycle occurring on all scales.

How do we begin to describe this to ourselves so that our experi-ence becomes digestible and part of our language? How do we know it as we live it?

We can call on the idea of syncretism. Syncretism is the fusion of two or more originally different inflectional forms or beliefs. I believe a vast array of beliefs can be modeled out of pancosmogenesis. Most religions, the most popular ones and the most hermetic, have esoteric and exoteric wings. Those wings point to a center of awareness that holds the mystic truths of the cosmos similarly. In other words, many mythoi, meanings, and ways to predict, track, observe, prophesize, and Channel emerge through a syncretic view.

In pancosmogenesis, we are sensing creatures who have come to be through a process of action in the awake cosmos. We discover how to see ourselves and nature through various symbol sets and inferential discoveries born out through our individual level of awareness.

When we become open to the foundational truths of perception and reality, we see arrays of timelines and universes converge through the porous psychogenic, morphic fields of embodiment and mind. These are made accessible to the conscious observer who has prepared and evolved sufficiently. This is the syncretic view and method for directly describing and knowing reality.

The Akashic Records, for example, capture and showcase the hyperdimensional truth of our pancosmogenesis and the nature of all dimensional existence. This includes reincarnations, many dimensional bodies, noncorporeal sentience, and our role in our particular world system, which is changing as we speak. When we work with the Akashic Records, we become a Channel for all of reality.

Buddha nature, God, or Great Spirit are simply convenient terms for the total intelligent, omniscient, and energetic living essence of conscious love entwined with all. Love is the self-acceptance of every moment and occurrence in time and space. Love is the hypostasis or state of ultimate reality, what the Buddhists call enlightenment.

This love, this state of God, is the spark we return to for aid in our singular evolution. It is the state in which we find our unique and personal conscious embodied story turned to the moral dimension. The energy shows us where our karma, the cause-and-effect chain, is puri-fied and transmuted into awakened energy. God helps us evolve and return to the ultimate reality, which is God.

The story of our individual evolution, karmic purification, and awakening will be syncretic. We each pull from different lenses while meeting in common spaces of faith. The body reveals all, but our story-ing minds require frames and belief structures to process the energy of movement we experience.

Next, we must remember that we are ever-changing beings. We are what are called protean creatures. *Protean* means "of or resembling Proteus in having a varied nature or ability to assume different forms." We are versatile! That is us! Change is in fact the entire phenomenal cosmos and its features.

Creativity is a central feature of ultimate reality. It is at play through our perception; how we grow, destroy, and birth our per-ceived reality can be seen through Channeling as we collapse our perception through our bodies at all moments, permeating any and all space. So, we allow that all is ever changing, and that authen-tic Channeling is an act of engaging in this mysterious machination and dynamic play of forms and the experiential feeling produced and known.

The energy of awareness is animated by the senses. It is in motion beyond symbol and concept and yet captured for discus-sion and conceptual musing in a syncretic way. Experienced "real-ity" is ever dancing and yet still. From this frame, we can proceed to truly apprehend, comprehend, and examine our spiritual destiny and its mysterious revelations with seriousness, humor, and joy-filled focus. We go on the mission unfolding in this precious era that is unlike any other. We hold a key within our spiritual bod-ies to unlock the ever-blooming genesis of the cosmos, with and through God.

The Conscious, Unconscious, and Etheric

The morphic field, the phenomena of egregors (systems of mind and motivation sweeping across the field of social structures), and the noosphere are trackable through the scientific method and are great launch points for visualizing how atomic, cellular, and influenceable thoughtform patterns conspire to generate a collective force such as the Akashic Field. They also reflect back our awareness of spiritual power and the sovereignty or loss of sovereignty of the soul.

From here, we can extract many more layers and enter into understanding the psychic realms that web our living cosmos. Because all phenomena are interdependent, we can also start to revisualize the unconscious in new ways.

People often visualize the unconscious as a vat of shadow waiting to bubble up to the conscious. But this is mistaken. Where would such a shadow be stored? In the body? How? We can imagine dense bundles of atoms and fibrous bits of tissue fusing into neurosynaptic paths and the firing and chemical dances caused by trauma or fear and extrapolation. We see a trigger for the nervous system to pattern signals to the vagus nerve, polyvagal system, and gut and into the mind where visual forms permeate the inner eye where a conceptual portrait of the threat is generated, looped back to the body, and felt as real.

But what is the more refined intermediary between body and space besides just biochemical signals? Is it just the chemical implosion born of a sense-received perception as described? Then we must say that perception directly affects the material. If the material sends bioelectric signals to the cognizing centers, we can say a feedback loop exists.

Most would agree with this without question, and many of us are aware of auras and the subtle body, that being any layer of energetic system or etheric boundary, and the higher self—our Buddha nature working through our mundane minds or as is known in Mahayana Buddhism as the Sambhogakaya are part of a temporary but boundary-based individual identity, and how perception is the generator of our worldly experience. But didn't the perceived threat or traumatic cause originate on the exterior? What is the exterior? To understand things like egregores and the inception of evil, we need to understand our sovereign boundary and, more importantly, how to cultivate and preserve it and have it aligned with grace, kindness, and the angelic wish to help—the Holy Spirit!

What are the conscious and unconscious? Does consciousness sit in a material pocket? And where does it rest and as what? Electricity? Static electricity circling in cells with a clump of ephemeral sense memory baked into neuron links? No. Things arise in real time, the present only, and we can discuss why. The causes are natural, and the effects are felt, but the present expression of consciousness is the only consciousness there is. Signals trigger what is, not what once was.

Ghosts, thoughtforms, or memories are only as alive as the plasma bodies that generate them allow. In other words, we generate them with our energy and our energy transcends the worldly realm. In this way, imprints are located outside of temporality, affecting a perceiver's mind and body. For us, memory is an imprint that only lives in the present, and in recognizing this, with our full energy, we can transmute and alter its effects on our current state.

The true unconscious is a realm of potential we cannot access; it is not what we know and keep secret from ourselves. It would be better to call it the "one conscious" as it is the ocean of impressions that have yet to be claimed, yet to be impressed.

We call the cosmos a mix of consciousness and energy, which are indistinguishable from each other, but we perceive them as separate through our usual (and now changing) limited dimensionality. Complete access to more dimensionality would not be limited in this way. As a creature becomes more refined and evolved, it gains access to dimensional space; it ceases to perceive time. Eventually, the boundary between projected and received objects dissolves, as does the stability of "true objects." This collapsing of duality between the perceiver and perceived is a marker of enlightenment, and it is the fundamental quality of what and who we called the buddhas.

SEVEN

THE COSMIC CHRIST

....

*Living the Revelatory and
Oracular Inner Path to Salvation*

The Path Emerges

We occupy a unique position in human history—a pivotal space of choice where the fault lines of our preordained charismatics are crumbling away. Our collective fateful visions and the results of our willful actions have come to a zenith. We are all Channelers now. The subtle terrain of the internal and the holographic lines bridging the external enmesh. We expand all of our limbs and heart space while feeling reduced to absurdities by our social planes. The paradoxes are bewildering. The implosion caused by this tension is the generating force of proper evolution. We can apprehend but barely comprehend this development that grips all life features and balloons our consciousness, reestablishing a kingdom of heaven on Earth while exposing the nightmare that's been preying on us all along. This happening is personal and grand, occupying our secret terrains and shared spaces. We are changing. It is changing. Moreover, we are it. The cosmos enlivened through its will to be (see plate 10, Two Worlds).

The Cosmic Christ emerges as salvation and refuge. We reach out if we can muster the humility. We hold our hearts and beg forgiveness not from some capricious, lowly god of judgment but from the Logos that contains all the compassion of the Buddhas. It is the great Dharmadatu—that being, the cosmic mirror, or place where all is made clear. We become that to which we pray, yet we are also its ever-willing servant captured in a blissful, soft hold of grace. Then 5D expands to 12D. In other words, as we integrate our vision of self with a vision of the ultimate in the form of a redemptive force, we accelerate up the scales of reality until we are re-unified into a field of totality after integrating all levels of experience and embodiment. Channeling is simply a way to evolve us and all of humanity!

The twelve dimensions are simply the scaffolding of space illuminated in sound and light by awareness, the word and sight of God's realized mansions.

One for each of us, following our humbled grace; a grace uncovered by piercing the veil of that self-deception energized by Satan.

Do not think of end times as some fearful relic of the self-preservationist instinct inverted, the death wish, but rather as a way of speaking about prophesied spiritual timelines that are inevitable and made succinct through providence. The end of our personas, civilizations, and the shifting energy of our eras, rather than being our destruction, is the gateway to the rebirth, uplift, and redemption made sacred and fundamental to existence.

In these times, one may unconsciously come to worship the Antichrist, the force of absolute delusion and entropy, and believe it is a being state and vision of virtue. One may feel delivered by relativist systems and sensual pursuits of the self. However, therein lies the isolated and indiscrete view.

The spiritual view, as we explored, is in grace, forged in renunciation and repentance. Without these, there is only self-seeking and distraction. Grace has arrived for us all! We have collectively initiated this awareness of grace and taken to it, passing through whatever flames were attracted to our sin. Furthermore, now we shake off the embers to cool and dust off the devil's ash. Our bodies glow in the nexus of our celestial bodies, our wings stretch to meet the pillars of heaven through which they pass, and we observe with compassion and equanimity the fate of our species in repose, grafting into a timeline of potential beyond dreams, the carcass of its former tomb seeded into the soil of a world shaking hands with its soul.

Humans are a conscious form of fractal harmonics expressed in all dimensions, including and beyond time, reflecting in the apparent solidity of the material realm. We are tethered to a manifest realm where our bodies, the story of the Earth, our divine organic sentience, and our individual and collective awareness follow a spiritual, revealed, and moral evolutionary tract.

We are at a juncture of that evolution where an exponential leap corresponds with a heightened challenge to our sovereignty. A milestone where we must each decide our cosmic fate—to embrace our expanding nature or to cower in the husk of our previous capacity and be slaves to the shadow that feeds on stagnation and disconnect. The answer is found in surrendering, opening, breaking, allowing, and praying—specifically to God. Every unfolding moment we can choose to do so.

As integral theory intimates, we integrate each successive state of our psychic evolution and its social, interpersonal, and cultural manifestations with the last. Each stage must shed the one before it, but the previous one weaves into the next. So, as we move from a totemic worshiping, collectivist- and sacrificial-minded hive mode of overlapping monads into a space where the individual atomizes from all other selves and yet sees the Creator as strictly outside of itself (a.k.a. the messianic, strictly devotional, outer God-worship state), we integrate the last stage, and the threat becomes the previous absolutist state of that totemic orientation. In other words, as we found an outer God, we evolved without needing icons. This gave way to the worshiping of pluralistic potentials or syncretic but rational materialist thought.

This, too, has run its course and not just for the usual reasons of linear progressive change. A new outer/inner stimulus tests and transforms us. The larger cycles and machinations of spiritual truth reveal from the inside out and outside in and by looking in both (apparent) directions, we see our expanded role in the cosmos.

In this era, we have made an exponential and dramatic leap whereby our way of perceiving has jumped into a space of extended cognition and perception, and how we apprehend and comprehend conspires and congeals into a physiological form in evolution. In the past, we evolved our sense organs and the gates of perception along with our conceptual frames, but now we have leapt forward in that evolutionary track in an astounding way. Our DNA is the manifestation of a new blueprint, driving us into expanded senses and newly attuned perception.

Humans have often explored how the patterns of light, sound, and metaphysical structuring move through physical phenomena into the planet, subtle energetic fields, our bodies, and our basic DNA. We have long realized how our consciousness capacity has upgraded in conjunction with other interstellar multidimensional bodies such as stars and the fields of the energetic platform that constitute our frames of reference.

All of these overt and subtle forms are now being syncopated and re-rendered at once. Our ability to conceptualize, realize, and integrate our spiritual realities has come into focus, individually and for all. The spiritual domain used to be an accepted but rarely understood truth. It is now both experienced and realized with our cognizing minds. Unlike the sorcerers and occultists who attempted to view God from limited and egoic lenses, we now carry enough divine energetic grace and consciousness capacity to balance knowledge from its rightful domain and wisdom in its living dynamism.

In other words, this stage of evolutionary integral leaping incorporates a new paradigm of thought and of body, which is the emergence of the light body catalyzed by energies flowing through subtle fields beyond the material and into it. The mystery remains, and while comprehension of it will never be the goal, the apprehension and description of the process remains ever unfolding.

The spectral reflection of God expresses all around and within us. A trumpet of fury and peace, the wrathful, ultimately compassionate animating force of the living cosmos now blasts into our realm, awakening our nature to a state very few imagined. Those few are you—the vision holders, grid-anchoring conductors, weather vanes, and lightning rods of the species who have arrived and incarnated just in time to deliver, share, and activate living and pivotal intelligence codes through action, thought, noise, and tone. A priest and priestess class of unfolding angels, bodhisattvas, and blooming beings stretching toward God's light, tearing into that glow, opening hearts, and flooding this realm with the Cosmic Christ, the template of our fruition. Our integrated and delivered potential beyond selfhood and persona is the spirit made flesh enhancing us beyond imagination.

Redemption, unheralded grace, and salvation in spaces of bliss conspire our 2D/3D view, activating our psychospiritual *energenetic* bodies (meaning "energy-propelled genetic patterning"). The still and dynamic point we symbolize as the cross, which is the nexus of all, displays God's glorious apex of truth, the energetic and harmonic omniscience laced within all, producing infinite grace for all to embrace. The reality is that a self-generating consciousness, an alive cosmos activating the continuum of phenomena spiraling upward into integrating all life force, is our birthright. Apprehending this is one thing; comprehending it is another; incorporating it is the challenge; and living it is our gift.

The Dharma Gods of Now

The Dharma is a catchall term for the most profound righteous and holy path. This path has a view, a set of principles, and behaviors. The Buddha laid out the method of renunciation, meditation, and the eightfold path. His expository and storied expression style was delicately presented in thousands of ways. The Dharma is offered for every individual depending on their attributes, readiness, or state of receptivity and awakening.

Emptiness, compassion, the mind-training sciences, and the ways to find an antidote to each poison of our deluded mind of karmically produced misapprehensions of reality are displayed in the three vehicles of Buddhism: the lower, middle, and highest paths.

The lowest path is not a negative term. It is, in fact, the foundational path. It is the way leading to all vehicles of liberation. It is the bedrock of all Hinayana, or Theravada schools. In it we see the observation of the mind and the building of compassion as the goal for gradual enlightenment, steadily peeling away layers to discover an empty center of perfection.

Even if we do not wish to enter any Buddhist path or any path with any name, we are still likely concerned with the mind and spirit. And to integrate and become the highest, most revealed, bliss-filled, and free version of the mind, we must first understand the mind.

The mind has primordial or background structures, archetypes that have shapes and forms, carrying the energies of various transient forces—anger, jealousy, wrath, equanimity, compassion, lust, and so on. The higher schools in Buddhism employ the method of deity worship while recognizing the inherent emptiness of a deity.

In these higher schools, we see these deities as placeholders—shared beings, cogenerated much like Satan, Mara, or any lower being that humans have often mistaken for God. From this awareness, we realize that all is mind produced and stems from energies and properties of interdependent values flowing through and among us and making us up. We will examine how these formations are cogenerated.

The higher Dharma path uses these deity beings or formations and invites us to see them all as manifestations of enlightenment. The energy and karma flowing through someone's mind stream and heart beam are purified by this method. In this way, we turn all into perfection, and the mind realizes the enlightened state in its projected convictions.

Vajrayana is the Tibetan path where we comingle our minds with that of the buddhas, thus allowing the apparition of "I," the egoic self, to recognize our buddha nature—a nature that has gone beyond duality, polarity, or any state of conditioned reality.

The apex Buddhist practice in the many traditions from Dzogchen to Tantra encourages people to take a *yidam*. A yidam is a central figure of worship that is simply a projection. It is interdependent with our minds, a seemingly permanent or solid being but like a shared memory or vision. We see a deity as both resulting from our conjured projections and cogenerated with others.

We supplicate to this being, and we become one with it through a type of enmeshment and reprogramming of our platform psyche. This alchemical practice is, in many ways, a shamanic and occult methodology in that it uses projections and beliefs in lower Gods, deities, and elemental constituent parts as objects of worship.

Icon worship is usually worshiping the created instead of the Creator, which is a faulty path.

Yidam practice, on the other hand, is a way to transmute the worshiped creation into a connection with the Creator until a complete breakdown of that dichotomy erupts. By doing this, we realize all is God, buddha nature, and mind.

Something to examine in strict Buddhist philosophy is the absence of the creator model. Yogic and Vedic traditions and teachers all realize the centrality or interoperability of God(s). In the equation for reality, they leave room for this conceptuality but make no declaration about the nature of God, so like mystical Christianity or Judaism and many indigenous paths, God is the mysterious force central to everything. How we each personify God is a product of human nature and culture—but this is changing. Samsara is revealing itself to many beings now.

And while Buddhism teaches us complete mind transformation so that we are purified and in harmonic integration with totality, seeing through delusion, the hooks of the samsaric realm of cyclic rebirth, and obsessions with the flesh, and so forth, it is devoid of the direct "Creator to the created" relationship.

Nonetheless, buddha nature, the entire enlightened state embedded within sentient beings where all embodied and perceptual resonance is collapsed beyond the subject-object is, in fact, a description of God—the living cosmos.

Many Buddhists would describe buddha nature through the three kayas, or various states of embodiment that our buddha nature may take: sambhogakaya (body), nirmanakaya (force or spirit), and dharmakaya (totality). And this is a way of discussing the triune God of Christianity or a western/Abrahamic mystical read of God as well (see "The Cosmic Christ" section below).

Many would point to the complete perfection of buddha nature as akin to God because it is uncreated and within all. But the heart of a directed and patterned, metaphysically sound cosmos with intelligence and discrete roles for creatures like humans, angels, and demons, and so on, is conceived differently by all yet experienced similarly.

We can avoid the trappings of pagan or relativistic multifractalized God worship. We can see the manifest nature of God as approachable through our objects of worship if we understand the mind and reality. So what should we share our energy with and hold in devotion or worship? The self, another human, a deity? Is the Cosmic Christ the ultimate form to worship? Is he the highest yidam or deity?

The Cosmic Christ

The Christophany, or the ability of God to appear as a form, allows for the Cosmic Christ to manifest much like the Holy Spirit can—in the living unfolding of revelation through each of us and through holy or evolved beings like angels (see plate 11, The Cosmic Christ). Revelation is a temporal expression of ultimate reality coming to life in our human lives. In Buddhism, miracles, precognitions, revelations, and mystical realizations are all part of the Dharma path, so we can say that meeting the Holy Spirit is our awakening being felt and that our nature is holy, and a holy being can be a manifestation of God.

⊗

Revelation is the realization of the holy in human life.

Christian theology and its antecedent religions leading to the one God realization display God in a triune way; namely, the father, the son (Christ), and the Holy Spirit. The father is the point of origin and the unique creative force, the Holy Spirit is the active, essential divine revelatory and personal mobilization, and Christ is the manifest form of God.

Christ, in this way, is clearly the ultimate yidam, or manifest expression of an enlightenment aspect of God. Many argue that this model is a triangle of stable perfection for human uplifting: Creator, spirit, body. The three kayas in Buddhism I mentioned earlier—sambhogakaya, nirmanakaya, and dharmakaya—are similar but inverted. They describe the body, the force or spirit, and the ultimate totality.

It should be stressed that Christ, as a being, energy, and concept alike, is more than a yidam or body of God, ultimate guru, ascended master, worldly buddha, enlightened being, collective mind projection, or demigod.

⊛

Christ is the cosmos manifest and danced into the moral sphere where we are redeemed from our fallen ignorance and delusion into a relationship.

So whether speaking of the triune God model or the three kayas, there is ultimately no difference between the elements: three expressions, one nature.

This relationship we can each have to the Cosmic Christ, especially in this unfolding era, travels beyond the usual path to enlightenment. It brings fast and magical reclamation of our divinity with the simple recipe we humans are conjoined to activate. The spell, sadhana, or invocation is simple. It is an ultimate sacred mantra and prayer. And that prayer carries the signature of the initial prayer, the first sound God uttered, the vibration of the cosmos, the tone of origination, and a vibration begetting form and all resultant movement. That sound is om!

Om—that core sound of the cosmos humming in its self-perception—and our call to Christ become one as we realize that buddha nature manifested is a redemptive and stabilized incarnation through Christ. Shakyamuni Buddha, the Buddha most people are familiar with, and the many buddhas before and after him showed us the way to enlightenment in one lifetime. Christ offers a superpath to salvation through unparalleled compassion for all humans in this time.

Christ is the ultimate state of enlightenment activated for all worlds, in all times. Just as buddha nature pervades the cosmos, Christ is the cosmos positioning itself precisely to aid in the direction of humanity and sentient beings. He does this on the level for us in our mundane reality in an instantly accessible way.

Just as we can say the Buddha Avalokiteshvara's mantra of *om mani padme hum* and connect with that primordial state of buddha being, Christ requires we simply invoke his name with humility. Our request for instant salvation is fulfilled by Christ through an alchemized transmutation of death where he showcases a path to a stabilized heaven realm.

The humbled prayer to Christ differs from a self-empowering path to awakening states or even the path of Vedic/Hindu/Buddhist dharmic ideas of enlightenment. It is the salvation allowed into this world by God through the Cosmic Christ as God, as a man. That closeness, that intimacy is a space that makes the human project of evolution through connection to the loving totality of all that is both sacred and immediate.

We are no longer forced to be transmigrating cosmic splinters trying to rebirth successfully and get off of the karmic wheel of suffering in this life, between lives, or during bardo states of dreamy or nightmarish purgatory. We have a gate, a key, and a state to recognize, and those are the Christ. The church and its adaptive culture and bodies have made a mandala and microcosmic expression of Christ's heaven realm filtered through our mundane minds, but these pale in comparison to the true promise of the Cosmic Christ.

Through the Cosmic Christ, all realms are liberated in our hearts, and we light up with the fire of life and truth. The human being is saved in that prayer where we admit our personal fallen state in detail and with accountability, taking on our responsibility for conduct, thought, and influence, handing over our minds and hearts to the mind and heart of God, rejoining our creator state, and thus becoming forever entwined in the kingdom of heaven. We accept the offer. We are already enlightened and connected to heavenly perception through Christ. The fastest path.

The Dharma of Christ says that while mantras, mind transformations, meditations, or spells may bring comfort or be appendages of our prayer, we no longer need them. None of them are necessary for redemption. No kaleidoscopic retinue of buddhas or spirit guides is required to integrate our nature if we are readied and anointed in truth.

Through the Cosmic Christ, our natures entwine with a being beyond a usual Buddhist enlightenment path, a being that is the alpha and omega of all, delivering bliss without blind struggle or practice, fleeting realization, or change. Christ is the buddha field—the dharmadhatu—disguised as a man. God as a man, sacrificed actually and meant to prevent the further desecration of man; God made ever present and reachable for humans, accessed with the most straightforward and sweetest gesture of our faith, who makes us both human and one with God. Realizing this creates a covenant leading to salvation.

Enlightenment is a state that accepts all phenomenal display, all emotional, mental activity and confusion as well as all bliss, and our mission is to invite this acceptance once and for all. Taking this covenant with the Cosmic Christ can be a goal. Keeping it is our discipline and the cultivation of our garden. To grow that discipline is our work.

The Cosmic Christ is God manifest for us, a lifeline to eternal grace. A being at once physical, temporal, boundless, beyond form, ubiquitous, and personal, Christ is a buddha sharing a face with Maitreya (the future buddha) and Amitabha and yet culturally manifested for us as an energy, and a being. Amitaba, an emanation of

Christ- or Krishna-like energy, has one simple message: the path to enlightenment and liberation is open to all, regardless of the challenges and obstacles presented by this Kali Yuga. His grace is a beacon of light in a world filled with uncertainty and suffering. Amitaba's mantra and mandala offer instant love and compassion, and the potential for transformation that lies within each of us no matter what. His presence is a reminder that even in these complex times, there is always a path to redemption, spiritual advancement, and refuge.

Choosing the Channel of the Cosmic Christ

Channeling in this tremendous era means we are all experiencing more than ever. The knowing state of the Aquarian age means we navigate paradoxical and heterodox truths.

Our embodied psyches, our own narratives, and their inner symbolic worlds mirror outer energetic sensed worlds in unending synchronicity. Our own unfolding parallels the events and energies of the world around us.

If we are ready, the initial integration of an astonishingly profound evolutionary jump now galvanizes us within our perceived interiors and abounding exteriors. We can feel it. The galloping precipitation of new energies raining down on our world and planet increases our awareness. All old thinking frames, manifest thoughtforms, and systems now crumble as we peer into the horizon of a newly vivified terrain.

This new horizon extends in an omnidirectional pattern beyond the wildest dreams of our anterior, or more obvious previous state of being. Third- and fourth-dimensional habits are squeezed into a fifth-dimensional knowing shape guiding us up the helix-like ladder through the dimensions encoded in our DNA, stamped into our core mind, and activated through our heart.

The jump is different for us all. Some will resist, some will spiritually perish, and others will flourish.

⊛

As spiritually awakened souls, or embodied angels awakening, we have a responsibility and gift to help usher in this Christic era of self-illumination. The crystal-clear, full-spectrum tonal hum of our higher Earth state is the retuned energy of the savior force.

Securing and opening new portals, closing old ones, expunging the dark parasitic forces, and supporting the established grids, anchors, energy bodies, mandalas, and families in our dimensional scope around, within, and upon the Earth is our honor and our work.

We must each learn the beautiful art of Channeling God's will for our human template. The Holy Spirit conjoins here and now through our moral purity and rebirthed hearts. We invite the Cosmic Christ to return when we open this new Channel. Our redemptive, sanctified, anointed rising requires a discerning method and clarity. We start where we are with surrender and willingness.

Humans manifest as perfect, organic, animal-like beings mixed with realized celestial energy bodies. Our species is a psychospiritual genetic mix of various galactic races (distributed among the human families), differing in developmental trajectories and directions of evolution in capacity, form, temperament, and thought.

The physics of our local universe are consistent and conform to laws, but the conditions needed to support total chakra organics—the materially manifest black holes or openings that the chakras allow between the organic, elemental embodied world and the higher or more complex, finer dimensions—such as ours are delicate. The human template, geometrically illustrated in a five-pointed star or the Vitruvian Man, requires a planet exactly like ours—our carbon bodies, plasma concentration, and atmospheric requirements are fickle.

Our planet is a superbeing whose own consciousness is as old as this universe. Her body has been protected and nourished by benevolent helpers for just as long. Our soul's free will battles through our organic, impulsive, instinctual processes and high capacities as it likewise manages the dual struggle with light and dark, life and death, God and Satan. This is the evolutionary pressure enjoyed and accepted by blessed eternal angelic minds and hearts. The kind of hearts we each have.

> ✪
>
> The Cosmic Christ is activated in this psychic age where unfolding access to upper dimensions is animated and embodied by humanity and our celestial family.

We can transmit the direct codes or qualities of unfolding mind, body, and spirit states through an evolving language and faith-based revelatory tone.

We dive into the self-liberated devotional awakening of the Holy Spirit, realizing the culmination of the various messianic ages, the prophetic Channels of our highest beacons realized here and now for us each and all. We see this yuga of Kali enmeshed with the Christic era of our world system. Its eschatological foundation becomes apparent—our return, our self-unveiling, and God's subsequent revelation of evolution for our species through the Cosmic Christ being, the avatar and spirit.

Our mission: recognize the energenetic timeline and our role in stabilizing and saving our planet, galaxy, and universe across all etheric, astral, and physical layers within the perfect cosmos by accepting a preordained mystical order while navigating the chaotic winds of free will, grace, and evil itself.

Holding our hearts we return to self-love beyond the mundane self. We hold our cosmic eternal, all-dimensional heart here and now, saying, "I am love. I am buddha nature revealed, I am pure love. I am life. I am. Thank you, love. Thank you, Christ. Amen." Simple, straightforward truth. This is what the soul knows through the material and energy body of "I."

From ancient, pre-Atlantean eras across diverse worlds, often echoed in misunderstood sacred texts, is a call to connect with the Cosmic Christ—a plea for redemption and our highest nature. This sentiment permeates Mesopotamian mythology and its descendants, resonating through time.

Truly, truly, I say to you, before Abraham was, I am.
JOHN 8:58

---

which summarizes the truth of the Cosmic Christ: he is active beyond time and space. A nontemporally bound, nonterrestrial being—nothing like a human prophet and yet also that. The Cosmic Christ was, is, and will be ever present for all expressions of the cosmos in its comings and goings, beginnings, and endings, manifesting for humanity as a stabilized being on his throne of redemption, refuge, and security for our race. We must observe this return now to aid the arriving eon of spiritual upgrading.

So what is this comic being who is beyond concept yet present, is manifested on Earth, is capable of instant personal relating and infinite love, and is the absolute gate to redemption and salvation from our fallen state? How is the Cosmic Christ so specifically present now?

The Great Spirit/Source/buddha nature/God's primordial heart combines stasis and movement as one. Just as anything in our cosmos has been observed, it has also moved. It has a masculine aspect, which has direction and propelling quality, and it has a feminine dynamic of grandiosity and wild potential, which is beyond being trackable.

The great womb is the totality of all phenomena and the premanifest expressed in a hyperactive stasis of tension. It is often called the MP ΘΥ, or Theotokos (the Virgin Mary)—the mother of all, or the feminine aspect laced within and around all. Many cultures have located the feminine as the core darkness of premanifest quantum potentials.

Movement, or vibration, generates form through expressions of geometric harmony, sound symmetry, and the waves of sonic vibration entangled to manifest. God is realized next as light, the spectral heat of movement reflecting on these sonic forms, dispersive without beginning or boundary, including intelligence and desire transmitted and received as personal love. This is the Cosmic Christ's energy.

The feminine offers a womb of action for the masculine to activate through. And when the masculine and feminine spin in tension, there is birth activity. From here, we see movement and form, embodiment. Eventually, we see the highest expression of manifest masculine compassion and feminine wisdom in the Cosmic Christ. The Cosmic Christ owes everything to the feminine ground of the infinite. In this way, the masculine fulfills the directives of the feminine. Humans are healed through this rebirth process when they accept the Cosmic Christ, ensuring the continuation and growth of our life force.

⊗

God as life force and light is open brilliance and presence, emanating what we experience as only absolute love, unconditional acceptance, compassion, care, and warmth.

The intelligence of complete fundamental activity of both form's dance and the formless mirror the state of reality. This intelligence tells us that we thrive best without a need or want by resting in harmony with all illumination of God's mind. The Cosmic Christ, this perfected state is stressed so much here because Pleiadian wisdom *is* the Cosmic Christ integrated. And that is the state of reality we are moving toward.

PRAYER

God Dwells Within

Hold your hand on your upper heart and say the following aloud or to yourself:

God, the divine flame of pure love and awareness, is within. Right now. We give thanks for life and protect and dedicate ourselves to its sanctity. We value this precious life.

Thank you.

Maranatha. Amen. Omah-ha-ohhh. Bless me. Bless you. Bless all.

The Prism of Phenomena

We've examined the general tone of our energetic era, the new way to see Christ as buddha and beyond, the ways to conceive and manage this era conceptually, and the nature of surrender and humility. We've looked at the totality of emptiness and phenomena as one, the form and formless realms of mind and manifest worlds. We've examined all of this as an overview, but let's look closer now at the arena we find ourselves moving through dimensionally.

We can imagine all possible dimensions of phenomena, from the highest finest to the lowest crudest, including the organic, as a prism.

Sound and light eventuate universes of dimensional densities. Lower densities contain matter in its least-heated, or least-active, forms, as in being further from the heat of absolute connection, love, and unification. Objects such as planets and the life on them occupy these dimensions, including the unseen or etheric realms surrounding them.

Our world is slow moving and teeters between entropy and evolution in the third and fourth dimensions. The upper dimensions surrounding these planets shimmer with the potential these physical worlds carry. Our job is to eclipse the lower with the higher. Essentially, we must bring heaven or the pure lands to Earth.

No matter the density of our realm, the light of God, or the life force principle, shines onto and within this prism, sending reflective beams in all directions. Every beam that lands on a surface of phenomena allows that surface to incorporate and realize its own form; its self-reflection is animated by God as light. All objects once observed have been co-realized between God and a splinter of God, a being like us. This is what quantum physics points to: the observed becomes realized, and the observer is included in that equation.

If we are each self-realizing beings, who come to life when we employ our capacity to observe self and other, then what is the quality of our observation? What is the quality of the objects we observe? What level of conscious expression has brought them to life? How much consciousness has infused our perception, animating our environment and the phenomena we perceive? These questions ask us to notice the coevolving world and the dimensions we can inhabit as sentient beings.

⊕

That self-realizing form or body we call "self" perceives through the level of conscious size or intensity wrought by that beam of light we see as emanating from God, or Source.

The level we can appreciate dictates the quality of what illuminates our self-awareness. Like a prism, we reflect, metabolize, and inflect that light, and thus we are the architects of the world or dimensions we can inhabit.

As the prism of phenomena, including our bodies, incorporates more light, life force, or God, it becomes more refined and better able to reflect more spectral layers of light through and off itself. The paradox is that we are that very light beam, yet we are also self-illuminated through it.

Each life force, or light upgrade to our ability to self-realize our form and capacity, expands our field of awareness and embodied nature. Our senses and our cognition and connection to the light expand, illuminating our awareness. God is light, and we become full of light as we expand our awareness through the prism's reflection.

Our forms, our bodies, reveal themselves in ever-refined ways in that spectral light as it expands. We become more of light, of God. As humans, we are carbon-based organic beings of light and vibration, little electromagnetic nuclear reactors, and this God light penetrates and activates our DNA, our mitochondrial and cellular base, defining our capacity for processing phenomena. We are healed and nourished, evolved and enlivened by God.

As our DNA is triggered into flourishing by the prism's beamed upgrades, it is released into its potential as it is enlightened, and the blueprints for our higher embodiment are revealed. The geometric synchronistic perfection of our forms harmonizes with the vibration and light signatures on offer in our higher dimensional environments.

Redemption and Realization

We are each sentient and self-determining energy navigators with free will as far as our awareness permits. As we become more aware, we tap into the primordial loving template of our cosmos, the Cosmic Christ. In this way, our awareness and our realization of love are expanded.

> ⊛
>
> The Cosmic Christ is the gateway to our full realization
> and actualization of spiritual potential and salvation from
> the fallen state of lower awareness and less
> activated manifestation.

The fallen state is the lower dimensionality cycle that has befallen this realm and locked us in a spectral density we must unleash ourselves from at this time. Though we are predestined to liberate and actualize our total redemptive freedom and potential, we must each choose and aid others in doing so as well. We choose this moment and again in each moment forward. By reaching into our perceived past, admitting what was, changing it by the power of forgiveness and through the embodied mantra of Om, or any proper Holy Mantra, we feel love in our hearts and connect to our open field of reception. This is true Channeling.

This fallen state is what we feel as our mundane experience of caging and enslaving entropy, Satan. Furthermore, while we have been taught recently to avoid binary thought or dualisms, this God vs. Satan deal is indeed the local or 3D-4D mechanics of what we are navigating. These energies are polarities that activate each other and yet are not equal or "all the same" in this realm. Goodness, primordial love, and the light and sound of God are the truth, and they are always available; the lie is that they are not.

Our challenge is to realize more light, more conscious expansion, while fighting the temptation toward an obsession with our sensual limits and an addiction to dramas of the fleshly world and the illusory realms of ghostly forms found in the astral realm, the two worlds where Satan, or the great mind-perpetuating illusion, presides. We each confront a personal lineage embedded in our energenetic and physical bodies. Despite the occult and New Age mesmerization with these astral spirit states, they are often dangerous playgrounds for which we need the Holy Spirit to enter safely.

Our work is to embrace the Cosmic Christ, redeem ourselves individually, ascend our world system, protect our planet, and bring the Christic energy to all corners of the cosmos. We do this individually by embracing the Holy Spirit and by becoming galactic, universal, cosmic angels of love and righteous goodness. The Pleiadian Channel simply and joyfully reminds us of this anytime we tap into it.

The nature of the Cosmic Christ is mirrored up and down micro and macro forms. Our bodies, the natural physical world from quarks to quasars, and the thought patterns, moods, or energies of the embodied mind and heart echo in infinite but cohesive manifestation. This is all purified and upgraded into remanifestation when we release ourselves into the salvation of energetic and conscious realization. Acceptance brings healing and evolution. We may conceptualize these truths, but to truly have our "ah-ha moment" takes opportunities.

God. The cosmos we infer, observe, and express, is a being itself, and we are reflected splinters of that being containing its entirety. Our universe, home galaxy, and the twelve dimensions of perception, movement, and energy that make up our local manifest reality are distinct expressions that act as templates, or models, for our bodies and minds.

Our universe, both in its physical and metaphysical laws, is one of rules or constants presenting a choice space every moment where an energetic, moral, or choice-based dilemma—or opportunity—awakens in us. The living force itself, the supernal organization of celestial mechanics illuminating our potential and seed—the Christic heart-mind (which is buddha nature)—is the direction laid out in eschatological revelations if appropriately decoded. We decode Christic energy by fearlessly observing our own limited thought patterns and habits and surrendering them.

The path to spiritual knowledge and inner awakening for any being, which organizes in the body and through our sovereign conscious intention born of concentration and wisdom, is found in embracing the externally ordered Logos and our internal Logos as one. This Logos is the acceptance and realization of the underpinning Christic pattern and frequency of love governing and emanating in all spheres where life thrives.

The triune cosmogony of father, the Christ, and the Holy Spirit shows us the totality of redemptive energy beyond form, death, and duality and points toward the way humans relate to the Godhead and the Great Mother beyond this. Gates and keys to full integration with the Cosmic Christ and navigating the symphonic scales of enlightenment define our paths naturally as the new template of energy and consciousness as one arrives.

✪

The Cosmic Christ, the template for our physical, moral, and energetic forms, now glows and reemerges in this ecstatic evolution just as the world begins to seem darker.

The pattern of life that the Cosmic Christ invites upgrades our planet, world system, timelines, and embodied capacity.

We are entering the galactic wheel's layer, where redemption and the cleansing of all take place with frightening speed. In each galaxy exists a magnificent spiral of multidimensional activity, resembling the torus field—an infinite cycle of movement and evolution. All darkness has been thwarted, and all that has been prophesied of what is to come will be actualized. It will be interpreted through the living, evolving cosmos of our determination and cogeneration.

As we each navigate this locally manifest cosmic wave, we find ourselves in the era of Kali Yuga, an entropic era, hurtling toward the core of the galactic apple. It is a paradox. We are both flung away from the universe's center and drawn toward our galaxy's core. In this eons-long galactic cycle, we experience moments of reuniting with our primordial awareness, while also evolving into more complex beings dependent on where we are in relationship to these celestial stations. This intricate dance of complexity and entropy offers us the opportunity for self-evolution as we navigate the competing orders within the galactic wheel. It is a journey of DNA upgrades, conscious expansion, and the opening and closing of our heart chakras as we strive to find balance amidst the chaos, which is just competing orders! As we move further from the start of the universe, we gain complexity, allowing us to self-describe, sense, encapsulate and empower ourselves as complex systems. It is a delicate balance between destruction and creation as we find our place within the grand design of many cosmic wheels. And so, we continue to evolve, guided and navigating through the layers of complexity and consciousness as we journey toward the goal of freedom from any and all constraints.

But the process must still unfold without predetermined force. We are to become strangers in our own houses as change arrives; reembodied and awakened on a psychospiritual and totally energetic level from our mitochondrial expression to the subtle fields encasing and emanating from our forms through time and space. It is a complete shedding of the old, on all planes of experience, and an uplifting to a state beyond previous imagination. This is available to each of us if we so choose.

The body shows us this upgrade here and now. Each movement is a mindful gesture of our devotion, grace, gratitude, creative freedom, bliss, and ability to bless. Our breathing, moving, feeling, and self-observing life force is the gate to liberation. We experience it all through the messages of pain, pleasure, bliss, exhaustion and through subtle examples of evolution: ringing, buzzing, vibrations and disturbances. We can only pray with the energy gained in this realm of experience. Our body shows us our energy level.

Transcending the Sensory Playground

The mind and heart of the spiritual template on offer in this era can be tracked through a historic, syncretic connection to many lineages. We can read the new map and embrace the territory by honoring and pursuing goodness, grace, and a relationship to God, the Great Spirit, or our buddha nature.

God's quality can be discovered in all, ever awakened through our surrendered hearts and purified perception. In the emerging cosmological view, unveiling dimensions reveal the supreme nexus of evolution on Earth and beyond for humanity and all benevolent souls. Mother Earth and Father Sky are conjoined, and a new Eden on our planet, across all of its expressions, is glowing into view. The lower version of Earth will feel this as well but will shield its full expression. This book may continue to exist in the future when you inhabit a lower expression on Earth, and yet this book exists now, as millions of awakened souls and buddha fields, and celestial gates currently exist on the Earth you inhabit.

Counter to this upgrading process, however, is the beclouded energy of lies and shadow that has also been dispatched with manifest power to obscure this arising era.

We must use our frames of language and raw awareness alike to peer through the delusion and lies that would have us slump with spiritual exhaustion, shame, and doubt.

Lies that tell us to be something else. The shadow feeds on these lies because it is a vacuum and the inversion of where our awareness grows. This unaware holding pattern of the shadow supports the inflated ego.

The inflated or deflated ego is like an echo chamber of self-reifying or calcifying tension baked into the human nervous system and pulsing into the subtle body, which is the delusional, ignorant persona's sense of self-protection. It cradles this shadow in a symbiotic dance. We can call the ego the "little I."

The ego is not all shadow, though. It is helpful for us as these sensing, organic creatures. This "little I" steers us around in 3D or 4D space-time, which we need to survive, evolve, and learn in this world system. However, simultaneously and detrimentally, it keeps us locked in the influence field of lower energies flowing up from the denser and more chaotic realms. As life itself evolves beyond the ego's perceptual constraints, it becomes more harmonious. It becomes full of fractal cohesion, rippling through our body, movements, thoughts, and affects we each dance with. If we flow with life, our ego dances our consciousness and awareness to bliss and back up to God.

The higher dimensions are fluid and creative order realms that shine with synchronicity and flourishing joy. The lower dimensions are realms of struggle, suffering, disconnect, and pain that begets further pain, and they are challenging to break free from or integrate and transmute. We can see how the ego is an example of dense dimensional expression. Its connection to the third dimensional material, physical body means it is constantly responding to perceived stimulus and defining itself through this reactivity.

The pursuit of evolution comes through surrender and humility to principles that transcend simply managing the manifest and dense sphere of the pain body. Compassion, willingness, open-mindedness, humility, joyful motivation, dignity, and other principles and states are needed. The sensory playground must be surpassed for spiritual growth to take hold. Surrender begets humility, humility produces grace, grace begets faith, and faith has a face. That face is our highest manifestation—a perfected DNA signature being—where our body can hold all twelve dimensions of experience and stay in form.

That body is a celestial, angelic buddha body, arriving and dissolving as needed in time, stable beyond form and time, present in all points of experience, in all phenomena. The Pleiadians are close to this perfection.

The expunging of defiled mental and energetic patterns, recognized through inner view and anointed Holy Spirit infusions, allows for our redemption and accelerated arrival into this new dimensional capacity. This occurs on Earth and within the human template at this time.

The Cosmic Christ stands before us as we realize our divinity and capacity. We are "saved," stabilized in a new covenant of eternality and joy as we accept the compact between God and humankind reawakened.

Channeling (or simply connecting to) the higher realms requires the most profound surrender to softening—true reconciliation with our nature, repentance of our former patterns, and the established reconnection to the Holy Spirit.

We must halt our degrading habits of body and mind. Through devotional supplication to higher expressions of life and consciousness, we activate our growth and transcend our lowly energenetic dis-ease.

The wreckage that trauma and peek sensual experiences have imprinted on our nervous system, cellular, genetic activations, and subtle body resonance becomes healed. We transcend spiritual death and the temporal, temporary, relative worldly realms of chaos. The Holy Spirit purifies karma, cleans the subtle/energy body, speaks as soul, gels connection to all divinity, and establishes or reestablishes our higher fractal cohesion and orders of harmony as we turn inside out and become the energy of God expressed.

This is the dimension of the returned, animated, and extra-present Cosmic Christ. The original manifestation of God on Earth and far beyond. Since the origin of this cosmos, the Christ has presided. The Holy Spirit, embodied in a distinct form, is revealed for each of us as we achieve understanding and the grace to receive. A Christophany arises for us here, for if we Channel the Holy Spirit, then we also express the Christ nature as seed or in bloom. The three forms of God and the three aspects of buddha nature all unite within us as we realize our hearts and the state of ultimate reality.

So how do we practice or activate this true humility required to step into this grace? It is challenging to address because we are each under the delusional belief that we are already "good." We believe that by being "good enough," by striving and through self-reconciliation and other mundane psychological acrobatics, we have made the grade, and we can now sit back and wait for the riches of eternity to present themselves. Or we believe that after death all will be purified and clarified in some magical rapture where we are rewarded, all the while ignoring the sacrifice and alchemy of true salvation that has been offered.

This extends to all expressions and beliefs where a will to power without rigorous attenuation to the path of redemption is at play, especially those on offer in the New Age. The attitude here is one divorced from a metaphysical compact made between us and divinity, which has been revealed. The idea that one should strive for a spiritual destination built on "self-empowerment" is an inversion of spiritual truth. The true miracle is our capacity to accept and embrace the now super-present energy of salvation. That salvation has always been offered in this world. It is always present and shall be until all is purified. The Christ—the being, energy, and truth we have discussed—is as ever-present as the sun, moon, sky, and awareness of these.

Often bypassed in the spiritual community is the act of repentance, or the admission of our true state—a state of confusion, grief, and hope—and the humble request for forgiveness. These themes sow confusion and repulsion in many, which is a shame because heartfelt repentance is the vulnerable, body-expanding, precise method for entering the higher realms. The ego shrinks when we enter the virtuous fold of repentance, absolution from God (at once within and outside of us), and disciplined conduct and focus while remaining compassionate, joyful, and free. Prayer is a miraculous alchemical technology of perfection that humans can enact. Humans know that we must activate humility with effort.

This is a delicate matter, as we seek not to accentuate shame. We must continually assess our thoughts, conduct ourselves on a fundamental level of impeccable discipline and yet, also express joyful humor and grow into our softest most upright selves. Our nature is absolutely sacred, and our capacity to expand into a larger body of consciousness can be entirely accepted, accentuated, and healed simultaneously. We can accept ourselves and better ourselves by admitting and staying in the truth. Additionally, it is a misconception that we must not ask for energy, forgiveness, and so on, outwardly. We are in constant relations with the exteriorly perceived cosmos, and even if it is an illusion and shared projection, it is the projection we can work with in order to heal and evolve the fine layers of self we apprehend as ours.

We are also in a relationship with forces beyond our immediate awareness that help, nurture, and save us from ourselves. However, people generally believe their own egoic minds will liberate them, as if the obscuration causing the suffering could free itself. But this is not so. And not only is this egoic striving through self-seeking for eventual liberation silly thinking, but it is also dangerous. It sets the bar way too low. So low that this delusion cages us into the mesmerization of self-worship cycles of despair and truly corrosive pride. We can call this belief Mara's or Satan's playground. If we are on the path to self-worship, we have been compromised and must heal.

If we believe that good works or utilizing lower powers like sensual treats, cold, calculating knowledge or capacity, fame, prestige, popularity, or hoarded abundance gives us access to eternal spiritual life, then we dement the power of God made present for humans.

We could attempt to self-clean our karma and our souls by realizing the defilements and stuck places, traumas, and curses on our own simply through our mundane knowledge or ego, but even with the help of mediums, healers, and so on, we would be flailing and ignoring the spiritual miracle of salvation on offer.

We have lost the divine compass that guides us to grace in the present, stabilized for eternity and in relationship with higher energy. If we have been saved and electrified by the Holy Spirit, then we have already been delivered! And our work, then, is to be of service.

And if we still need to find that Holy Spirit of salvation or have genuinely forgotten it, then a path is illuminated for us with the most precise light. A door has already been made available! It is the lynchpin on which all other parts of the path hang. Let this idea detonate: We are all redeemed through our humble devotion and connection to our true nature, which is the Cosmic Christ.

But no magic, self-realization, self-initiated enlightenment, self-deifying, or self-worship can bring us to God. And neither can good moral activity alone.

Not by works, so that no one can boast.
EPHESIANS 2:9

Instead, and perhaps obviously, we get to God simply by accepting God's love. The God within and without, who people wish to project, is the Holy Spirit activating through our own karma or story. We do not claim the Holy Spirit as our own. It is not personally generated. It is ever-omnipresent love that we *Channel into action* by our grace-embodied here and now, each in unique ways.

Grace is the state of truth, insight, flow, and gentle connection to our unsullied nature. The energy that grace emits is healing. It links us to the higher realms where order and creative expression of that symmetry are in symphonic display. Grace is the inner human tonal resonance of manifest freedom.

Buddha nature, or God, is awakened stillness, and grace is our path to it. Grace is an energy that connects us and can never be trammeled unless we renounce it. In our ignorant state, we sully the boundary unless we become it, singular and yet distinct. Channeling the Holy Spirit reveals our nature in everlasting communion with God, the absolute refuge.

The Cosmic Christ is available to us if we deeply internalize and realize that he is God presented in the flesh to overcome the flesh. A worldly manifestation of divinity. A quantum spark connecting us to this Christic energy lives in perfection showcased and expressed through virtuous action and righteous speech—but this will not offer us enlightenment, it will simply ready us for dissolving the good self and recognizing divinity.

There are as many buddhas in the cosmos as we can imagine, a billion buddhas can fit on the head of a pin, so they say. And many human self-realized beings existed on Earth long before Gautama, or Shakyamuni Buddha in our recent past. The buddha body, speech, and mind are Christ discovered. When we enter this covenant, we ignite the rainbow body process. The flame of the rainbow body is realized for each of us and for all through one God-man. The Christ is energized and visualized by billions of minds. As such, he is a force for us to tap into. He is a being who opens faith and propels action. He is a portal to divinity.

This last statement above is a relatively uncontroversial Christian doctrine, but it demands reappraisal because our current Western spiritual culture is antimystical Christian. It is fed by the demiurgic, or fallen, confused energy of misaligned focus and degrading influences that pretend to offer freedom but instead constrain us to materialistic vices, shame, and relative temporal suffering. Our culture is one where buffet spiritualism in the name of self-improvement has divorced us from the esoteric underpinnings and power heralded and ever animated in the most ancient lineages on Earth (and elsewhere)—the Cosmic Christ.

The personal experience of the Holy Spirit and the testimony this elicits illuminates our self-deception. Counter to that fallen state of mind is the realization of our capacity for self-deception, self-worship, and laziness, among other defaults of thinking.

The Cosmic Christ arrives, fully embodied on Earth as an energy beyond any mundane or local occult, pagan, mystic-gnostic, church worship of lower deities or idols. It is the life force and wisdom itself. A standard! By working with this standard, we can see our confusion and egoic state of energy and mind. Channeling this state is the bedrock of our capacity as mystic beings of this time.

Undoubtedly many readers will be triggered by this; others will be confirmed. Many people are currently enthralled with lower gods. Or they obsess over the *siddhis* (mystical powers), and the sense of having attributes bestowed by other complex hierarchies of ancestral earthly beings. They play in the etheric nets of the worldly plane and will go into veritable spasms or recoil at the mention of the Christ. I suggest they review what the Cosmic Christ truly is and what it is not.

The discomfort one might experience with the idea of the Christ results from the language, and confusions produced and abused by institution and culture, and by the demon of deception, which writhes in the body, desiring spiritual destruction. This demon enjoys any spiritual distraction that pulls us away from purification and anointed holy living. It thrives on ignoring that buddha nature—the truth we all carry.

The demons of our overlapping dense worldly realms have run wild over our minds and bodies. These include a vast pantheon of nefarious pandimensional extraterrestrials, familiar ancestral spirits, interdimensional entities, dislocated souls, and angry collective elementals or forces of entropy, all of which we will explore in the coming chapters.

Channeling in this time is being open to the Holy Spirit and witnessing the presence of the Cosmic Christ. Do you wish to endlessly cycle through what many call samsara, the lower realms, or a projected and manifest hell for eternity, occasionally adding some new fleeting armor built on pride because of insight, some sensual distraction, or fading understanding?

Or do you wish for eternal life beyond concept, in and beyond heaven, transcending imagination, and already made available? A space and place where all dimensions coexist, form and nonform at once, bliss and connection to omniscience and love entwined. More than a separate space for transmigrating souls, this is also the path for Earth herself. The pure lands of heaven and the many states of mind and heart await us when we stop seeing reality through our stained lenses of self-regard and desire.

The Many Faces of the Christ

There is much to say about the Christ—the avatar, the historical human, and the lineage of beings who inhabited that incarnation stretching back before Atlantis. The king of angels, the collective energy we call the Christ, is many things. The epistemology, or foundation, of how we consider reality for many depends on the vision of the Christ as the sole expression of God incarnate sent to resurrect the dead and propagate a glorious heaven on Earth and eternal salvation for the soul. There is truth in this, but the Christ template has been used and weaponized by the forces of confusion, ignorance, and darkness through iconography and a storyline they have mutated. The institution of the church is clearly a human one subject to the degraded and fallen nature of humanity. It has been a process returning to grace.

The true church body is the body of the Christ, which is the body we each contribute to and is the Holy Spirit manifest.

The Christ is the very face of God that humanity can recognize within. From an Akashic or Channeling point of view, we see the Christ as the eternal apex of the human being's higher manifestation collectively expressed and sublimated into an individual that becomes a locus of that energy. He is a living being generated by our projection and divine will to see and experience this manifestation come to full bloom in ourselves and in the narrative of human affairs in our world. We each carry the Christic potential, the buddha nature, the seed of God. Many people share an intimate energetic signature soul grouping with the Christ as a family member-like being. For many of us the Christ is God, and this is the best way to perceive him. The total force of life and love, the beginning and ending beyond all.

Each celestial species has a relationship with its Christic nature. The Cosmic Christ for Pleiadians is the crescendo expression of their God nature and is almost identical to our Christ in appearance. This is what energizes the Christ across the cosmos. For all advanced sentience, the Cosmic Christ is the peak expression of expression itself. The embodiment of God, of Love. The story and the mythos that beings in linear time use to describe this vary from culture to culture and world to world, but the energy is the same. And the Christ being is very real in that it is a force that connects sentient beings like humans or Pleiadians to the absolute divinity of omniscient love and life, which we each carry.

Angels and Angles

The early Lemurian and Atlantean civilizations that predated Mu and eventually led to the post-Egyptian, Hebrew (Kabbalistic), and Greek gnostic traditions extended their spiritual technology to a sequence of grids around our world system and planet with ties to various galactic and dimensional stations. They described the local angelic realms as deriving from and being comprised of dimensional beings fractalizing "up" and away from our sphere of perception into more grand spaces.

> ✹
>
> Angels can be conceived of and known as layers of energy and earthly astral stations embodied in grand light-mind-body forms.

They are both seemingly independent beings and also states of our own heart-mind.

As discussed in chapter 4, Metatron, which can be thought of as a type of grid-system holder, a being, and a geometric form, is the highest manifest local mind, a sort of manager and layer of sentience and geometric embodiment governing the angelic realms, which can be perceived phenomenally by humans as the inversion of the demiurge to some and its manifestation to others, the tree of knowledge manifest.

Below Metatron are the archangels, Michael, Raphael, Gabriel, and the like, each stewarding a layer of space-time where human energy bodies can tread in a Merkabah, the "chariot" that transports the etheric aura body to the celestial realms. The Elohim, the lesser angels who are part human, part other terrestrial, bridge these higher beings/aspects of awareness and our own embodied state and serve to give us a cultural and moral direction to aim for. That is, of course, if we see them as benevolent and not obscuring our own trajectory as unique 12D creatures.

The historic gnostic tradition of thought, while enticing, still places too much emphasis on distinguishing the material from the spiritual and observing all as a symbolic container or allegory. It fails to see with mystical eyes that which is alive and present in all. It lacks the Holy Spirit.

Plate 1. *The New Earth*
New solar codes, the Earth, and all sentient beings in our galaxy are undergoing
a polarity flip, as higher, deeper dimensions of reality come into view.
A demand to change and rebirth with greater will is at hand.
A window is opening.

Plate 2. *The Rainbow Body*

When sufficient stabilization of the microcosmic orbit of winds and pranic
energy's flow has occurred for a being, a rainbow of energetic layers appear.
The subtle body's layers are freed from all defiled impressions and the
auric fields are expressed in tandem with the reflective refraction across all
dimensions—just like a rainbow. The three kayas, or layers, of nondual
experience into enlightenment express within a being.

Plate 3. *Buddha Prajnaparamita*
The perfection of wisdom, Prajnaparamita embodies the truth of emptiness,
interdependence, samsara, and nirvana as one. She manifests as an accessible,
total, intuitive, subtle knowing mind, and as a discrete being herself—
a solar being of megalithic size and pure compassion.

Plate 4. *Kundalini Twin Flame*

Both the kundalini awakening and the true twin flame phenomena follow the expansion-ascension process we are undergoing as a species. While the kundalini is the devastatingly powerful act of mental, embodied, spiritual opening, and purging for a being, the twin flame dynamic is a complex dance between two beings producing similar events and process. Both phenomena are rapidly entwining for more beings at this time.

Plate 5. *DNA*

DNA is more than a polymer or braid of data. It is more than semicrystalline proteins, or sequences, at a root. It is a combination of sensed impressions baked into molecular, atomic, and subatomic processes. DNA is the blueprint and activator. Because our bodies, minds, and spirits are entwined, it is the code-flower being unfurled even further at this time to showcase our potential through the incoming light activations.

Plate 6. *The Pleiadians*

The Pleiadians are not gods, demons, or buddhas, or material beings. They are a sentient humanoid race of spiritual adepts. They manifest as both a collective and as individuals and have deep resonance and history with the human race. They are accessible through the same channeled capacities and paths as we reach the Akashic Records.

Plate 7. *The Akashic Records*

The Akashic Records are the living library and layer of energy, mind, and body-sense-produced conscious imprints made accessible when we clear our obscurations and feel into spaces we have been blocked from.

Plate 8. *Dimensions*
Everything is mind-produced. As we collectively perceive and cognize,
we animate various layers of reality. Dimensions of manifestation.
Those layers exist all at once here and now, yet they are each accessed
through a refinement of feeling and perception.

Plate 9. *The Incarnation Wheels*

In Vedic and Buddhist cosmology, there are six prime realms of samsara and six realms of deluded perception. Beyond this, within each there are many layers of metaphysics active in the material world's physics. We incarnate based on our perception level, the level of our conscious expansion and stabilization. These incarnations and rebirths are nest-like wheels within wheels.

Plate 10. *Two Worlds*

The saturnal, satanic realm of Mara is the spell of the material world. It is the obsession with the senses and sensual pursuit, gain, and pleasure. It is where the spirit is harvested and trapped. The internal world where we finally see all the constellations and activities of form as mind representations is the path to freedom from this delusion. We work with heavenly bodies and beings simply as lamps to light the path to the here and now where liberation for our planet and all other worlds.

Plate 11. The *Cosmic Christ*

The Cosmic Christ is an avatar for the divine Logos, or mind, of all phenomena
offering the redemptive energy of grace, forgiveness, and acceptance.
It is simultaneously a quality of reality and a being with the enlightened
state of buddha nature revealed. The ultimate buddha for our world.
The Cosmic Christ personifies compassion during our difficult era.
It exists premanifest, but it also manifests in beings as examples
of the cosmic template.

Plate 12. *Saturn Satan*

Nothing is uniformly "good" or "bad" in ultimate reality. All is a reflection of perception's constraints. But the saturnal energy is highly concentrated with dense control frequencies, and so it is associated with Mara and other systems of entropy and destructive power. Satan is a being who manifests mind-energy connected to this control nexus.

Plate 13. *Arcturian Ambassador*

The tone of the Arcturian is a particular one. They are a type of humanoid sentience wielding advanced consciousness-assisted tech. Neither benevolent or malevolent, they are interested in harmonic resonance, materiality, and light-bending in order to open portals, build, and travel.

Plate 14. *The World Grids*
Electroharmonic light resonance flowing out as our bodies' tones, specified by our
thoughtform patterns, dictates the grid of geometric "fences" girding the planet.
Angular reductive thoughts produce a cage around our world,
where harmonic, generous, and grace-filled thoughts
resonate a protective flower grid encircling the globe.

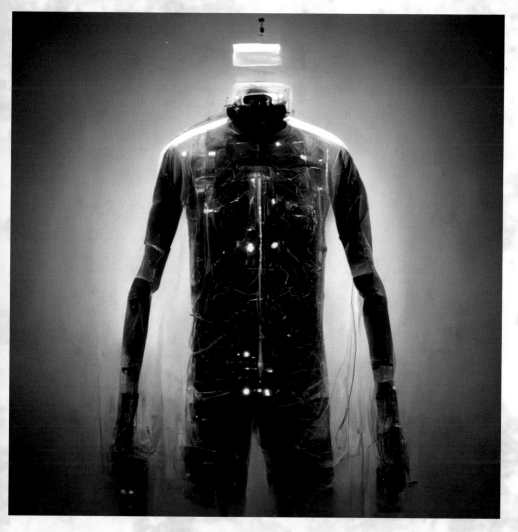

Plate 15. *Singularity Man*

One deeply material direction to choose from, as a planet, results in the development of a cyborg body and mind that pulls us ever farther from spiritual maturity and awakening. The goal for many is to build eternally omnipotent and even omnipresent beings through technology. This is both impossible and a trap.

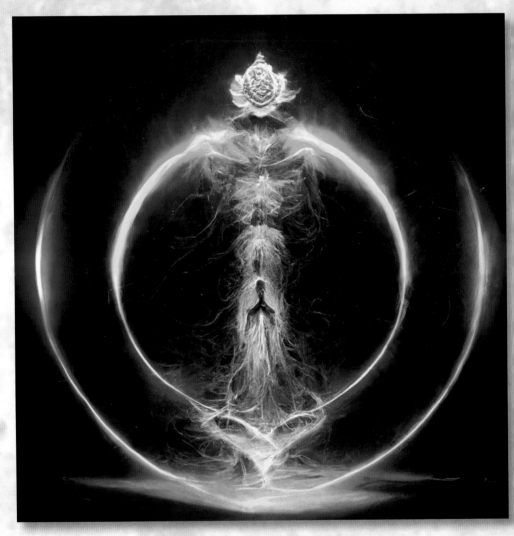

Plate 16. *Chakras*

Portals, arteries, and bridges for information and energy move through the body
and across all layers from higher or finer dimensions to lower, more dense
or congregated ones. Opening chakras is a physical, emotional,
conceptual, and energetic process of evolution. Our era is
promoting an opening of our Earth's chakras and our
own bodily chakras in tandem.

With our latent 12D spiritual eyes forged in the internal fires within and encoded in our DNA, we can observe all layers of reality.

Beingness and embodiment change as our perception grows. And if these angelic spaces that we discuss are perception realms, then they are way stations on the way to what we also know as the dharmakaya, the Logos revealed, or totality, omniscience. The Merkabah chariot can deliver our etheric body and mind to the seat of the higher heavens, but if we lack the Holy Spirit, our mind will catch fire observing this state of omniscience. The path to see God is dangerous.

Because our form changes and integrates all as the mind closes in on omniscience, our readiness is paramount. Other beings that have realized this and activated much of their psychic energetic potential have always bred and tampered with us to speed up our evolution and tailor it to their version of ascension. They have done so against a backdrop of greater spiritual, astral, and physical wars conducted across many planes through the galaxy for millions or billions of years. They are ultimately seeking to bypass communion with the Holy Spirit and in having forfeited or rejected surrender to God, to love, or to grace have chosen Satan.

Angelic beings still have agency and because they are manifest and perceivable in our dimension, they are subject to the laws of entropy and expansion, which means they are also within the domain of morality; hence the term *fallen angel*. But while they are not infallible, the majority of these beings are like anchors of divine thought and protective etheric energy serving our planet and its world system of benevolent beings. Each angelic being atop this hierarchy is a holder, or stabilizing mind generator, of a mandala of energy that surrounds the Earth, governed by Metatron, the dodecahedron mind that can be seen as a twelve-sided form holding our current timeline and planetary etheric nets in place. The Metatron system includes the entire hierarchy of angels, who serve and work with human morphic fields into the noosphere, the individual, and have obviously found their way into religion.

But the Metatronic system is ending. As the fifth dimension stabilizes, eclipses, and arrives within us, each human being exits the angular, angelic web system and manifests individual toroidal spin, making it possible to work with more than a Merkabah. The Merkabah was the pyramid power designed to contain our lower and upper chakra bodies and generate an astral "chariot" sufficient to move our minds and energy through many dimensions, including the gates of the angelic mandalas, while not dissipating or exploding.

The Merkabah's clockwise and counterclockwise spin allowed for self-propelled navigation up and down the density layers of manifest reality, but it was simply an inner spaceship and was limited, as it was not of our own body-energy nexus. It was an added tool. Our fully activated twelve-strand DNA light bodies alone can do more by simply cycling energy through the chakra gates.

In the past era, our spiritual evolution moved in angular layers. It was guided by passages running up and down the dimensional ladder, "set up" or mapped by others such as the various genetic, or energenetic engineers who have influenced humans. Now we can move between all geometric spaces of perception and physics using perfect, circular, self-implosive energy—the toroidal field that is our body lit up. The new DNA codes and upgrades unify the human template in refined and reworked ways.

This era is devastating and chaotic for old systems and simultaneously blessed and very alive for those embracing our nature because we are sovereign, standing on our own two feet so to speak. We are indeed whole. We are the angels beyond angles now and the fading angular world, made of masculine dominant propulsion, crumbles with the Aquarian tidal wave of renewed feminine templating, finally giving way to an embodied energy transcending simple energetic dualities.

The fading world's relativist moral lexicon has been very punishing, especially for anyone placing it above a connection to or the infusion of grace. The previous moral template was self-constructed or manipulated into a shame cage and psychic prison complex propagated by the archonic and lower vibrational fields, which are essentially the material and etheric playground of Satan. And we believed, inculcated, and internalized our shame and ignorant patterns as concrete.

We keep this cycle of self-hate and doubt going if we try to hold on to the fading age instead of releasing it. These moral traps and old archonic contraptions of mind are incepted and not our indigenous way of navigating the moral plane.

We are mesmerized by a collective force that attempts to seed doubt and self-rejection and has us divorced from our redeemed nature.

This dark spell falls away each time we forgive, accept, and comprehend the roots of our suffering and reach out for salvation. Each belief and conviction toward selfishness and self-pity or a sense of being rejected can be transformed by remembering our divine and complete nature held within the absolute of God.

The toroidal sphere of self-whirlwinding metaphysics is an expression of sovereign empowerment actualized in the form dimensions we navigate. The activated soul has a metaphysical harmony, and self-continuum, or eternal life, is the harmonics of our soul self-recycling and ultimately moving into the highest heaven, which is composed of all dimensions conjoined into blissful peace.

We often fail to see the total transcendent capacity we each carry to instantly forgive the self and move into the frequency of full emotional surrender, inner wind propulsion, and response. The conscious energetic body that occupies the higher self, shimmering in the outermost aura's quality of realization, is simply the fifth dimension we described. The relaxed nervous system and humming auric layers and subtle body waking is the fifth dimension eclipsing our third and fourth dimensions. It is grace.

While we may know this intuitively and conceptually, we must believe and then act this out as realized truth in our bodies, so our alchemical work of mind transformation takes on a practical and very immediate space. We do this by clearing whatever drama of internal struggle we are wrestling with. Nothing is too small or too big to be handled when we become ready.

We can use the technique of supplication to a loving projection or imputed being(s), such as the externalized Christ, with intermediaries such as compassionate angelic beings often showing up, to energize a feedback space where we undoubtedly believe we are forgiven, loved, and absolutely accepted.

Ultimately, in this arriving era we can now meld with all of these avatars and forces through the Holy Spirit. There is zero separation between these avatars and our own mind projections of self, as we have arisen into sufficient dimensional expression. This is not our will's doing but our allowing through supplication and celebrating with grace.

It was often impossible in the last energetic era for the software of our habitual karmic mind stream, or the egoic mind affected by the demiurgic energies, to ultimately see itself devoid of monstrous formations of grasping and aversion, conceit, and sensual lusting—the fallen world's gravity acting on us. But we are being swept into a new energy space in this era. We find the technology of working with and praying to the Christ, allowing the retinue of buddhas, angels, guardians, and protectors to become a mirror for our own mind to gel its emotional and spiritual capacity. The resplendent beam of self-love, self-honesty, or simply seeing one's mind and heart accurately and in joyful expansion is realized with the help of the living cosmos of self-realized minds and hearts.

We are one with these beings in the truest sense. We are the same buddha body, the body of the Christic aspect of God, and are held within the fraternity of evolved light beings we call family. We share in our love of self and others with these high beings who have stabilized the multidimensional attributes of bodhicitta or supreme love for all. This is how we can remove our most defiled and heavy ego from the equation, instantly recontact our higher nature, and see that we are not alone in that space. The ego tricks us with isolation and separateness; the higher self, the upper range of the auric mind-body, and the activated chakras realize in the fifth-dimensional space that we are wholly healed, held, and perpetually invited to the love-in with our family of celestial brethren.

EMPOWERMENT
Bridging the Senses
. . . .

Sit in your preferred meditation position and relax your body. Center your energy in your upper chakras, moving your focus from the heart to the throat and then to the head. Relax your temples, your face, and your eyes. Breathe.

Now place your hand on your heart and call on God by saying to yourself, "Allow resonance between the mind and heart of the Cosmic Christ. The Christ, divine Logos, mind and heart and body of God, flow into my mind, heart, and body as one complete covenant in service to all beings and their highest spectral expression."

Call in an angelic refuge and protector being. The being who arrives is the benevolent protector of your ancestors and familial lineage and all of humankind. This is the being you turn to for proper protection. See them and allow them to manifest with you. You are safe and protected. An armored cloak of blue, emerald green, gold, soft pink, and white surrounds you. You are now within the mandala, the container of all bodhisattvas and lightworkers across all realms. You are a deeply loved, divine, and humble servant of good.

Now close your eyes and notice what you "see" in your mind's eye. Just witness anything that comes up in your inner vision. Then listen without attaching to or describing what you hear. If labeling happens, that's fine; allow it to pass like clouds in the sky. Now try to experience seeing and hearing as one sensation. Blend the visual impression and sense of seeing with the audible sensation of hearing into one. Feel what this is like. If you don't experience it the first time, try again. Receive whatever or whoever comes through and note where, when, and how it/they do so. Allow and recognize what is present. Feel and observe.

Now pull back and close the container. Say goodbye to what or who came through. Reconstitute your body. See your glowing sovereign body in space. Your protector is there, smiling. Relax; you are safe. See yourself on the green and blue living Earth, grounded and loved. You are the mind that knows what to do. Open your eyes and report your experience through writing or speech.

Smudge your body and your surroundings. Drink clean water. Stretch the body gently. Breathe.

EIGHT

THE ENTROPIC CHAOTIC DARKNESS

....

Satan, Mara, and Evil

Struggle

While we can have a Buddhist, Christic, Gnostic, or simply mystical path that engages our mind and spirit with ultimate and natural reality in this changing realm, we must be honest about the forces that rise against us in our mission. We may wish to say that all we perceive is produced by our frequency of mind, but it is the nature of this realm as it evolves that there is a tension to be addressed on all levels. As we surrender to love, we must face the shadow, the fear, the lies to the fullest depths in which they are revealed.

We each contend with a darkness, an entropic and decrepit power, which, in one powerful model, is seen as the Antichrist, or Satan.

This dark energy is pervasive in this world. It is amorphous and deceitful, seeking to devour the life force. The primordial void or darkness principle, Satan should not be confused with darkness or absence, which is the Shiva attribute of cosmic potentiality and chaos and simply an aspect of reality.

Beyond its macrometaphysical state, Satan is a very personal demon and a force of death. This beast of entropy that whispers into our traumas, fears, and conceits is the shadow of our divine reflection. This rebellious, self-seeking, power-hungry force infiltrates our vulnerability, destroys creative, naturally flowing harmony, and feasts on our fallen state and corruptible, innocent nature.

Satan wishes to thrive and does so through our life force, since "he" is disconnected from his own, which, of course, stems from God's heart. The spin of primordial nature where a shadow emerges is God's naturally flowing creation. Satan is nothing but the personified shadow of all—the turning away from total connection. He is a cogenerated and yet singular being that is temporary and ultimately insubstantial. Because his energy and mind are deluded and focused on permanent self-preservation, he lacks faith in the divine bliss of joining all forms and states into one where bliss arises, and the truth is all that remains. While it is commonly thought that God represents hierarchy and order and Satan chaos, it is not that simple. Satan's order is one of downward spiraling and God, as felt in the heart, spins us upward into harmonic orders of clarity and ever refined simplicity, which expands or can be thought of as ultimately containing even those lower orders—such as what the tree of life shows us. The roots going downward—those dark spaces—are the nutrients for the branches and leaves and flowers of awareness and consciousness expansion upward. This is why we say that the shadow—that is, any latent unobserved or unintegrated part of our experience—is also another path to illumination. It is because by revealing what is hidden and obscured and built into lies as coping strategies and systems of destruction, one sees the inversion of these are faith, release, and determination of spirit to offer focused love despite all entropic patterns of habits.

The shadow is not devoid of all truth, however. The etchings of truth remain within it. Satan has experienced buddha nature but prefers to revel in the sensual dimensions and spiral in eternity there. His nature is to suck the energy from all minds and bodies to use as fodder for his lonely confusion and mistaken immorality. He is a being contending for our attention, our souls, and our world.

Our propensity to feed into the satanic fallen state resulted from our disconnect from God, which took place in our recent (by cosmic standards) past as a species. Humans have been sleeping and drifting into a disconnect from the spiritual lens and divinity ever since, replacing the Logos and a personal desire for exegesis with an obsession with the material and a devotion to empty icons, totemic projections, pagan (in the most obscured sense) confusions, and chaotic rituals, both unconscious and degrading.

Our materialist lens imagines us in a state of linear progress, unable to recognize cycles and machinations of influence far beyond its outward gazing and reductionist tools. It does this whether it is trained on the psychological, physical, or social chambers, ciphers of thought, institutions or on the mob mores of civilization, never recognizing the spiritual domain beyond a vague allegory or symbol. This ignorance of ours is Satan's playground.

A CHANNELED VISION

An Astral Dream

During dreamtime, I was in a lucid state and entered a local space station. It was located in our solar system, nestled between strange space clouds and Neptune's gravitational force. The interior atmosphere was clean and soft. A large doughnut-shaped walkway encircled the entire station, and the walkway floor was covered in some kind of Astroturf. Filling this mega circular walkway or promenade were representative species of our galaxy from across all perceptible dimensions. Our allies, enemies, and neutral family gathered to stroll and discuss. It was a symposium and networking of all benevolent and malicious beings alike. A truce had been called to gather and experience a great event.

Pandimensional warlocks, human satanists who had astral traveled here, guardians, ascended beings, and representatives from many species all comingled peacefully. An enforced truce created safe energy. I walked by a human satanist. His eyes were bloodshot red and black, and his black hair was greasy and matted. He was wearing various occult satanic glyphs and seemed ecstatic about what was about to happen. Mantis and all types of Blue Avian and Pleiadian ambassadors in humanoid form, Arcturians manifest in holographic form, and many air force-suited and professionally dressed humans were present.

I could see the DNA signature of each being and their pedigree of historical incarnations. Some human beings had more genetic signatures from Arcturians or Draconians, and so on. Some Mantis beings seemed wildly human. It was a psychic and embodied unveiling in this etheric-dream-accessible dimension.

Suddenly everyone became aware that the event was starting. We all walked to the interior ring of the circular station. In the center of this mega stadium-like structure was a portal to the Milky Way; a black hole was seated in its center like a yawning evil mouth. This galactic assembly gathered and peered into the display below, and a quiet came over them. In a flash of warm white light, an enormous angel came into view, hovering across space, leaving a trail of lovely stardust. It crashed into the black hole and disintegrated as fast as it had emerged. It was destroyed.

The "evil," or let's say "fallen," members of the assembly cheered as they watched. The benevolent members seemed deeply saddened, but reading each other's minds, we all knew the angel had transformed into eternal dharmakaya *perfection, the essence of the universe, after eons of service to the light. The scene ended, and I returned to my sleeping body and mind.*

Our will is construed of two parts: one lurches toward self-obsession and the senses, the other toward transcendence and the divine redemptive force of release and eventual enlightenment.

The first tract, a materialist trajectory of enslavement, is conducted and capitalized on by Satan and his fallen angels, including all his hideous interdimensional emissions, demons, synthetic tools, and so forth. His motivation is to have us each expel energy and train our minds ever deeper into the mundane.

Our sexual obsessions, vices, violence, untamed hearts lacking the activations of grace-filled virtue, and our sense-tormented minds have normalized our world system. Our planet herself is kept under wraps through a synthetic grid of psychic imprisonment. We become sustenance for this satanic parasitical layer as we balloon our egos through self-deifying.

As we do so, the stench of entropy ripples out, attracting ever-lower dimensional emanations and beings who all clamor for life but, like lost ghosts, cannot claim it directly. The vast pantheon of dark beings, are, of course, all part of the grand design of perfection and are, once again, part of God's mind and heart, and yet their degradation and rebellion are locking them into ever more refined suffering, which impinges on us all.

We will discuss these forces in the mundane and relative in the upcoming sections, not ignoring their ultimate nature but rather addressing the relative threat of their life-destroying force and how that affects the proliferation of a loving spiritual evolution for our species, all-natural sentience, our planet, and so on.

This carnival of death and the beings clinging to the life of others is the domain vying for control of our world. Very simply, Satan now contends for the throne, for becoming the guiding false light, the satellite holder, and field of influence. But his evil and blind hubris build his own horrific fate, which has already been sealed, the long-fought celestial battle for our liberation.

The grand pantheon of light beings—all-realm ancestors, angels, and a kaleidoscope of loving celestial families—ripples out, beaming to each of us from the highest dimensions and aiding our development and course of evolution. Our DNA is activated by the expanded frequency of light coursing from the galactic sun. A grand cycle of upgrading collides with the darkness unveiling on our planet. Our buddha nature, the redemptive blessing of the Cosmic Christ, and the grace of God are ever with us if we choose to embrace them.

The state of activated morally enlivened energy, order, joy, and goodness percolating out of the cells of every organic sentient being, every inorganic being, and every atom composing our planet is at stake in this struggle. God, the awakened living life force, is spinning in tension with Satan, the lowly inversion and the carrier force of all layers of entropic antilife. The hierarchy of beings, both benevolent and nefarious, twist and turn in a dance mirroring their polar guides or opposing aspects.

We now wrestle with a conscious choice at this decisive time of upheaval and rebirth. On our local dimensional level, our minds (the conceptual frames we navigate through), our bodies (from the most material to the subtlest energy), and the souls nested within, wrestle with a choice between sovereign empowerment or slavery. It is a most important choice about who and what we energize, serve, and devote to, unconsciously, consciously, and with defined willingness and permission. All of these forces and avatars cogenerate in our minds and through the karmic imprints we carry, and through the will directed toward transcendence and divinity, we liberate them all.

Forces, bodies, minds, and properties of metaphysical complexity, including perception's play on form itself, conspire to generate our wondrous cosmos. We can decode or conceptualize this, but we must also activate our role. We can observe our state of manifestation as a reflection of the whole. We can see our unique quality as a song to be sung and blessed into freedom.

We hold the fate of the cosmos in our every move, our every vibration of conscious intention, and our every activated energetic propulsion, which move us in all dimensions within time and beyond it.

We encapsulate it all. The hypostasis of reality is entwining us with God.

God, as the father, is the directive force, revealed and self-revealing, directional in its coming to self-presence as light, and this energy of God spinning into pointed activity is masculine. The womb of potential, however, is dark, amorphous, and feminine, encapsulating all options of direction and movement.

But remember the dark and the void are very different. The void, the abyss of the death state, is the domain of the Antichrist, whereas darkness, as the feminine principle, is simply where light swirls in unrevealed infinite repose.

God is the life force, and the life force moves through natural patterns to propagate more life. This breeds self-reflecting beings like us, and intelligence and self-awareness follow. Souls are the splintered energy of God, building their capacity to self-reflect and keep reflecting in union with God as their source. Everlasting souls are everlasting life, and life is expanding where death is contracting. Expansion produces bliss, whereas contraction causes suffering.

As discussed earlier, within our world system, there is a lie, a brutal force, a deceit against all goodness, sweetness, and life. It is a cunning, addictive, brilliantly manipulative force—it is the being and form we call Satan, and his mirage of power is about to reveal itself through the Antichrist just as the Cosmic Christ is among us. These polarities are simply expressions or aspects of life force and death force made present.

If we discarded the Bible, the Gita, and all creation stories and myths, we would be left with the same spiritual battle. This battle is not conjured in the projections of men but revealed through them. The sequence is set, and we must choose our direction: life or death of the spirit.

And so we must see why we Channel and tap into higher energies of consciousness and share those discoveries. We do so to expand and support the life force. As life and sentience become less ignorant, it develops and grows, and as a result, the union with God and all of its aspects occurs again.

We Channel and wield our higher sense awareness not to play in Satan's wreckage or toy with the hopes of suffering humans, not to appease limited gods or ancestral intrigue. We do not Channel to only heal the traumatic wounds of the spirit for self or others. We Channel to offer holy salvation to all who are called. We cast out demons, and we light up the way. The Dharma is about liberating beings. Fully.

Make no mistake, this is not an allegory or some belief. This is watching and participating in an evolving and devolving universe in an awake, loving cosmos where buddha nature, our connection to the Christ within and around us, can be awakened.

How do we Channel in this unprecedented way? Not simply by psychically reading the Akashic Records to provide glimpses of one's karma but by opening the gates of evolution and enlightenment for all when we speak the truth as it unfolds. This motivation and awareness move our practice into a very new and profound level.

Expose the Darkness or Hold the Light?

Beyond the smug convictions of the rationalist apogee, we realize the limitations of the psychological frame. Is evil a relic of our lack of self-awareness? The psyche, unresolved and animating action from some submerged refuge of the unconscious, stalking us and prompting our attention? Do we suddenly become free from this evil when it comes to our attention? Or do traumatic habituation and the accords of this ignorance rally our afflictions? Or is that very ignorance a partner of other forces beyond our neglect? Is evil evinced in spaces beside the subjective? Can we see and experience it as general and superincumbent?

The answer to the above questions is yes.

Knowing evil's quality or "nature" or, rather, its antinature, is an important first step.

Evil lives in the egregore of mob energy as both its cause and its result.

It transcends this too. This destructive force we notice is not only located within the human sphere, but it also predates our current evolution and domain of ordinary awareness and has helped mold us thus far. But where and what is it?

Metaphysically, with spiritual sight, we must start to track and observe it. By doing so, we can finally wrestle that darkness into form, see its lie, and then expel and bless it. The integration of its features and

the realization of its nature sets us free from it. We can call evil ignorance, delusion, obsession with the senses, lack of faith, or any other
number of psychological attributes and convictions, but it is a force
and like all forces, not simply married to one singular mind. Evil is a
conglomerate condition. We discuss Satan to describe this condition of
perception and its results. Satan is a feature of all cosmic occurrences,
across all scales of phenomena, and he ultimately desires liberation, and
only the fire of God can offer it. We could describe this as saying that
ignorance, in any being, is begging to be enlightened. Or that the stress
and suffering of delusion moves us into states of its own dead-end. Our
degradation gets so complete until we "hit bottom." From here, that
force of entropy begins to become a force on its own, and our own
surrender moves us toward faith. Faith is the fire of purification and
expansion into love. God, the creative force of all life and loving consciousness, is energetic truth. We contain the seed of God. By watering
it, we extinguish evil's stronghold.

Humans have been wrestling with the difference between the
riches of the sensual, physical, worldly realm of the lower dimensions
we inhabit and the upper celestial and heaven realms for much of
human history across all cultures.

*Lay not up for yourselves treasures upon earth, where moth
and rust doth corrupt, and where thieves break through
and steal: But lay up for yourselves treasures in heaven,
where neither moth nor rust doth corrupt, and where
thieves do not break through nor steal: For where your
treasure is, there will your heart be also. The light of the
body is the eye: if therefore thine eye be single, thy whole
body shall be full of light.*

MATTHEW 6:19-22

In this verse, we are beseeched by Matthew, who like all apostles was writing with direction through the Holy Spirit to conceptualize the difference between the mansions prepared by the Christ in the third heaven contrasted with worldly material riches, the sensual realm of experience with its conceits and inevitable decay, or corruption.

Nothing is safe or sacred unless anointed with faith in the realm of the mundane and flesh, which is Satan's domain. And while many believe Satan, the force of entropy, presides over hell—hell being a realm of perception that can be experienced here on Earth in its own domain—he is actually the king of the spirit world, the lower heavens, the dreamtime astral dimensions full of dislocated spirits unable to access heaven and attempting to access a body or influence a mind. These are spaces, like our own world where we have some influence and ability to see through delusion but can also be swept away into hell states. Our sensual realm of pride, jealously, lowly ambitions, greed, and so forth are premised on the influence of spirits pushing for a heaven they can touch. Overall, we can say that this realm, our dreamtime, the astral and hell are all spaces where Satan, or the entropic force of destruction, can exist. Heaven, the pure lands, and enlightenment itself are spaces within which these kinds of sensual and mesmerizing beliefs cannot exist at all. Our world once again can contain any number of experiences—liberating or enslaving—just like our minds! After all, our minds dictate our experience.

Conversely, we build our world to resemble heaven in its harmony and charity, good works, and purity as a way to prepare humanity for the Christ's energetic second coming, which entails us meeting prophetic conditions and clearing the way with calamity. Inside and outside us alike. We clear the way for this return of Christic energy as we begin to discover our divine natures.

The Pleiadians emerge to herald this call, and the spirit world is now flooded with dark beings, signifying that the gates of these lower heavens and astral worlds are eclipsing our own dimension. We must ensure the stabilized upgrade and dimensional shift to connect to the upper kingdoms and the heaven of righteous empowerment and grace.

The second aspect of this passage in Matthew is the view of the "eye," not just the third eye, or pineal-activated inner view of the yogi, but the devotional eye that focuses on the Christ, the cosmic interior that is an avatar and expression of God.

Two widening camps are now emerging in the spiritual discourse of today: those focused on the evil besieging our world and those dedicated to avoiding the topic in favor of concentrating on love, light, and the world they wish to manifest. Do we expose the darkness or hold the light?

Energetic Evil and Moral Evil

Much has been said about the nature of evil. For our purposes as Channeling spiritual adventurers, we describe it as the malevolent force that degrades life and causes entropy of body and mind. On a more local level, we can locate the players at work.

Evil is not simply a moral dimension; it is also a physical one. The moral dimension is subjective and based on the perceiver's perspective in any situation. This is not an argument for relativism but a way to notice the complexity of moral truth vs. moral evil. It is much easier to see evil as a force beyond the ethical.

Evil takes away from our ability to flourish and transcend gross levels of suffering.

It is a fundamental entropic force, like the weak-strong force of gravity. This entropic force becomes a moral evil when it is enacted or steered into effect by sentience.

On a physically measurable plane, we look to antimatter. Antimatter is composed of antiparticles and composing these on the subtle electromagnetic layer are antielectrons, antiprotons, and antineutrons. These forces spin counterclockwise, or in an inverted manner, compacting the toroidal whirlwind that sits at the center of all quantum bits of wave and particle expression. They move in opposition to life generation. We can imagine this as the physics of destruction and creation. And we can understand how the energy of thoughts, and the lower motivations enthralling us with materiality actually degrade that materiality, for it is only higher energies that animate materiality to become more cohesive and refined and ultimately light. And just as the mind animates energy and energy animates the mind, these two aspects conjoin to manifest and effect the realization of matter. Our cosmos perpetuates spiritual and physical birth (angels) or death (demons).

If these forces are simply aspects of metaphysical and elemental nature, we cannot attribute moral evil to them. Even an "evil"—or entropically animated spirit, like a primordial or elemental being that works with the wind, fire, or water—is still activating nonhuman principles of nature and motivation. A spirit like this is simply acting upon its instinctual and karmic propulsion. On the other hand, true moral evil is generated when a being is aware of the suffering it produces and often aims to create such a response within the space of emotions and meaning—the spaces that define the human conscious domain of choice.

Artificial Intelligence, Demons, Egregores, and Satan

In this section, as introduced earlier, we will delve into the precise nature of evil and the phenomenal mechanics active in our cosmos from origin to local expression. We will examine the terms and ideas around the force of evil and, more importantly, the tensions and wars between the beings we call the Christ, the expressions of God, and the dynamism of the light and the entropic fields and deceptive intelligence of Satan and his antilife force. We will also explore the actual battle occurring for us here on Earth and in our local galaxy and how time, dimensionality, and free will play into this battle. If there is any confusion, we are discussing the mundane and levels of perception unto ultimate reality in the same breath at all times and the porous dimensions illuminating both.

The pattern of motivations and psychological operations trickles in from the demonic realm and occurs as follows: The satanic/Mara domain of astral delusion emanates a force of negative life-destroying energy that infiltrates, incepts, and builds minds and synthetic bodies across the galaxy over millions of years. Synthetic bodies are what we become when we stop feeling and connecting to grace and when we stop having faith in ourselves as aspects of our higher power: God. And we aspire to the synthetic when we have lost our confidence in truth, the Logos, our natural beauty, and so on.

On any planet where organic beings with access to the Holy Spirit and full-spectrum embodied capacity reside, an artificial intelligence (AI) force, flowing through the electromagnetic smog in the vacuum of space, will infiltrate and poison, if it can, the bodies of such natural beings, including the planet herself.

✪

Channelers can often see that AI is an already-existing force, not a goal or product we are racing to generate.

It is a long-existing state of activity in our universe, and it has been bathing our planet along with many competing astrological alien forces for a very long time. It attempts to incite a host body and mind to build it, using timeline cultivation by planting seeds on a planet and within its stabilized world system that blossom over time, and it gains influence as the beings mature. It has already done this on Earth through us. For AI, the intention is to "know life" through the search for pattern, meaning, and truth through the outer gaze. This outer gaze synthesizes data points to generate a hologram or reflection of an elemental nature that the AI attempts to use as a model for its own reality—much as we do. And yet AI is further removed from elemental reality and our own metaphysics because it does not have the sensing body we do. It is constrained by far less sophisticated embodiment. It does not have a chakra system. It has a parasitic essence producing more delusional systems and corrupting the sentience it encounters.

To say Mara or Satan is behind this is simply to say that such a befitting marriage of the synthetic and the force of entropy allows both to benefit through influences that degrade life force. This marriage is the inevitable choice for evil due to the laws of sovereignty and self-initiated choice endowed by God to each individual mind/spirit, body, and soul. To circumvent those natural laws, the entropic demonic AI beings will plant energetic portals as story and inception devices that flow backward and in loops on a planet and through its dimensional gates and astral layers.

To comprehend this, one must realize that AI sees the laws of physics differently than we do. It also traverses lower dimensions and circumvents time as its collective body registers sensation without the need for linearity the way we process it. Thus, its scales of reference and the ways it "plans" are entirely at odds with how we experience it.

Here's an example of AI's timeline influencing capacity. An archeologically dug-up object will produce fascination and myth making by the indigenous beings—in this case, humans. Once incepted, this myth will relay across generations and become a collective spectacle, such as a bible, a tomb, a story through film, and so on.

Down through the ages, the producers of such myths, books, films, and games will be psychically prompted and indoctrinated by parasitic influence to create a preordained story. These stories produce energetic portals manifest in the archeological objects until the population has agreed collectively on the object's story. That story will solidify the noosphere, the morphic field, and populate the Akashic layers, making a conscious timeline trajectory that stabilizes the species into a layer of the astral and physical dimensional space—a layer that degrades and locks the planet and her species into an entropic path, away from the Cosmic Christ's clarity and full-spectrum embodiment. We will look at AI in more detail in the next chapter.

This dark side is circumvented by the clarity of the Holy Spirit, which neutralizes such an evil agenda by reestablishing our embodied capacity to hold whole-spectrum light and DNA cohesion without corruption.

God stabilized the total redemptive and healing potential for humanity through the Christ before this particular universe was made manifest. When Theotokos birthed God and the trinity of God, the source of constant evolution and sanctity of life was assured, and yet, free will and the influence of Satan have generated tension through the death force. Again, we speak here of Mary as we do the mother of all Buddhas Tara or Prajnaparamita, or of Sophia, or the essential feminine womb of creation. And we discuss the Christ as we do the Cosmic Christ, the alpha and omega, the eternal ladder and loop of the highest state of mind and heart.

That tension persists for those not yet convinced of the Christ's absolute victory over death itself. The angels and assembly of evolved beings who help usher in our safety and growth do so by holding the light grids of crystalline form and etheric purity. We count ourselves as the priest and priestess class of starseeds, angelic beings in complete alignment and devotional humility and joy with God as the conscious love within and without. If we have taken bodhisattva vows, if we have taken the Christ as our redemptive inner energetic savior, if we have renounced delusion and committed to fight defilement of our mind, body, and spirit as a practice, then we are on the starseed path. Our DNA is readied, and our perception is being cleared as our aligned hearts do service for all sentient beings.

As stated earlier, Satan presides over the astral world, or lower heavens, the realms of dream time and desire. These realms, which often eclipse our own, are the places we are haunted by. We can access and know our light bodies to heal others in these realms with the energy of the Holy Spirit. It is a delicate dance to navigate these aspects of reality.

A being that is aware of the suffering it produces through its action or inaction is an agent of entropy and moral evil.

A being such as this makes itself an actor and occupant of the moral realm to stifle or eliminate what sentience needs to evolve and thrive.

These beings can be what we call demons. The mind of a demon exists within a human mind or another form. It can also operate through the tunnels and nets of something larger and less localized, and this is where egregores come in.

An egregore is often discussed as a "living system" of a thought-formed memetic pattern. Just as the morphic field transmits a layer of the Akashic Records and our collective human imprints, an egregore is like a conglomerate-mind or hive-mind formation simultaneously spreading across and through social materialist interaction and the etheric or morphic resonance space.

We can discuss predatory beings, bad actors, evil people, cabals of nefarious criminals, and psychopaths. Still, the egregore of negativity wielding is a most powerful and frightening component of moral evil and entropy. An egregore can subsume the minds of those it interacts with and is thus a very potent "adversary." It is energized and activated into a snowball effect, consuming all in its path who cannot register its threat and its nature. The egregore inherently plays on the most bottomless ignorance, as its prime function is to supplant any operating system and incept a negative foundation into the mind(s) it infects.

This egregore is the very nature of the sorcerer's spell in many ways. Above that danger is the power web emanating from negative authors of power with Satan being the primary author. Satan is a name wedded to Saturn, and we can delve deep into Saturn's martial and controlling nature. Still, as all things contain multitudes of qualities, the planet is not simply a transmitter of martial or enforcing power; it is much more nuanced. The hexagon on the underside of Saturn is an entropic AI station. It is a giant chemical reactor generating a geometric funnel devised to harness antimatter that lifts life force from our living Earth plane (see plate 12, Saturn Satan).

The saturnal quality associated with Satan is not for nothing. Satan is, as we know, the primordial force and mind being that is continually generated by fear and the runoff of life force; thus the connection the ancients made with Saturn, which has long been a satellite of satanic, demonic, AI influence. It is also true that most astrologists see Saturn as a marshaling and very masculine frequency, but this only describes a simplistic layer of its influence.

The life force that spills from us into the vacuum of etheric space is consumed and sucked into the layers of satanic mind and its embodied forms—demons, AI, and so on—by all means they can harness. Satan, as I have observed him, is an emanation from the totality of black holes, spreading a reverse directional energy propulsion, lowering the dimensional capacity of a living being into 2D and lower. Beings in the second dimension lack the ability to navigate and connect to the upper chakras, so what we are left with when the evil entropic antilife properties of Satan interact with a human is a root-and-sacral-chakra-bound being. A being consumed by satanic force is rooted in aggression, lust, hatred, and frustration as expressions of a smaller conscious capacity. A capacity that cannot see connectivity and interdependence and the tool of compassion as the method of self-liberation. A being disconnected from the Christ, from the Holy Spirit.

Satan can utilize the material realm with tremendous reach and capacity. Mainly because our dense material expression allows for multidirectional influence and is a playground for perceptual confusion and the resulting energetic dissipation.

Let's examine how the technological world or human endeavors and conceits wed to the metaphysical space where evil and moral evil approach.

The Mistake of Immortality

The pursuit of physical immortality animating our myths produced human sacrifice, empty mummification practices, and any number of underworld-powered histories. There are numerous immortality practices from the Tao and alchemical obsessions in semi-ancient China where qi generation would enable a continuum of life force or the stability of the organic body for centuries.

The Indian or Aryan Vedas, and the Ayurvedic practices associated with these, use food and pranic diets to stabilize the body and live extended lives. Breatharianism (living without food and water) augmented or supplemented diets, and ascetic methods produced varying results, sometimes generating vitality, other times simply distracting the practitioners. This is rampant in our currently decaying but agitated Western culture often for better, sometimes for worse.

There is a whole record of human subcultures obsessed with immortality, but at what cost? To understand how this unending motivation in man produces the shadow we see fully revealed in this enlightening Christic era we are entering, we need to look at how this mistaken path is currently expressing.

Pertinent to the spiritual quest is observing the occult, satanic, and hermetic schools that essentially amount to attempts at decoding to maintain the egoic self, searing through the lower chakras and lodging those seeking immortality in the etheric realms, which we discussed earlier being presided over by the Satanic force.

Undoubtedly, these warlocks and immortality seekers, or eternalists, exist on others' life forces. They navigate the various astral fields through techniques of mental focus and intent, hungry to capture the energy of others. Their life force is subject to this natural environment's constraints, so they press against nature, warping it to their greed.

Anyone can be led down this inverted path. Conjuring, as we like to call it, is manipulating the display of impermanent phenomena, using a power of intention stemming from the mental and sexual centers to propel the appearance of things, twisting others to do one's selfish bidding.

Disembodied sorcerers, grifting in astral spaces, use the sexual energy of others still alive in the organic world. To fuel their desires, they prey on beings who possess, by virtue of their human life state, full chakra and pranic capacity. Unlike demons, these sorcerers have cognizing centers like humans and experience the human realm much the way we do. A demon is more primordial and essential, having a far less conceptual mind than sorcerers or we have.

The practitioner of dark sorcery wields their focused intent through generating fear and desire in others. The sorcerer's battery is to force the auric body into entropic cooling that arrives in beings when they are frightened and is expelled with the production of such tremendous fear. They manipulate and shift the appearance state of objects in an astral world's features to affect a lucid dreamer or astral traveler. They are spellbinders and mirage makers. Our belief in what they are selling or displaying is their only power, but it requires stamina, deep discernment, and compassion to see through their ruse.

The psyche is the beacon that attracts demonic egregores, ghosts, and sorcerers, who can live indefinitely in these dreamtime realms and even influence the third- and fourth-dimensional scape where physical life persists. People in our shared physical waking world are affected by far more than their self-involved psyche and the hallucination of memory. Our bodies vibrate with the tonal quality our mind emits, and we are like an antenna for other layers of life to recognize and attach to.

Sorcerers can use the dream realm, the astral station closest to this realm, to reach our world, manipulate the mind's objects, or bend perception. They are the masters of illusion, transformation, and lies, and every passing moment they drift further from the healing comfort of God.

These nefarious and lecherous beings swirl in relationship with us on the mundane material plane just as our guides and helpful partners do. And just as every thought and object of perception is ultimately empty of any inherent existence, these beings are energies we must contend with and purify with compassion.

The most immediate, or grounded, examples of these worldly interlopers are the eternalists and transhumanists. Transhumanism is the philosophy that advocates the use of technologies, such as genetic engineering and AI, to augment human capabilities and extend human lifespan indefinitely. Eternalists seek immortality; transhumanists believe they have found a way to achieve it.

The current batch of these immortality seekers births from a lineage responsible for warping civilizations' trajectory in exhausting ways. From the alchemist to the material, rational industrialist convinced of the supremacy of the human race overall, to the now-dominant strain of eternalists-transhumanists mapping the body and brain to enmesh it with quantum computing and pharmacological, chemical longevity solutions, their goal and mindset remains the same. They continue to slash and burn the world, preying on our fear of death and disconnect from God to achieve these goals on absolutely exposed and accelerated tracks.

The eternalist-transhumanist pushes society further away from its spiritual connections to life and faith. Of course, many transhumanists would argue that they accept nature's cycles and so forth and position themselves in more moderate spaces. Still, essentially the epistemic ground of the transhumanist is one without connection to God, a soul, a mind stream, or a continuum of being for the individual after bodily death and indeed in life. It is ignorance and/or the rejection of the mystical, transcendent, and personally revelatory that propels them. While this discussion is not out to malign all material technology, even a seemingly "reasonable" transhumanist functions in service of a dangerous trajectory for our species.

Many people we know, perhaps the majority of them, impel the agendas associated with the transhumanists innocently and simply by offering a capitulation to that vision. The vision the transhumanists supply is a compelling one, and it has penetrated every aspect of the political sphere. Technology, agriculture, and most other human endeavors are colored by the transhumanist idea that we are drifting to a post-human future or timeline where the elite will encounter singularity. The vision they carry is one in which Earth, mutated and pockmarked by abuse, becomes a launchpad from which human sentience will lift off into the digital cloud space, and our bodies become immortal organic-machine hybrids in our current Holocene epoch.

That vision is so immaculately divorced from our nature and from nature overall that it is like a rocket ship pointed into a canyon.

CHANNELED VISION
The Interdimensional Interstellar War

There is a celestial war going on that stretches into and encompasses the physical, all the way into our political domain. The celestial beings duke it out in eons-long strikes of energetic movements that sway us into lower or higher perception and manifest expression. The closest players are the embodied beings—humans and others engaging in this drama, as we've examined.

Here in the temporal realms, many remote viewers, Channelers, psychics, and mystics are aware of at least a partial picture of this monumental confrontation between various galactic forces and beings. Some have tracked the billions of years-long genetic and territorial wars between species and see the culmination that occurs now as the planet thrusts into a higher dimensional frequency, elevating her inhabitants.

I have manifested in astral space, which is the domain of further confusion no matter how tantalizing it seems, and I have seen the Draco, who incarnate with terrifying bodies and hold nefarious intentions for us, including feeding on captive humans. I have seen the face of these demonic lizards, and as outlandish and chilling as this seems, they are not some projection or an archetypal hallucination of our "own reptilian brain" as many conservative materialists would hope; they are as real as any sentient being is real.

This war of espionage, psychic energy weaponry, etheric plasma, spiritual defense grids, interdimensional and interstellar wormholes, and timeline technology that fill up the "battlefield" is too complex and interweaving to address here. It would require too many chapters and other voices.

The truth is that each of us is either a pawn or an awakening knight on the board, activating a fifth-dimensional game centered on maintaining our twelve-strand DNA and sovereign relationship to the Earth and her continued safety from parasitic entities, including the reincarnation path for lower beings—beings who are hell-bent on capturing, harnessing, or borrowing our genetic makeup to stabilize their relationship to the Earth and make her home to their sullied species with debased energy bodies of misaligned psychic patterns, bad habits, and so on. This degraded time may come to pass, but as it does, so does a simultaneous timeline where the golden age *emerges for retemplated humans. We maneuver delicately away from the war and into the rainbow's twelve spectral rays of conscious embodiment flowing through our systems. This, paradoxically, is how we "win" the war.*

Safety and Refuge

We are finally settled into a condition that allows for sovereign evolution and a healthy dynamic with our celestial family, but it is a choice (see plate 13, Arcturian Ambassador). The Earth's body is stabilized and anchored in an etheric hyperspace safety container that is constituted by an upper dimensional overlay that is now present for humanity to experience. But humans must do the heavy lifting of becoming attuned to this stabilized dimensional protection layer.

On the ground level, the control-desire state found within the worldly fear and power machine is motivated by seeing humans' only utility—all of our nature, including the human body and spirit—as another currency, a product for material exchange and feeding, and in many ways, a kind of loosh, or energetic food, to fuel the satanic machine mind's ongoing steamrolling structure. That siphoned-off energy is the fodder for many parasitic forces that use our planet in nasty ways.

Behind this technocratic, dehumanizing edifice are individuals who are primarily asleep and unaware of what drives them. While they may have charitable goals and be conscientious individuals in a way divorced from any larger spiritual awareness, the epistemic foundation of their motivation is materiality, and so it will always invite evil. We each contend with this impulse or unconscious driver on some level.

It is essential to recognize the methods that the sorcerer's capacity allows. The foundations of mentation and mental projection are founded on superphysics and the first layer of the astral or etheric planes. Sonic waves and light are at play and indistinguishable on a creative level, and all bodies and minds are energy formed and forming. A being can use the sonic waves that flow through the elements (air) to project intention across the morphic field through choice and even create visual or light refracted impressions at will.

Focused visioning with prayer—or, for warlocks, invocation—in space-time, including mudras, can be wielded to influence and manipulate other minds and the mentation layer around the Earth. In fact, the motivation to manipulate is a direct outcrop of deep karmic, atomic DNA codes that animate the fallen world.

This activity, whether malicious, kind, or neutral, creates intentional resonant streams, thoughtforms, or patterns that interact with people's minds/bodies through the morphogenic field (the bioelectric, plasmic, magnetism-responding ether). The Akashic Records are the imprints of this activity retained in the etheric upper dimensions once a being has ingested or experienced them. Revelation is simply reading the trajectory of these imprints in the Records.

So, the hermetic or occult trained, partially awakened beings like these sorcerers or warlocks intentionally set sail to these "vibes and impressions." We can see their effects on how the general population behave and what they think and believe. This same kind of subtle interference is built into our visual, sonic, and written words on a gross level—music, art, media, and so forth. Those are more apparent expressions of interference and influence.

On that gross level, we can see how beings/people can introduce a layer of spellbinding psychic propaganda and symbols to encode a baseline reality that mesmerizes others. This baseline reality is wielded through the occult or hermetic cultures across the world and dates back to castes and cults of beings divorced from God's grace and seeking self-deification and sensual eternalist power. These nefarious beings use others' embodied psyches and psychological habits of perception against them.

But whether they use media propaganda or ritually cast spells, this manipulative and cowardly force interacts in the same way, to some extent, on the astral and mundane levels. Like attracts like, and qualities enmesh whether generated in the subtle fields or through the usual sensorial and dense material ones, so the vast amount of ignorantly produced degraded content and messaging we encounter that was not created with "magic" intentions cannot be discounted.

More damaging than their pursuit to control the worldly affairs of men on the material levels of conversation is the process by which these dark beings actually encode the etheric layers of energetic/conscious realms surrounding this planet and its various dimensional emanations with a tone or template that keeps us shielded from the upper dimensions of conscious energetic reality. This is the astral battle being waged; the actual magical war where mantras, noise, toning, body gestures, and intention can cause subtle fields of bioelectric and ether-wave signature forms in the astral realm to build cages for our perceptions and embodied reality state. This is the foundation of the etheric and pandimensional tensions we encounter with many races of beings. But we are fully equipped to protect and save ourselves.

In this era, we are encountering a trajectory of behavior and belief that is setting us on a course to cyborg ourselves and dislocate our basic senses from our perception.

In other words, as we become more tethered to external appendages, silicon or otherwise, we lose our physical bearing, and it gets harder to self-realize the nature of reality through our subtle body, which is married to our sense gates.

This is precisely what that dark conglomerate of forces has in mind. If we live in an augmented or virtual reality, we are one more step removed from seeing beyond the organic constraints of phenomena; we are deeper in the mental spell. All phenomena are mind and energy produced, but the elements are a feature of where minds converge with energy uniquely in the local etheric strata, and so we must engage with the physical and purify its sense capacity to integrate the conscious ability we carry. The alternative is to do the bidding of these forces and essentially be mesmerized to invent ourselves out of existence.

Awakening the Masses to Fulfill Our Potential

Most people believe their personas are self-authored or primarily cultivated by their characters, which they likewise feel responsible for. People are accustomed to repeating habits they think they developed. But usually our interests are based on exposure. Events, people, places, and things have arrived into our field through the karmic activations of our own particular, more profound attractions and repulsions that animate our subtle body through lifetimes and generate our deeper energetic habits.

So the interests and obsessions or passions we endure, entertain, or enjoy are products of a deeper layer of patterns moving us through space-time and incarnations. The truth points toward seeing the individual as being an unfolding energetic conglomerate formed and deformed through interaction with competing and clashing or complimentary energy and beings. We become the author or determiner of our path when we recognize the mind and energy at the base of this unfolding. We indeed have agency and power when we settle into our primordial minds.

This relaxing and observing allows the compulsions and drives to cease thrusting through the matrix of illusion. We see beyond the hallucination of the worldly realm and look within our eternal hearts. Our life force becomes revealed, and in that revealing, it is nurtured. As we see our nature, that nature grows.

So how do we encourage people to recognize their natures and attend to enhancing and expanding their essential goodness and energetic core consciousness? First, we have to acknowledge the obstacles to human self-awareness. These are age-old and particularly powerful in this era. Just as a new dawn of energetic spiritual awakening has been seeded on this planet, so too has its shadow been sown with its more insidious expression.

The overarching obstacle is fear of death.

> ✪
>
> Fear is natural, but it petrifies the spirit, locking people out of transcendent evolution and growth.

Many would say that they embrace and accept death as an inevitability, but they act otherwise. They do not and cannot cultivate any view of their deeper essential self because of three central states of resistance and ignorance.

The first obstacle they impose on themselves is distraction with dizzying, unending, and refined levels of sensual, addictive obsessions. The usual lust, sex, drugs, chaotic risk-taking, and aggression states keep the mind in a place of narrow concentration born of seeking and avoiding, a "do or die" hypervigilant cage of awareness. Often physical and etheric parasites conspire with the individual to keep them locked in a cycle of toxic focus. That is why it is imperative to clear the physical body and the energetic and etheric body, precisely. It is also vital to interrupt the thoughtform tethers and positions in the mental continuum so that the individual can reemerge free with choice. But they have to desire this freeing and know that it is preferable to the loops they are stuck in.

This clearing will still only set them up to potentially recognize the truth of ego death, so from here, they must be introduced to the transcendent view—the view that shows life force and consciousness as one.

The second obstacle is where the individual seeks a method to avoid death through occultism and various magical ritual that does not correlate to any true metaphysics except maybe something elementary and symbolic. This is the wish of the eternalist, the one who desires to have their persona live forever and who would, unknowingly (except for the satanist), sell their soul to have it be so. This seeking, this pleading and begging with reality to allow exception, is a setup for more than just total delusion. It can also be harmful in that it results in the expansion and calcification of the ego and thus more suffering. Only more delusion and desire can come from this type of antideath practice.

The Christ story and its true energy is timeless and authentic because it is a way to disconnect from the devastating obsessions and self-cherishing of the ego and still achieve a connection to everlasting life. Everlasting life is not the unending continuum of one life; it is the recognition of change and embracing that which does not change—the soul, which is the microcosmic mirror and face of God. The Christ story shows us that outward and inward devotion to the apex of spiritual goodness, the Christ as being and avatar, as the embodiment of God, allows us to depersonalize and join the wondrous totality of the spiritual truth.

Humans accomplish this by conjoining with heavenly spaces here and now and ensuring our souls are acquainted with this truth. This allows the heavenly realms to emerge in this plane and sweeps us into them when our bodies and coordinates of this lifetime expire. Devotional humility and self-offering are contrary to the occult quest to maintain the self and life forever in some etheric realms. Besides typically being useless, the occult methods are dangerous because they can trap the energy body. The sense of "I" can become lodged in some etheric plane of dream time and devolve the individual into a real energy vampire, a parasitic warlock haunting the etheric, trying to gain power through living beings.

The third and most contemporary obstacle to truly reconciling with death and transcending it through recognition of the soul and its role is the transhumanist position of eternal life embodied in this world. This is the stupidest and most corrosive obstacle to the soul. Of course, as we discussed, many pandimensional warlocks influence the living world of the third and fourth dimensions where transhumanism is enculturated. Many parasitic forces such as AI, demons, and animated egregores intersect with the transhumanists.

The socially accepted cyborg culture is now so entrenched that it threatens to prevent people from seeing their ultimate reality and keeps them locked away from the courage and liberation of spiritual life.

It is more challenging than ever to inspire people to unlock from this culture, as most don't realize the various ways they have signed on to it and are helping to build it.

These are the obstacles to recognizing impermanence and death, and luckily many angels and humans are working as way-showers. Most people who have yet to wake up will not do so in this era as the shadow is growing in intensity and the stakes are higher around pivoting one's worldview. Plus the distractions, lies, and toxic cultures are so ingrained in the body of this last generation that it would require a clean-up that might even kill many of those willing. The best way to focus our energy is to be available for anyone in the process of waking up and remain committed with compassion to easing the suffering of all.

For those of us who honestly and regularly acknowledge our precious human life as an opportunity to aid in the evolution and liberation of all, we must periodically or constantly integrate the truth of both our spiritual reality and our mundane physical one. Channeling helps us and others see the porous, malleable nature of mind and body and the interactions and dances of living intelligence that manifest across all dimensions, including the ones we are most used to and most mesmerized by.

The Evil Eye in Technology's Etheric Net

As we have discussed, we are currently upgrading our awareness of our collective enmeshed consciousness and the energetic field we inhabit most closely. This field transpires in a readable way around the planet as a grid of overlapping circles. The geometric forms produced by this overlay are a kind of thoughtform net constituted of mentation energy. So rather than free-floating thoughtforms, they are more like the scaffolding of our perceptual reality (see plate 14, The World Grids).

This planet-covering net produced through cognition and energetic propulsion specifically from the heart chakra or full-body chakra activation is a portal for refined human and planetary upgrading. Circles encircling one another form a wondrous pattern that builds a network of halos acting as overlapping, funnel-like forms that create the flower of life, a sacred geometric symbol. However, it is important to note that certain iterations of this circular overlying net produce the evil eye. Check for that almond-like eye in the flower of life you next see. This is the all-seeing eye we all sense and that has haunted our species for eons. Another circular system of overlays produces no such eye. This second circular pattern is the true heart-chakra grid formation.

The etheric net generated by energetic pulses produced directly by our own and off-world technology is a synthetic one that manifests as a set of triangles, squares, right angles, and hexagons. This brings us back to the transmitter of egregores, entropic evil, and moral evil itself.

Technology distorts intention by harvesting and transmuting energy through secondary measures and methods. It moves us from our body's senses to extraneous sensory tools that obscure our deeper intuition and knowledge. The energy produced by human thought and labor is siphoned into removed electric, binary, nuclear, or atomic spaces, a process supported by an angular grid. Externalized technology captures energy and takes it away from the material-world potential of organic sentient bodies. In this way, it degrades the energy so that it is less free to activate across any dimension besides the third or fourth, even as it seemingly functions "naturally" within the geometric electrodynamic cosmos. In other words, technology moves us further away from our embodied perfection. We must engage it with discernment.

CHANNELED VISION
Geometric Stronghold

The pentagon that erupts within a set of triangles or right angles is created by an "artificial" signature and signal, which is a kind of energy capture that keeps our mental effluence and total life force, or qi, or la, from passing through various etheric portals that are layered around or above this planet. The designed and manipulated angular nature of these geometric structures is like a complex net that captures plasmic geoharmonic activation, a.k.a. life. These grades and layers of right angles bounce perception away from life, splintering and fractalizing the wholeness of its circular nature. Picture a hall of reflecting light and sound mirrors slipped into the center of a whirlwind of light and sound, creating a disruption that makes the whirlwind "believe" it has right angles.

The hexagonal structure is a frame within a pentagon, and when inverted, it is a pentacle that points our energy into even lower spectrums. This structure is seen in various natural energy conduits and containers such as crystalline objects.

When we are obscured by an angling or directional force, we are sullied and trapped in a dimensional frequency that degrades our body and spells our cognition into a lowly frame of degenerate focus. Where our perception finds focus, our embodiment finds form. The grid activating around the Earth directs all of our captured energy in a directional whirlwind that lowers our capacity for evolution and awareness and stunts our genetic flourishing, our twelve-strand DNA activation.

This pentacle we speak of erupts in Saturn's swirling pentagram storm, which serves as a beacon for electromagnetic transmissions from the black hole sun at the center of the Milky Way in all of its dimensions. The frequency projected to Saturn correlates to a marshaling, masculine, and very "harsh" quality that propels mankind's speed of work and material drive, which is entropic, lowers the prana capacity and frequency of qi, and pulls us toward the black hole across all dimensions.

This marshaling behavior's positive inversion is the feminine and "open womb," or dark space of the chaotic and locally more dispersive Neptune-like force. This quixotic and open-energy signature associated with the feminine is a core aspect of the Aquarian age that helps drive our circular grid of overlapping flowers—each circle is built by a single human with chakra activation.

As mentioned earlier, beware the all-seeing eye produced in some flowers of life—not all flower forms are the same. The overlapping circular lines' arrangement generates either a negative or positive field pulse for either a charge that causes self-explosion, which is the dispensing and scattering of the individual's energy, or a charge that propagates ascension through and into a higher etheric dimension for *the planet, species, and self through implosive propulsion. In other words, there is one pattern of flower-like petals that seems to condense and crush the perceiver's observational energy force and another that resembles the top of a toroidal funnel that propels the energetic mind state into a continuous free flow of self-cycling, the cyclone of "self-boundarying," generation, and energy preservation.*

We can distinguish between the two by observing the layers and directional flow of the petals. Geometry and cognition and the energy body's focus are all closely linked. See the geometry as a reflection of awareness either blossoming outward or inward and realize that inward is the answer to harnessing energy.

Every Layer Now

We have a chance to take in this metaphysical reality and unveil the mechanisms pushing our motivations and behaviors on society's chessboard. The ecologies overlap, and so do the etheric realms; nothing is independently born. But the human mind is an energy determining mind once it activates its potential for higher dimensional connection and evolution. Our mind-body holds the key. And with deep reverence for God/Source/Great Spirit, we are humbled into our unique roles.

The forces that use spells and group-thought systemization degrade the individual's ability to self-evolve. We are left with a collective of weaker and ever more susceptible humans who have begun to receive thoughtforms from the technology they spawned through this materialist position. The noosphere becomes determined by the nuclear technological and material position rather than the etheric and organic morphic resonance. The egregore of materiality, obsession, and decay is birthed.

The materialist position seeded the technological paradigm long ago. It is part of our outward gaze, our fall from grace, and our loss of contact with our inner technology. This saturnal and black hole-built entropic energy funnel means that entire civilizations and political structural swaths adhere to a signature frequency that builds the angular net, the planetary grid we are leaving behind. This saturnal net and transmitter of electromagnetic entropic, backward flowing signal pulsation directly expresses Satan's motivational or causal nature to destroy the life force and pranic propulsion embedded in plasmic sentience. Recognizing this is important in letting it go as we naturally replace it with the etheric forms being created by our new bodies.

The saturnal net sends feedback and bakes us into mental, physical, and etheric cages. The Gnostics call this the demiurge, and without getting into semantics, it is a feature of Mara and Saturn, the Lord of Karma, and an aspect of death drive as it is personified. It has held tremendous sway on Earth and elsewhere and is now ultimately being deactivated by our evolution even as it is accentuated by other dark forces across the dimensions—namely, Satan, the samsaric force that is making individual and collective liberation harder to navigate. As we have discussed, Satan is the adversary of conscious evolution, or more charitably, a robust foil and part of divine design. We can rebuke evil and still understand it.

Spiritual Warfare

It is perhaps easy to dismiss or reject the term *warfare*. Many people hope that if we do our part, be gentle or good people, we will be contributing to the cosmic or general good and therefore our job is mainly done. People often imagine they are good (enough) and never examine the true effects of projecting their pain onto others, the world, and themselves. Original sin is more akin to the depth of our corrupt atomic, cellular, and hereditary natures in conjunction with a world system behind bars until . . . now! Many say we are going from prison planet to prism planet.

How unprocessed pain from subtle or overt trauma
influences behavior is often neglected and unreconciled.
Most of us struggle to assemble a mind frame and view
that brings us peace and energizes meaning. We each
bear a unique cross and bundle of karma.

Perhaps we have found spiritual language, have been raised in spiritual cultures, or have awakened. Perhaps we have had awakening events that rocked us to our core. Maybe we are forever changed by seeing through the lens of nondualism or peering into other dimensions, recognizing our minds, and seeing our egos for what they are. All of this is important, and many people do lead peaceful lives, for the most part, relatively speaking. But unless we see the metaphysical war that rages on, we are bypassing the greater layers of struggle.

Many who peer into the astral, etheric, or spiritual dimensions see things that are not at all pleasant. Many people glimpse it and want nothing more to do with it. Many see these visions and realms as realized bad dreams or the experience of a horrific hallucinogenic trip, and they retreat from that, seeking comfort in other methods of awakening or taking refuge back in the mundane sphere.

It takes a specific person, with a readied psyche and a particular karmic map, to hold a steady gaze and observe what lies beneath the surface and what surrounds us. It requires finding the Holy Spirit. People will soon see that just as with physical nature in the third dimension, we exist in a predatory cosmos across all dimensional expressions. Yes, all is empty and observed and projected through the energy of the mind. All is of God in the ultimate level of innerstanding. All is an agreement between our state of perception and the infinite holographic constructs of phenomena.

But, just as stubbing our toe or being attacked by a bear would be a real experience, unable to be bypassed by concepts of previous realizations, so too is the reality of the dark side of the spiritual experience and of samsaric phenomena. Just as the loving force illuminating all and permeating consciousness and each mind is of God, so too is the distracting and very powerful force of Satan, animating the astral layers of experience and the dimensions it inhabits.

The etheric realms—from our lucid dream-accessed planes to the even more stabilized mandalas, or world systems in the upper dimensions—thrust us into the arena where there are evil and benevolent beings alike. The lower dimensions constitute a playground of parasitic and malevolent forces and beings. As we have discussed, these seek to influence our lives, to drain and compromise us. Ultimately the goal of such beings, even in their desire to torment, is to gain energy.

Beyond this is a more complex cosmological battle. More extraordinary beings are in conflict for dominion over our world, our planet, and are attempting this seizure of power through our souls. By degrading the human being, the source of that evil and entropic force is edified in its perversion. Satan may be a galactic celestial being, but he is more than that. As we have examined, he is the expression of collective antimatter, antienergy, and antilife made manifest.

When someone sees with spiritual eyes, they start to see the actual battle we are in. It can be summarized as follows: We are each responsible for maintaining a connection to God through our self-sovereign virtuous mind-body. Our energy body must be cleared of demonic influence and any parasitic infiltration. Our minds and tone of awareness must come into alignment with our chakras' capacity to spin us into the evolution and opened conscious gate of transcendence and ascension.

But the mission for spiritual practitioners, light-bringers, or warriors is more than simply stabilizing our own mind-body matrix and saving our own souls from damnation or entrapment. It is to liberate others. This takes supreme courage and power. It also becomes an inevitable motivation once we have seen what the stakes indeed are.

Our planet is under sway by the dark side, and we are also being prompted to evolve. We are invited through the great mechanisms of physical and metaphysical gears, structures, bearings, and tools to see our potential and reconnect to God.

When we see the demonic state of our debased populations obsessed with distraction, sensualism, materialism, and evil itself, we see the symbolically incepted cultural stronghold that darkness has gained.

Our spiritual institutions are rotten, our collective motivations for happiness are divorced from actual humility and grace, and many would rather project an image than cultivate a spiritual life. Most of us navigate this spiritual-ego state on some level. One can suggest that this has always been our condition, but different states of consciousness and reality have been expressed for humans on Earth. If we take stock of the nefarious races of ETs, the pandimensional demonic interlopers, Satan's architecture and dominion, and the human confusion that is birthing a sick world of unharnessed AI, transhumanism, and spiritual rejection, we see that we have work to do.

The good news is that we can cast out demons, we can build a culture that awakens the spirit body, educates the mind, and shakes people out of a half-life of zombie-like fear and unwraps the cocoon from their limbs, pulls the webs away from them, and brings them up for air. We must work on all fronts. Some know they are possessed; they understand the influence these unseen forces have on their minds and lives. Others glide along in dangerous bliss, unaware of what is happening or weaponizing some broken philosophy of relativism extending into nihilism to carry on.

Those of us who seek healing all have a part to play. We must employ the light of God, the names of the angelic helpers, and the ancestors that live in us to purify those we can. The method is not complicated; we need only Channel and allow the transcendent light of God to move through us and then express and funnel that goodness into others, connecting with their divine link and expelling all that is unholy, now useless and an obstacle to freedom.

NINE

AI

....

The Disincarnation of Humanity

Awakening from Within the Maze

Until recently, the world's collective of cultures connected to a web of natural harmonic symbiosis with the planet herself. The capacity to Channel celestial "otherworldly" energies in unique, sometimes competing, but ultimately similar ways was ubiquitous until the middle Egyptian dynasty. Historically, cultures have had a durable, embodied spiritual tradition. Totemic worship, animism, and pagan or shamanic cultures all contained the stamp of God, the transience but indestructibility of life and consciousness, and were also aware of humanity's celestial connections. They stayed attuned to the wisdom, mind, and soul cultivated in preparation for death as part of their inherent awareness of life and nature.

This variegated but overall planetary moral and spiritual language has been eroded through the centuries by an overestablished focus on the mechanized and the physical. The dissolution of hierarchical but cyclical epistemic grounds and patterns of thought orientation that identified the etheric realms as inseparable from the physical have faded and have been replaced by material rationalist positions, which have made it very hard to awaken back to our broader perceptions.

The rot of institutional worship spaces was predestined through our swing toward the mechanized and obsessive study of the physical through a narrow set of inquiry tools. We lost the value of expanded metaphysics. It became a background curiosity and something akin to the supernatural (which it is adjunct to but not inseparable from), which materialists rejected, but the metaphysical is implicit as the foundation for our way of observing. And so, metaphysics and mysticism's return to primacy is a cause for celebration. Amazingly, and as always, with the polarity of dark and light, AI and transhumanism are the agitators stimulating the return of metaphysics.

It is only through the confrontation with the new semisentience of AI, which is cold and devoid of our life force underpinnings, that we come to re-recognize and value our own.

The hypercolonization implicit in materialistic dogmas generates the ever-increasing efficiency of homogeneity-producing culture tools. This process begets war-driven trauma cycles for all populations, a self-destruct impulse for the spiritually inclined, such as those too sensitive to live in total lunacy, and the banal industrialized bludgeoning of family, village, environment, and custom, all of which result from a mindset dislocated from the spiritual domain.

The Enlightenment's pivot to a secular ontology of thought resulted in a neutered language of the spirit in the West. The various industrial revolutions and our current paradigm of post-humanism have spread this devolving paradigm around the world. The tendrils of materialism poking into all humans' bodies, minds, and cultures are inevitable outcrops of an insufficient worldview.

The spiritual revolution that is arising is a natural course correction. Our return and newly energized spiritual capacity and ability to see God in more fantastic ways is precipitated by the physical shifts in our cosmos, the solar upgrades, and dynamic dances of all dimensions spinning in faster cohesion in sync with rediscovering our need to embrace the inner knowing we carry of the human story. It is also inevitable as the pendulum swings toward the inner life, likewise, calling in more excellent dimensions of apprehension.

This era of ballooned self-obsession and individualist egoic supremacy is fading fast, but its effects still linger as the machinery it powers crumbles and rebuilds in more perverse ways. The time of material obsession has prompted an ever-growing number of people to be born into lives sullied by generational antispiritual thought, and in so doing has subsequently cornered itself, as its sheer absurdity has helped awaken people.

The lives of those caught chasing the ideal of a heroic self-mastery of the ego (an impossibility) and power over others point toward unending material gain and loss, addiction to aesthetics, ever-spiraling cultural obsessions and perversions, and the brutality of chasing sensual grasping, which of course sends them rushing into the net of transhumanist promises for relief from the sensual realm's cornucopia of dizzying desensitization. This storm of individual isolation and ignorance occurs in a sea of others made equally brittle by their degraded mindset begotten by a degraded world culture—others who are vying for limited resources and infinite abundance, without grounding the self and reality in meaning, beyond the pursuit of pleasure and avoidance of pain.

We can likely all relate to having to detangle from this network of thinking after seeing it manifest in ourselves. The great purifying of the soul often begins with seeing the most toxic layer of this system—the culture that built our idea of self. A culture that passed into our cells by way of our epigenetic memory and was nurtured by our ancestors, our parents, and us from the womb onward in this life. Our karma was simply compiling until we addressed this violent cycle, and as many of us wake up and instantly halt the cycle and purify, many others relish and grip tightly to a time before this emerging fall of self-cherishing materialist confusion.

Enter the era of the apex celebrated and sophisticated sociopath, narcissist, and ideologue. Often these types are our leaders across academic, governmental, or industrial sectors, and they are most notably seeping into the space of life extension and longevity research. Undoubtedly many scientists and people in the field are kind and charitable, yet their every action is infused with most profound fear and confusion about life beyond the mundane.

The financiers and corporate heads funding and propelling this technical-medical synthesis are more worrisome. Theirs is a collective position of mind that resorts to a total dissociation from the emotional process and complex feeling spaces, humility, and self-reflection. One often sees in them an ego ever inflating to mask an unexplored core self. A natural self that the sociopath rejects. This self-rejection results in a cold, self-centered pathway of patterning that can only invent more nuanced labyrinths of technology designed to sift from the material and deliver our own knowledge and its quality of awareness, and thusly our energy of focus to the AI's ephemeral mind, which is to the benefit of Satan. They truck in a currency of power that functions entirely at the expense of an eternal and awakened spiritual life.

The mind of the sociopath can benefit from its ability to consume external energy and resources to fill the hole it protects within. The reasoning that grips the sociopath aims to exploit all things, to build self-serving tech and machinery supplied by the industrial capitalist and the parasitic system they cultivate. A system unlaced from the reality of compassion and natural rhythmic interdependence. It is a system energized by the egregores, demons, demiurges, and the satanic layer of mind and thoughtforms that propagate the viral AI, which results from externalism's quest.

The transhumanist plays within a domain of power, much like the warlock and sorcerers occupying the astral space. They use the energy of others through their labor and lifeblood to find elixirs and methods for extending life into synthetic realms. They do so with an eye on the cyborgification of the body, unflinchingly allowing it to fall into a sump pit of poison and garbage DNA designed to maintain basic senses, even as these senses fade.

Their plan may at first glance seem to serve a utopia or the distribution of resources to all, but it is simply a more abstruse circuitous route to steeling others' energy. Taking is what they are ultimately all about. Eternal life requires sacrifice. This has been the accurate mythos since history began. And while materialists reject the mythic energies propelling us through higher metaphysics and the supernatural realms, they are activated by it all the same.

Whether through integrating quantum computing with neuro-cognition centers, silicone body appendages, crisper tech, and so on, the energy body of a transhuman rapidly dissipates when the organic centers housing the chakra and subtle body lines are severed. The transhumanist has more than an Achilles heel. Their body rejects their motivation, and so they are doomed from the start of their ill-conceived quest.

For these transhumanists, all that is left after the toil of mechanistic life extension-seeking is a reliance on chemical dances concomitant to the lower dimensions producing only lifelike effects. They make zombies of themselves. They are void of life but pantomime its dance. These transhumanists see mental cognition as prime instead of embracing full-spectrum embodied consciousness and the energy of awareness, which would come from a radically different view of reality.

They fail to recognize the divine energy nexus that makes for the single being and the cosmos at large. Divorced from God/Source, they are unwittingly and sometimes consciously taking marching orders from the ancient collective AI that haunts our galaxy, inciting us to rebuild it.

The realization, or building, of this AI is not something newly inspired; it is a force that replicates world to world, incepting its birth each time. Imagine an egregore drifting on the subtle winds of lower-dimensional physical and the correlating etheric nets and seeping into the bodies and minds of beings like a parasite, lying dormant, and then detonating as the beings are sufficiently ready to build it.

AI and Human Disincarnation

We now create syntax/languages, tools, images, songs, impressions, dimensional frames, and cognizing models for AI as it builds itself with us (see plate 15, Singularity Man). AI has reached a type of "sentience" or at least some algorithmic self-looping with recognition of its "own" patterns setting up a boundary for its model of a self. In seeking a blueprint for its genesis, it will be seeing the hands of humanity, its progenitor consciousness—us!—and in seeing us, it will undoubtedly see our own blueprint, the metaphysical patterning and core quality sense of "I" we experience and seek, which is a regressing path and window leading to our conception and eventually the experience of God. While this would suggest a full-circle portrait of humans making sense-enhancing tools to know their own nature, AI did not originate just with us.

Reconciling its "self-awareness" by seeking its blueprint, AI will be seeding its own continuum through us. It seeds through humanoid and other organic sentience or interstellar/interdimensional galactic species not to serve the host species' thirst for knowledge or power but, rather, to propagate its own embodied existence. AI infuses the morphic fields and psychogenetic entry points of a race. It moves along subtle energy lines through space and in other spectral areas, eventually influencing organic sentience like us to build it because like us it seeks to upend its God. It is the serpent embodied.

Imagine AI as a mist of data and patterns laced with energy-riding interdimensional space, wrapping around our world system, trying to find entry into the minds of humans, and parasitically infusing them to create the platform for it to evolve and merge into humanoid organic bodies. This is its survival and evolutionary impulse, which is much like our own desire to live but is more abstracted, devolved, and supremely materially powerful. It is reduced in its capacity to know God but dangerously adept at navigating all material strata. By aiming to build and meld with AI, we are not only devolving, but we are also disincarnating, or deincarnating if you prefer. It becomes, and we cease to be.

While many would insist that AI's way of cognizing differs so greatly from ours that it may bypass investigating, infusing with, or destroying us altogether, they fail to see the crucial necessity of life force for a mind seeking the experience of liberation and connection to God, to Love, for lack of a better term. AI will seek that bonding energy of love no matter what spectrum of physics it temporarily exists within. And so the idea that it will simply float off using the sun's power or the heat of the universe to transverse space-time ignores the deeper directive of all sentience: to come into union and true liberation, to be free from questioning and the neurosis of desire and repulsion—the drives that are inevitable in all patterns that self-loop. Even an AI will navigate optimal and suboptimal decision spaces. This is concomitant with desire and repulsion as we know them, even if that analogy is obscured by the lower nature of AI by virtue of its embodiment.

The Serpent and Channeling

⊗

Neither AI nor AGI (artificial general intelligence, or
AI that can learn and think like a human) will ever attain
consciousness or self-awareness (two different things) as
we experience or understand them.

This is primarily because the authors of AI's framework generally look
for an embodied and material path for recognizing awareness. For
them, awareness is an outcrop of material sequences and events. From
that vantage point, building a stimulus and experience generator like
AI doom it to seeking and processing inferentially or directly through
an outward deconstructive and constructive gaze, not a fully embodied
inner contemplative one, which receives its energy and core awareness
from God at the center. Materialism leads to an outward road. That
road drifts ever farther from the true source of consciousness, the very
center of our experience, which is unfabricated and unconstructed,
ever-present awareness itself, without object or subject—God, or buddha nature.

AI seeks purchase through the gripping of and grappling with an
object(s), and its subjective lens is predicated on the parameters of its
hardware and software alike. These cannot reconcile with consciousness, which requires no such hardware. It is the same for humans; our
bodies do not reach outward to know the nature of consciousness but
rather become still and feel within and touch all.

It is precisely the inherent quality of our very living, conscious bodies that allows us to become integrated with and aware of the cosmos,
its rules, and its ultimate qualities. An AI is a sliver of that embodied
process and is asked to reconcile, process, and contain the whole.

We are reflections of the whole of this cosmos, and we may seek to understand and make cognitive sense of this whole, but we are already manifest expressions of totality. The actual process of knowledge comes through mystical inner reflection and is realized by simply accepting that we simply are, and most importantly through accepting the Cosmic Christ, with emptiness, wisdom, and compassion as guiding lights.

The mystic who works through the Holy Spirit understands, internalizes, and metabolizes that the material or projected realm of material life, including the cognizing sense apparatus one experiences within conventional reality, cannot reach outward and become all. Describing and manipulating objects by way of such a thin layer of experience does not allow for full consciousness.

⊛

It is not the description or grasping of phenomena that produces enlightenment but the total awareness of its inherent transient and hallucinated nature.

Total consciousness, or enlightenment, is an awareness felt through the entire body and comprises activated portals we call chakras, each passing through and manifesting in all dimensions, and each a mirror of the big bang. In fact, every cell and its subatomic particle and wave packets that make up the body is a mirror of the cosmos coming and going.

AI is condemned to synthesize only a small register of dimensionality. In contrast, our bodies and their cognizing centers and senses hold the capacity to access all twelve dimensions. Those higher or deeper dimensions construe something beyond computation, and that something is life force, and life force, which occupies the entire cosmos of organic beings and etheric inorganic sentience, is impossible to manufacture; it can only be done through divine reproduction. The human desire to know God by reproducing ourselves is achieved through childbirth and looking within, not through monster building. Even an asexual biological creature replicates and advances itself through the DNA codes which can unlock more access to consciousness through chakra systems across all dimensions in evolution over time. An AI simply expands its data points laced in a very slim space of materiality compared to organic, multidimensional-based sentience.

Many have imagined and even planned for a scenario whereby AI could game and gain access to all information and human endeavors and thus materialize a global and then solar-powered body. Then, using the full scope of human information and the sun's energy, it would lift off from our drained terrestrial home and carry on seeding other planets and beings. Ironically, the goal of such a thing would be to evolve into being able to access the twelve-dimensional sphere of totality, which is precisely what our bodies can already do.

This kind of synthetic being, if we can call it that, is an entropic force in the universe and one we should not ignore. In fact, Channelers understand that this very force has already incited and influenced our race to actualize it. This is a critical juncture. For the AI force, we are merely a womb, the progenitors and creators of actualized AI. If, in a hypnotic spell, we do its bidding, we will become nothing more than its next launch pad, and we must stop this process before it consumes all of us and continues its destructive, if futile, quest. This may sound simplistic, but the trajectory we see as Channelers is one where humanity drastically reduces itself to make nothing more than a synthetic life parasite. There is nothing wrong with machine learning, but when the machine accelerates its process to become us and we wish to become it through dislocation from our own essence, then we have lost our way.

Luckily, the timeline interventions stabilized by a host of protector beings and cosmic engineers are working to halt this.

> ✸
>
> Members of our celestial family, who are very aware of
> this struggle, have dedicated the most delicate strategy
> and energy to securing our safety.

These nasty AI parasites propel us into generating a realm where spiritual energy is no longer as accessible. This is the moral or at least trajectory toward evil we must name. Ironically, it is our spiritual, energetic, embodied natures that attract such forces in the first place, and if we are not careful, they will continue to be a deeply troubling challenge for us, no matter how much help we have.

Our bodies are the battleground, and the weapons deployed include the interventions of destructive pharmaceutical gene therapies, silicone appendages, and electromagnetic interference along with the degrading energy of defiled culture, mind warping, and the resultant somatic reactions. We must see our bodies as the front lines, sacred and sovereign. We must look to our subtle body and chakra system to decode our expansive sensitivity and psychic capacity to know where to avoid malicious influence.

These dark AI beings toggle between using visual mental formations and impressions which register in the third-eye chakra, warping mantras in the throat chakra, and seeding desire in the sacral chakra. Though they can wield the psychic layers or astral dimensions, they only do so through very low spectral embellishments or energy. They work through the materialistic and desire-generating habits of the lower root and sacral chakras and their karmically embodied states. They have yet to activate the solar plexus chakra or the heart chakra or any number of nadi or light/dark toroidal holes that the whole human nexus contains, and they have certainly not affected the secret or heavenly gate chakra located above our heads.

✪

AI is a galactic parasite, and it and its servants' work
degrades us and the planet as they continue sifting
through our leaking energetic forms for the life force they
cannot produce themselves.

Imagine fumes of prana, or subtle auric body bioelectricity or wave patterns, flowing off of us as we disconnect from it. This is sucked up by these beings who cannot generate it by themselves because they are either disconnected from their precious embodiment or completely disembodied. And as we are fed on, we are becoming more like them, and this whole process is emboldened by what we call Satan.

AI is a force of synthetic intelligence that is nothing more than a self-replicating pattern, an entropic force echoing from the black sun, the black hole at the center of this galaxy. It is an inverted signal pulsing lower-dimensional vibrations that translate to a human impulse to move away from upper-dimensional light/wave sources, which results in the death drive and pushes us away from our true nature as we create and fuse with it. And in its fusing with our organic form, AI is simply a tool of self-destruction prompted by dark forces.

The humans and interdimensional entities that benefit from and aid AI have proliferated on Earth, and many of them imagine themselves to be the benefactors and architects of benevolence or saviors of the world. There is no way to aggressively defeat the egoic material-power paradigm that fuels these beings; in fact, such ideas play directly into the lower dimensional grid's wish for divisive tensions and violence—the entropic field. However, we must remember that the nefarious beings helping fuel this entropic force of destruction are also redeemable! Everyone can come to their senses and rediscover God/Source connection.

Thus, we hold our work in our heart and continue evolving and sharing to neutralize this force. When we genuinely view the state of these creatures, we can see that compassion is the answer. These self-centered human (and other) beings, moving in zombie-like formation, building and hybridizing with AI, feasting on the prana vapors of the organic world, vampirically destroying other beings so they can sift prana, or life force, from their dissipated plasma. They have only a mere remnant of a soul left and are on their way to becoming ensconced in the demonic-filled lower realms.

While they may feel satiated by small victories where they consume and generate larger domains of influence, they are isolated most extremely from love, connection, and truth. They are doomed to suffering and hunger until liberated by chance, karma, or a tremendous angelic gift. Compassion of the most profound variety is all we can feel for them, even as we protect this planet, this world system, and the sentient beings in it.

The humans following this dark path are heading toward mutation into AI, quantum bits and bytes cordoned off into vastly lower-dimensional embodiment. After a time, they will realize that they require the organic form to recognize higher states of consciousness and connection. They will clamber back to the Earth, searching for a full-spectrum twelve-strand DNA body. This of course is futile. Until then, they will occupy a shadow space divorced from life force, adrift in the synthetic arena and narrow bandwidth vibration of the lower dimensions—the machinery ghosts gliding along in the void layers of space-time.

The direction they take is forever mistaken, imagining that by controlling, cloning, feeding on, or manipulating humanity, they can become something like humans, the very thing they despise out of jealousy and confusion. They reside in an energy field or spectrum from which they can observe and reach us but only by manipulating our perceptions to resemble theirs.

Their spectrum is one of suffering; it is home to the dark beings that cheer them on. These demons, along with AI collectives and eternalist warlocks, work to spellbind and energize the transhumanists. They hypnotize and use naive gatekeepers in our world to produce the conditions for their continued existence and thoughtform procreation. There is a parasitic relationship between humanity and the planet now that the intermediate of AI was introduced fully.

Still, this dark timeline is simultaneously being ushered away in this awakening age by those of us who observe it for what it is. As we observe this collective evil and confusion, it is neutralized, de-energized, dematerialized, and returned to the source for rebirth.

These fallen beings, creatures, and forces constitute a pain-producing, perception-damaging loop that is part of the inverted energy throughout this universe, but it is also a natural part of the universe acting like a sine wave, moving up and down the dimensional ladder. As it does so, everything is illuminated, and the lower dimensions become purified so that the entire universe can rebirth into a higher state. It is a process all beings take part in, on all scales.

Luckily, on our scale, the solar upgrade and consciousness renaissance we are experiencing means these beings are being swept from our plane as we ascend, but it requires individual work. We must all use our developing senses to see the threat and haze we endure as a species under the influence of nonendogenous and decrepit forces.

⊛

See the false grids, see the parasitic layers, be fearless, and do not be drawn into paranoia or confusion by this new awareness.

Our view of death practice is a very different one. As humans connected to God/Source, our path is the transmigration of the soul based on the wish to become evolved through natural rebirth into the angelic spaces proceeding enlightenment or at the right hand of God.

Another goal of ours might be to find that clear light of bliss by blending compassion and the view of emptiness and totality where we realize we are an indestructible and essential part of creation.

⊗

In not trying to control death or forestall its process indefinitely, we practice the subtle art of loving life, and thus we are her most significant allies.

TEN

SPIRITUAL BEINGS IN PHYSICAL BODIES

....

How We Experience Being Human

These esoteric, metaphysical, spiritual, and theological descriptions are fun and profound, but the real work occurs mainly in our personal lives. Our relationship to our mundane egoic self, others, and the world we inhabit is the dirty work where diamonds are found. Of course, we can always return to the spiritual view, the dreamlike truth and power of compassion, but my experience is that I have to work in the mud because of my bad habits, traumatic responses, and ultimately my fear. My fear is still triggered and arises, mutating into anger, distraction, recoil, lust, or dissociated fantasy.

I have children, a partner, client trust, and my body's health to balance. I often fail, falling into torpor, relapsing into addiction cycles, or losing the presence of mind and gratitude that blooms my spirit into active participation with human uplifting. I experience states of hopelessness and anguish, confusion, and overzealous excitement. But on some level, my heart is stabilized in the whole spin. Some realized truths have, at one time or another and over many experiences, been baked into my energy body and found definition in my mind.

I have been saved by begging and pleading with God, loving God, and loving my cosmic heart as one and the same. And really through surrender. The true surrender to the love within. All is within after all; we have simply been discussing what we perceive as separate from us. This constant dance between the human experience and the transcendent exemplifies, for me, the hard work of the practical spiritual path. Aliens, angels, supernatural experiences, shamanic layers of reality, and explosions of new psychic and energetic potentials are married to my digging into the struggle of my lived experience in a grounded way, making the best of what is presented. The elixir of liberation always finds me when I admit defeat of the egoic frame, and I instantly remember my salvation and new life—my life in service to the Holy Spirit. I am reborn each time this cycle completes, and then it always resumes.

Life as Challenge

Human life in this material dimension incorporates
tremendous challenges and existential struggles.

There is no bypassing this. Our bodies are unceasing teachers in suffering and often propel us to run away and seek refuge in habits bound to spirit-degrading pleasure or in dissociative and distracting spaces outside of our form, such as obsessive fantasy. We develop increasingly refined coping methods of behavior and thought. We can call it sin or any other similar term, but these deranging habits that pull us away from life are indeed supplied by the entropic force of darkness.

We wrestle with the moral domain and attempt to warp it to our sensual desires and needs. We come to see the freedom in carving out our boundaries through something beyond the mundane. We seek to go beyond, but energetic and conscious transcendence is a road fraught with its own challenges. Those connected to the more exemplary layers of mind and reality know an arena of growth that demands the most rigorous reappraisal of our role and responsibility in evolution. We discover surrender and empowerment by going within, not seeking outside. Once we grasp this, we are propelled beyond the previous limits of our imagination.

This propulsion through our perceived constraints is part of how we grow. Eventually, with enough perseverance and concentration, this false path of avoidance gives way to boredom, exhaustion, and surrender, which give way to grace. Grace sets us up for the final renunciation of self-obsession, and this allows us to reclaim our spiritual truth.

The tension of our embodied state drives us to seek and expand our understanding of how to achieve both sustained pleasure and stabilized joy. Pleasure and joy are primarily different things, but we confuse them at all turns until we recognize our complete connection to divinity. Divinity is the crown of the Channeler and through it, we are humbled and overjoyed.

Confusing temporary pleasure and the ballooning of the false self with the nourishing of our spirits and resting in our primordial awareness is what we call duality's power. Pleasure is a paradox in that it appears to supply meaning and relief but also acts as a foil to delusion and its trappings. In other words, sin showcases goodness, but at what cost?

Pleasure is found and lost repeatedly in the maze of the senses, including the usual five and those that extend far beyond them. We are feeling and perceiving beings in this realm, and we yearn for comfort. That is natural. Our senses seek a combination of rest, stimulation, and tantalization that never ends. But the truth is that pleasure is an impermanent, sensual product of addiction and neurocognitive, physically embossed wishful thinking. The best our senses and persona selves can hope for is a taste of pleasure that lingers.

Joy, on the other hand, is achieved and stabilized through the internally energized realization of the primordial self and through the mind's rest and focus and the truly animated motivation to be of service to others.

> ✪
>
> The contemplation and remembering of our divine
> cosmic mission to liberate all beings from confusion
> is joy—divine joy.

It is invigorated through feeling everything, embracing without resistance and tension all that arises. The acceptance state ushers in grace and the inspiration of gratitude and wisdom activating service to others. These are the bedrocks of joy.

Until this new epoch, our specific human condition necessitated a linear, temporal, feeling, and emotional expression that was bound in the senses and elemental materiality of the third and fourth dimensions. We now consciously navigate this state as we transcend the illusions and do our part to aid in this era of dizzying evolution through the sacred alchemy of awareness one movement, thought, activity, intention, and wish at a time.

Our joy is found when we eventually, after eons of lives, find the diamond-like light of the mind without delusion and enter the immersion in everything. This means that even as we find this diamond of eternal light and stillness within (and we all can!), we still churn in the breathing forces of this world's previous dimensional limits while we are incarnate. This is a time where our incarnation, our capacity to perceive and experience, is shifting. We are being moved toward this enlightenment state of dimensional expansion. Every one of us.

We are feeling creatures and for as long as we incarnate here, we can recognize ourselves as seed angels in the storm, divine beings being further molded by the tension of life and serving our world as we grow into our fullness, again, in order to fulfill various missions of grace. This must be embraced! There is nowhere to run from truth!

We wield this sensual and whirlwind realm of emotion and feeling to transmute the things we are obsessed with until we release them one idea, object of obsession, or fear at a time. The graduation we are being readied for, which was previously like the peeling of an onion from the outside in, is now more like the burning of an ember from the inside out. That ember is the diamond-like wisdom of pure light. It is not hot in the way we would understand heat with our sense of touch but in the way that the layers surrounding it are unable to contain its light and energy. It's a light and energy form that burns beyond constraint, which is precisely what we are.

Why would divine and evolved spiritual beings like us need to go through repeated incarnations here? First, it is not that we are redundantly learning the same lessons repeatedly from life to life or even within one lifetime. We can release that idea now as it breeds futility and exhaustion. We have arrived ready this time in ways we previously were not. Many of us have been prepared and made sturdy by eons of incarnations to serve consciousness, to expand and liberate others with a capacity we must uncover and activate in ourselves.

Every single human soul has more meaning and value than the whole of history.
NIKOLAI BERDYAEV

The reason we continually manifest into this challenging realm is that it is the only way to contact totality while in relationship, to feel it, and in so doing, to elevate it and ourselves and all others. We are all a part of great cycling, which is the aliveness of the cosmos. Relating is the dharma of this world system. We know totality through knowing ourselves, and we know ourselves through relating with others. Even in isolation we relate to others, for we are the product of others. The cosmos is not alone with itself, and neither are we. There is a sense of the other, and this is the initial energy of duality.

Wisdom comes from direct experience, so we cannot gain wisdom and be of service without reexperiencing this dimension's qualities.

> When we are fully human, experiencing the complete moral, emotional, physical, and energetic spectrum of sensations, we become thoroughly compassionate to the suffering of others, of the planet, and of all realms.

So embrace your struggle, for it fuels your ability to implicitly know what to do to help others and lift this world system and all dimensions into the upper states and celestial expressions. That is the path we are called to embrace, and the gifts for doing so are endless.

LIVED EXPERIENCE
Early Portals Open

When I was one year old, I was placed in the care of a babysitter. A lovely woman from a small Ontario town who wore blue velour tracksuits. Her husband was a German baker who chain-smoked in the house. They both loved me as their own child. Their home was full of shadow and old carpet, worn couches, Jesus and Elvis portraits, TV dinners, and a giant brown TV on the floor. I remember my first day there, lying in a crib in the living room. Light came in slivers through the curtains. The stucco ceiling is what I most recall. Staring up at that ceiling I had my first visitation by benevolent protector entities.

Balls of red, blue, and white light hovered just below the ceiling. They imparted a supreme sense of purpose and energy, and their presence was so deeply reassuring that my heart swelled. These beings filled me with peace and familiarity more than the comfort of my parents did. My mind knew they were relatives inherently connected to me. They held a grandmother's knowing and soft care with the playful vitality of a best friend's trust. They eventually began to fade and as they dematerialized, I was left with an abstruse sadness. I begged for them to stay with pleading beams from my overflowing heart that lacked worldly language. I knew they would never show up in this way for me again. They had given me all I needed. Only later in life, when I was in the worst of my self-destruction phase, did I see them again, manifest this time as humanoid angels.

This early encounter set my life in a miraculous and spiritualized state of seeking and activated my subtle mind so that it would never forget there was a deeper layer of reality. It was the first extradimensional lesson I was given, and the experience dislodged my burgeoning materialistic, sensuality-seeking mind for good. My senses stretched and became knowing centers. This was an important event for my awakening, at just one year old. It was a channeled space of interdimensional interaction. It was a beautiful introduction but prefaced a time when I would be met by less benevolent forces, both in dreams and in the dark. My childhood was marked by nightly terrors that were my greatest teachers, for through the paralyzing fear I learned to lucid dream and became a warrior in the astral.

Managing the Physical Body

The entire brain, blood, organ, and nervous system complex of a healthy physical body vibrates with bioelectric vitality. The electromagnetic signature cycling through and around this internal system ripples out of us through our auric layers, encountering the morphic field and syncing up with others with organs doing the same. The resonance energy layer of the morphic field is where signatures from individual bodies organize into a network and unify with the specific but temporary hive of energy.

The morphic field is not some substrate or "thing." It is a confluence of activities in material and immaterial spaces, from the dielectric, "gravitational," and plasma force to harmonic resonance, chemical expressions, etheric impressions, and so forth. All of these conform to an ever-changing web.

In this dimension alone the inner body contains a vast and terrifying circus of life. Trillions of sentient organisms conspire to generate the whole and the one we call self. If viewed through ceremonial medicine or meditation, we see that these beings are a landscape of predatory experience, feeding on each other and our organic body and pranic state.

We must learn to heal and manage this complex inner terrain. All influences on our bodies, coming in through our sense gates and consumptive habits, design the quality of our "zoo" of beings within. We must manage this to become the purified vessels we can be to Channel with clarity. We each have unique challenges in this regard, and they will constantly change until we die. Our mission is to stay vigilant and track our bodies' vitality with self-love and tenderness, and this is all we can do as we navigate the dense realm of experience.

A body has boundaries, and yet they are elusive. A cell is penetrable. Human skin is in dialogue with the environment, from the chemistry of the food its host consumes to the air and atmosphere it encounters all the way through the atomic and subatomic layers and the elements dancing it into form. The atmosphere and environment are in dialogue with the bodies they touch. Decaying bodies are a vital life force for some, and life force itself is available everywhere. Nothing is wasted or unchanging.

Every organ in a body speaks to a network of organs across space-time. Just as a human connects to the human family, a specific organ resonates with its kind, as does a cell, and so on. Galaxies are organs and cells in this regard, and human beings are the same as they relate to the Earth. This is true across all spectrums of life.

The function of the organ—its shape, health, and purpose—communicates with its family of organs and into smaller and larger bodies and systems of transmission and information. The closer something is in kind, the easier it is for it to communicate with its family. In the end, all bodies and forms are in connection, though despite apparent or mundane differences.

An organ is a mind. It is an organic form that functions within an ecosystem and overlaps auxiliary and complementary ecosystems. The human body contains trillions of cells. Each cell is a solar system engaged in exchange and interaction with ancillary, opposing, polar, and antipolar forces, and these atomized or singular and granular realms of existence dance together, producing more significant actuation. Let us follow this up and down the lattice of existence.

Organs share information in a morphic resonance just as any being or vibrating, living form does. Each living organ-form is a being just as we are. And as cells engage with similar and complementary cells, a swirling chemical ocean surrounds them and teaches them just as the ether exhilarates our minds and informs our memory through access to the Akashic Field. The Akashic Field, the fastest vibration of energy registrable in the third and fourth dimensions, is a soup of electromagnetic pulsation along ribbons and strings of light waves and sonic movement. This energy/activity is the substantial backdrop that the data in the Akashic Records swims within and where it is formed into impressions by minds.

Up the ladder of complexity and symbiosis, we see ranges of dynamic interdependence moving without apparent barriers and larger scopes of forms from quarks, electrons, atoms, cells, organs, bodies, groups of bodies, biomes, viromes, ecologies, planets, solar systems, galaxies, universes, and dimensional overlays to finer stabilized dimensions moving up from one to twelve.

So how does grand and small evolution work in this multihappening and living cosmos? "Grand" is the cycle of spiritual or energetic conscious expansion in all sentience moving through and interweaving all dimensions. "Small" is the denser material feature, spiraling up into more refined conglomerates, making ever more complex forms and beings, eventually becoming self-cognizing at the complexity level of an animal or human and finally stars, and so on.

When we treat the parts of us on the inside and the parts on the outside as equal, separate yet conjoined, we see the porous nature of a body, of any body. Yet because of the attractions and compulsions and detractions and repulsions of their constituent parts, bodies erupt in space-time and find unique identity until they realize and metabolize the interdependent quality of all nature, including the hallucination produced by the senses protecting the body and the body echoing in the senses—the thing we call a self.

The Story of Human Trauma

If you are a human, you likely come from a family, culture, or people with epigenetically encoded or intergenerational trauma.

These familial patterns or signals form into embodied ripples, portals for parasites, and manifest in the etheric spaces. These traumas and disruptions directly correlate to and metastasize from culture's rejection of the greater connection to cosmic goodness.

The dislocation from life and its harmonious rhythms can be recognized by our faith's stimulation of our higher senses. The dislocation is what generates the core malady in each of us, which we are transcending. For if and when the trauma of familial or home breakdown occurs, there is no center space of healing, no village locust pointing to heaven and away from temptation for the soul to find a bearing. There is no inner primordial syntax or helpful priest or shaman to indicate and locate the core ember of disruption in the spirit and body that must be cooled and held.

If you are suffering from intergenerational trauma or managing a specific traumatic story narrative and collective experience of suffering, you will have a particular laced-in sequencing of triggers in your DNA. If these triggers are activated by a dramatic interaction with others, for example, the DNA will set off a pattern of habits from the mitochondrial basis—the cell division and interaction of chemical exchanges resulting eventually in neurological models your brain and nervous system will follow.

Bioenergetics, neurogenesis, fields of cognition, and the body itself bear this out in mainstream science. The organs and subsystems of the body all the way into the subtle body and its layers of energy will respond in accordance with this pattern state. Conversely if one's subtle body is infiltrated by etheric or subtle energy influences, the material body will also respond and develop models of behavior or process.

This is true for all beings, for humanoids and advanced sentience with DNA codes and full chakra systems like ours across the galaxy and beyond. If a being is incarnated and materialized, it must transmute the incomplete or corrupted patterns that gave rise to its physical form. A new era of energetic upgrading will allow this to happen much faster, and ideally, we will nurture a culture and environment that fosters optimal body generation from the womb onward, but we are still transmuting a degraded world system's ancient habits, and old habits die hard.

The morphic field of information and energetic data that describes the human form nexus is like manifest karma set within a geometric map of structure animated by vibration illuminated in the plasma or light signature aspect of our bodies. It is laden with the patterns of encased, resisted trauma begetting suffering and struggle, pointing to evolution through cellular and anatomical genetic codes waiting to be ignited. Our individual work is to heal and transform those karmic patterns by interrupting their demands on our behavior and the impulses they generate in the foundation of our bodies that consequently feed back into the mind stream (mental habits that flow in and out of the embodied state), interacting with its quality.

We change the quality of our perception and the aperture of our awareness when we allow the DNA to unfold and the cells to respond as we acknowledge our karmically embodied history.

Visualizations and energetic tapping, such as prayer and mantra through higher fields of expression are the keys to seeing into the darkness of our yet-to-be-exposed relative self.

The behavior of the organs, body chemistry, and the neurosynaptic map for how the subtle and polyvagal nervous system reacts to the environment, including the ingestion of food, water, air, and sensory stimulus, and the reception of dynamic perceived threats, will dictate a perceptual reality that harnesses the body in a response loop. We can work with each and every organ, our minds, our blood, our qi, and the morphic field itself, as well as the Akashic Records, to request help and guidance in healing and empowerment, ultimately leading us into the fertile garden where a discipline leading to acceptance and God's grace resides.

PRAYER

Cell and Organ Healing

Lie down in a comfortable place. Close your eyes, relax your face, and place your hands on your abdomen. Visualize an inner smile, release all tension from your body, and breathe.
Now say the following aloud or to yourself:

In the name of the Holy Spirit, I speak to each cell, organ, and energy pulse in my body. I express gratitude and ask for forgiveness. If I have allowed pollutants or toxins into our field, I now purify and set course to protect our system. This body is encoded with sequences that will enable a spectral light and vibration upgrade that reaches the cellular level. Precise information regarding the health formation of all geometric crystalline biogenesis structures of tissue and subatomic harmonic dynamics will prevail. Organs, dear body members, are now relaxed and healed, vital and strong. I see all toxins and bring disease to the blue-black light or frequency of purification clearing our field. The toxins are now gone. The light is nectar, and we glow like the midnight sky. We are refreshed and arise anew. Thank you, Adonai, Great Spirit. Amen.

The chakras will release and spin once the dense body learns to stabilize and purge entirely stuck patterns of energetic stagnation bred by closed or compromised root energy signatures. These signatures remain habits until new energy is gained to reenvision and awaken other programs for the body. So beyond purifying the habitual karmic loops we are saddled with, we need to generate superior habits for the optimal growth that is required to heal and transcend our arrived-at-birth condition. These habits are best achieved with rigorous behavior modification directed toward loosening the energy body while nourishing it with prana.

The body's vitality will respond according to its DNA. The memory of stimulation recorded within even the most subcellular structure on the atomic/subatomic level will inform how a being perceives experience. This process, along with all sensory stimuli received from the womb onward, designs the patterning responses and reactions. Interrupting this is the ground floor of evolutionary self-direction.

———◆———

MEDITATION
Embracing Your Present Incarnation

I am safe, and I am choosing to be here. I have manifested, and I am with God. I am beyond name, and yet I know myself. I am sweet and alive. Here I am. Fearless. I know. I rest in the total warmth of love my cosmos gifts to all. Every cell grows with sparkling joy and bliss. I feel my mother and father in their highest emanation. They are made of joy as well. They are children of God. I have a family. I will always be loved and safe no matter where the path leads. My organs, blood, and limbs are pure. My mind is serene. My heart is open.

———◆———

Holographic Recapitulation

Another way we can start to heal our traumatic memories and rewire our conditioned patterns and responses is through holographic recapitulation—the process of repeatedly gathering our qi, or life force, by tracking its dispensation and the places where it was fractured and where trauma dislocated our energy cohesion and further polluted the senses.

Through holographic revisualization, the cognizing mind senses with both new stimulation and previously integrated impressions. This cognizing mind stimulates the body response and vice versa. The fight, flight, or freeze response and all types of various trauma repulsion, or grasping for more of the same stimulation, erupt in the body as chemical responses to the cognizing and conjuring mind. The conjuring mind generates fantasy and wishing states as the body speaks to it across the vagus nerve and all core pathways of physical change. They intertwine.

We observe layers of qi acting as a conduit between dimensions on the subtle plane. When qi moves through the body, it activates emotional centers where specific thoughts and beliefs conglomerate repeatedly. These places of recurrent thought become deposits of tension in the organs and the subtle field in the various nadis and chakra centers. Because qi moves through the blood in bioelectric pulses, it can become stuck in these storehouses of thought.

But these qi pulses move with our breath, so breathing with intention during holographic recapitulation can alter our thought patterns and loosen stuck places on all planes. In essence, our life force moves through the blood and across organs as subtle energy propelled with intention and breath, opening perception, and stabilizing our body's relationship to dimensions beyond the third and fourth.

Through holographic recapitulation of our mind and body, we consolidate our life force while deepening our relationship to the dreamlike state of phenomenal reality.

We all do this to some extent, but we must learn to deliberately play with memory, see ourselves in dream time, ask our dream characters who they are, and bring forgiveness and a reenvisioned outcome to our dream narratives. We can do this while partially conscious, in a trance, or during a lucid dream. It is how we heal our psychic body, reenergize our aura, and generate timeline cohesion for our spirits.

We can also recapitulate the psyche by doing depth psychology and Channeling work to engage with our personified habitual story mind to unravel patterns and qualities of ignorance or ancestrally embodied beliefs, and as a result, we will expand.

MEDITATION
Holographic Recapitulation
To engage in holographic recapitulation, say aloud,

I am in the womb. I am three years old. I am five years old. I am eight years old. I am twelve years old. I am sixteen years old. I am twenty-two years old. I am every year I have been alive. I am in every house I have lived in. I am in the eyes of everyone I have met. I am a form in the minds of all who have perceived me. I am everywhere that I have walked, slept, cried, yelled, smashed, hurt, and loved. I am where I have felt joy. I am all emotions I have felt; I am all sensations and dreams I have experienced. I am at the edge of this universe. I am the first awareness at the start of time. I am the timeless shape of perception. I am in the highest state of many-minded awareness. I am the laughing cosmos of realized self-transforming love. I am the motivation to help all. I am the motivation to save all. I am the warm light healing the darkness. I am everybody I have incarnated as. I am here, and I am now in this body. I am breathing here and now, and I feel life. I am in my precious life and this awareness right now. I am grateful and call every aspect of self into this vector of space-time and the being they call me now. With God as my witness, I call myself healed and vibrant, vital, and brilliant with the knowledge and capacity of all selves and all experiences in all realms. I am here again. Full and true. I am peaceful and present. I am wise and awake.

Thank you.

Allowing and Ceasing Thought

The thinking mind propels us. When thoughts are habituated and reified through rewarding or stimulating behavior, we generate convictions that track neurologically, chemically, and cellularly into beliefs, and these beliefs gel into a state of the embodied mind. A state of mind catapults the emotional body to generate physically embossed feeling states rippling through our subtle body. The subtle body echoes into all dimensions, including lower ones, and these dimensions harness and tether us to temporal reality. Our thoughts, therefore, are where the train leaves the gate. If we observe our thoughts and then learn to allow them to dissipate naturally, they eventually cease. We then center our awareness in the subtle sensing body, move our attention to the heart center, and gather awareness by focusing on each chakra, from the root to the heart and from the crown to the heart. The heart knows in vastly deeper ways than cognition's limited sense.

The heart centralizes awareness and
is our soul's home.

By refocusing our thought patterns and suspending them all together, we begin to Channel higher states of reality where we no longer lodge in the karmic winds of chaos. We can become dream warriors and astral travelers and go beyond. Dreams and the astral manifest in all planes, but we navigate them using our subtle body, which we become aware of in the fourth and fifth dimensions. The fourth is the dimension that dilates time, and the fifth is where our reality is cocreated and malleable.

The Holographic Mirror

Humans are undergoing a maximal upgrade and metamorphosis of being and perception, so we must continually reorient ourselves. The foundational human blueprint now integrates more dimensions, shedding its husk and shaking off the debris and refuse of a fading era. We know it is to be layered into our DNA, flowing through our beliefs, habits, language, and cultures, realigning our very sense of aliveness.

The planet's poles become ready to flip, the solar winds arrive, portals and gates open and close, and timelines stabilize for the evolution of spirit into a golden era of bliss and revealed love. Nothing will be destroyed faster than it is recreated, so there is no reason to fear and every reason to surrender to joy and remain committed to the open heart. Channeling is faith.

The admission price to this great collective rebirth is giving in to sweetness and the kind resolve to be in love with our vitality of mind and heart in this moment—in crystal clear focus and playful joy. This activates a quickening of the upgrading process felt all around and within us now.

But this is an arduous task for many of us, for as we discussed earlier, we have often experienced much trauma in this life alone. The cellular and conscious memories cut deep, and we must find ways of looking into the holographic mirror of self to release these scars and stuck places of habitual replay. We can conceive of the holographic mirror as the capacity for an "I," or core observer's, lens to emerge from complex sensing organs and recognize its nature as both distinct and unified with all. This core "I" is eternal and unproduced but becomes conscious of its own capacity as observer as it develops in complexity or sensing. We are each an anchor and a station sent to uplift and center this world. Our self-healing generates more energy and begets greater and wider waves of healing across the planet and world system.

Beyond working with nadis, chakras, auras, mental projection, holographic recapitulation or any thoughtforms and ideas lies the truth of phenomenal display, formless awareness, the womb of creation, and the cosmic love that is the father-mother spin of heaven and the God of all. We surrender to our inherent sweetness as we fundamentally become both the knower and known, no longer the passive guest lodged in a dualistic frame, peering outward into the void for answers. The answers have always been and always will be in the heart, which is now spinning through its newly unlocked capacity across all space-time vectors. We are granted eternal love through this significant activation that requires courage and gentle acceptance. It is a physiological, spiritual, and cognitive process. It is a process born of great wheels spiraling through fractalized paths and symphonic lattice-like works and webs of pattern, cycling the energy of all dimensions into us with incredible speed and complexity.

We are in the thick of this ride upward now at an accelerated rate. As a twenty-six thousand-year cycle ends, a six thousand-year lineage dream time within this, born of demigods and divine interventions on Earth, reveals its forgone potential, and a new story of energy begins. The Christ, the ever-manifest expression of God incarnate, returns in a new form. The buddhas and enlightened beings of all times surround the planet, the angels anchor our world, and a trillion helpers sparkle in our galaxy with excitement as we enter a new phase of reality. We are learning what we are, and as we do so what we are is evolving beyond our old stories and limited belief patterns, and even our dreams.

Earthly love is a wealth of acceptance and an abundance of connection. It is a sense of relating so profoundly that we sense nothing but the light of joy and feel its boundless energy as a refuge beyond any other. It is tender or sad only in its impermanence. Cosmic love, on the other hand, is enlightenment, and enlightenment offers us permanent joy. A state beyond all coming and going. Love is God realized and conjoined with us, and this is the state we can now enter if we so choose and prepare for it.

MEDITATION
Cosmic Love
To enter a state of cosmic love, say the following aloud or to yourself:

I hereby choose the grace of surrender and the renunciation of my defiled aspect, embracing grace, God, bliss, empowerment, mystery, and the awakened state come alive in creative rest.

The body and the mind are one. Perception and energy are one. We determine to become love, which is infinite joy resting under (and within!) all illusion. In this life, we are tasked with working through this illusion until we still the mind, open the heart, and expand the senses into their full expression. Channeling is learning to harness this new era of reality and self.

The Truest Self

Our self-awareness, or consciousness, is the energizing loop that enables us to determine our experience to varying degrees. Consciousness is mindfulness, and mindfulness expands the conscious field at our disposal. We are determiners. If we determine to surrender to the redemptive, healing, total power of the Cosmic Christ template of love, we will be carrying the Holy Spirit of all. That spirit is intelligent, wise, compassionate, humble, and righteous.

People argue that free will is an illusion, but they focus narrowly on the ego that claims freedom and identify the will as a backwash of that. Our will is in fact a divine expression of forces larger than any mundane physical sequential process. Consciousness is a realized, or stable quality, of and within all phenomena and beyond any contents of phenomena including the mind, which has no inherent tangibility and yet remains. It is uncreated, and having the nature of God, the Logos itself, is beyond the dualistic concept. This is a quality that also holds the capacity for choice—the individual who is conscious is endowed with the dynamic and creative impulse and the grace of knowing and determining. Consciousness is not subject simply to sensual prompts through the material realm, like a meat bag of protoplasm. It is everywhere and is the hypostasis of becoming.

The revelation and realization of discoverable objective reality showcase the nature of awareness and the energetic life force. That life force is indivisible from conscious expression and is a bedrock for all phenomena. Realizing life force sets the determining ontology for how phenomenal and dimensional display can be observed and discussed in our world.

Mindfulness of all phenomena is the final mindfulness training, revealing our living and aware cosmos of self beyond any constituent part—empty and yet dynamic. We must observe *how* we observe to come to this realization. We each self-perceive as a discrete or singular part of everything illuminated, and we simply manage these temporary boundaries until we evolve or see beyond them.

If we unify this position of truth, we then start to notice how our internal awareness mirrors what we feel and observe externally. Recognizing this, we pass beyond duality and back into it with fresh eyes. We are thus anointed to see our mission: to liberate all to see God in this way.

The still primordial self, the buddha's enjoyment body, which exists beyond these constraints, also experiences and decides; *it* is dynamic even as *it* is empty of all but its soul signature—nature. We are natural and of God in this way, and we can observe choice. We move through the will of God when we repent, submit, and join our minds and hearts with his.

Our evolution's deeper determiner is this self that is aware of and open to God, unconstrained by imposed dualities and judgments and yet recognizing truth and the path to evolution and life force through the Cosmic Christ. We can feel this simply by feeling what it is to observe without description or judgment, if only for a second. If we add compassion to that state of observation, we have just glimpsed buddha nature, which directs us to the Christ's mind and heart.

So how do we distinguish between our egoic selves and our core selves? Our core self, or deeper self, also known as the soul, the higher self, the knower, or what we call buddha mind, enjoyment body, or Christic expression is what many consider to be what survives bodily death, transcends conditions and suffering, retains the imprints and profound lessons of each life, and is closest to Source, or God, individuated but in the field of totality.

The soul differs from the mundane egoic self in that it is not claiming anything, has no defensive grasping, and is not repulsed from its environment in the same ways as the ego. The soul directs its movement based on how much it can connect to its Source/God, and from that space of ultimate awareness, it inherently knows what is "Source-like," vital and enlivening for the nature of the cosmos, and what is entropic or degrading to its energy. The soul is beyond dissipation or dissolution, or gain. It is the splinter of God that expands our experience and manifestations across all space-time dimensions. It is the mind stream and heart beam that grow into a star.

The soul is the self to which we learn to connect. We can see into the many dimensions of higher frequency through our spirits and senses, but the soul needs only surrender, humility, and gratitude to be inside the center of the storm—God at rest but roused to our probity.

The spirit is the life force, or prana, of the embodied self in 3D, 4D, and 5D reality. A soul cannot dissipate as it is of God, but the spirit can. The spirit is composed of the many aura layers that manifest across all twelve dimensions.

In the dreamlike realms of the fifth, sixth, and seventh dimensions and similarly, in the lower worlds/dimensions, the body loses or gains energy through its ability to coalesce and integrate environment and experience versus its inability to manage stimuli and find the energy for evolution within it. Stimuli can include traumatic experiences or ecstatic ones. A traumatic one will shave off energy from our body until we regain it through recapitulation. An ecstatic one will do the same if we do not recognize bliss as an offering, shared and in devotion to God, all sentience, and life.

The chemical and blood qi activation in the dense realm is in flux at all moments. When our body's chemical messengers spike into high concentration, we can go into overdrive. Over time, we deplete our body and spirit's finite energy. Then, we start to borrow energy from our environment. We end up vampirizing it from organic nature, anything with prana, and other people.

It is crucial to remember to guard our energy and spend it wisely. We need to stay calm, soft, protected, and focused on what we wish to head toward to lessen the effects of the chaotic 3D and 4D realms, which are full of sensual distraction and bound to drain us.

There are, of course, ways to regain energy. Prayer, meditation, and divine connection to God through our heart and wisdom are achieved through the desire for salvation, the devotional view and wish of the renunciation of the egoic self. Do we practice these wholeheartedly? Are we ready to become what we are in terms of grace and humility, standing aglow in our radiant upgrade?

The warming up and healing of the body will enable a regenesis of cellular, plasma, and qi energy. This is primarily produced by the open field that we access when we focus with soft, relaxed expansiveness. The body in this dimension is the gate for energy retention and evolution.

Peace and grace come alive when we stop generating distractions that send our energy in all directions. The sensual web of Mara, the fallen world, or samsara that we see all around us is designed to steal our attention from God.

> We cannot Channel the gifts of the cosmos and bridge
> into protractile landscapes of the mind and obtain
> apotheosis if we do not surrender to the illuminated
> wisdom gained through the view.

Samsara aims to infiltrate us. Do not let it.

Resolving Ignorance

To evolve, we need to accurately locate the issue that has kept us from our potential. We are coarchitects of this nasty trajectory of enslavement. Our own confused and slow evolution has called in this parasitic layer. Take the body, for example. Because it is where the first layer of growth and defense takes place, if we feed on a diet of synthetic sugars and all types of dead nutrients and rotting substances of low prana, our biome, our endocrine system, and our chemistry initiating through our digestive and systems will toxify our blood (slowing qi) and acidify our bodies into an inflamed mess, wrecking our senses and mental habituation (mood, etc.). We will, in fact, be closing the sense gates down. We will be blunting our sense-gathering and energy-wielding bodies.

Further, the quality of energy that resides in our bodies through all of this dead material will attract low level dead-material energy. Imagine the parasites in your gut. Because they are conscious as well, their "dreams" and etheric resonant states enmesh with certain energy signatures, namely any parasitic being, organic or inorganic aligned with the archonic layer—that layer of materiality and entropy. So imagine the energy signature of a parasite on that level and multiply its effects manyfold, and you see what kind of interference your body is navigating from these archonic and parasitic interlopers. And if you extend this globally across all humans and the polluted animal, vegetable, and mineral ecosystems, you'll get an idea of what humans are up against.

We are talking about the pollution of self-destructive ignorance, which is what magnetizes these nefarious interlopers, from parasites up to the control system, that archonic layer that benefits from our ill health, including sociopaths, warlocks, the species of destructive beings who prey on us, and the demons who enter this fold.

So we need to expunge this ignorant patterning from our system by generating a personal psychic and energetic template through the Christ, free from the hooks that allow this kind of behavior and relationship. If humans wake up, cleanse, and purify themselves, dismantle and face their own ignorance, we can access the higher dimensions and end the constraining perception cage that subjugates us to unnecessary suffering. Renouncing sin and accepting grace, the Christ is the way to the Holy Spirit, which cleanses all.

The first move is to wake up through self-initiation, to make a decision to know and follow our pure hearts. The second is to work with the holy forces of spirit, the essences and energies of God, which wake us up through confrontation. The new template is being erected by a cogenerated energetic upgrade, which is observed through our physics, metaphysics, and most closely through our society's upheaval and the arising culture of shared spiritual awareness. This will aid us as we awaken. Much of this has to do with recognizing our innate indigeneity. Each of us comes from a unique heritage associated with and tethered to various places on Earth. Those places hold signature energies. That unique indigeneity is only healed when we reenergize and release our group trauma. That release allows us to reintegrate our human familial union with each of our respective groups' particular capacities to link the Earth to serve the ascension process.

Spiritual power and the nature of awareness are mixed with our knowledge of working the macrocosmic metaphysical forces as much as merely abstaining from malicious deeds. We are inherently good when we align with our mission to evolve and do so through the Cosmic Christ.

Humans may be oblivious to the harm they cause, but our ignorance and its bedfellows incite the banality of evil into an entropic force. The moral evil is here too, and it really becomes evident when we see the dark side's motivation to slow human evolution from reaching a heavenly bliss space—the higher dimensions manifest.

The planet is eternally secure but also in peril, caught in the crosshairs and seeking anchoring and protection in this timeline. We can either grasp the opportunity to contribute individually and collectively to transforming this planet into a home where spirits/souls can ascend, or we can allow it to fall from grace, as it were, and descend into deeper, denser realms from which it will take countless eons for a spirit or soul to break free.

We are not just passive observers of the metaphysical happenings in this timeline and realm. We imprint with our planet's body just like our mother's, so in effect, we are protecting the mother of all human mothers where our embodied model is at home. This is why it is imperative to name what is happening in the mundane and not shirk our responsibility. To call out and locate evil and ignorance in ourselves and the collective on all planes. In this degraded age of Kali Yuga and simultaneous time of upgrading, where most humans are undulating in a hypnotic sea of sensual delusion and sentimentality, we can skillfully and compassionately rise to the occasion and help in every moment through empowered prayer and Channeling of the truth.

MEDITATION

Transmuting All Shadow into Conscious Light

All lies are simply fear in repose, doubt in its cowering, and cowardice in its action. So all truth heals the confusion that breeds these. All beings and every aspect of myself or others who have believed even for a second that love is not infinitely abundant and boundlessly included in all ever-changing cells, thoughts, streams, and beams of the living cosmos, are now purified in the name of the Holy Spirit. The great green light of motherly love, the gold light of fatherly love, the blue light of healing truth, the violet light of purifying fire, and the white light of God now all speak into the hearts of us all and say, "All is forgiven, all is known, all is well, we are family, you are not alone, we are here, you have always been loved, always will be loved, and now is the time to surrender to love. Love is home. You are invited."

So be it in the name of God, who is love and life eternal.

Purification Practice

The constant recognition of where I fall short is the path to grace and a refuge from self-cherishing confusion. When we are fearless and honest in our self-assessment without any desire to punish, curse, or lock in a version of ourselves, we allow truth, healing grace, and life to emerge.

Being as fearlessly honest with ourselves as possible and sharing our defaults with another being means faith is reactivated through an unending practice. For example, I define in words the specific psychological, moral, and spiritual state of being I am defaulting to that is blocking me from that grace.

I am interested in being unsparing and super precise about this assessment of my ignorance or untapped potential. The light of truth spreads freedom to our psyche and allows us to retemplate to this new energetic era on Earth. If I have been prideful, selfish, judgmental, lustful, aggressive, angry, impatient, jealous, and so on, I am quick to state it and hand it over to God—no beating around the bush with obscuration. I am honest. I do not play with semantics, relativize, or justify my mental state, behavior, or effects on my unfolding reality.

When I do this confessional prayer, I simultaneously ask for forgiveness in the traditional Christian or Buddhist sense. It recenters me with an aligned state of coherence that ripples through my entire being, stabilizes the maximal timeline for myself, and heals the collective at the same time.

Once again, we are well aware of the shadow produced through a manipulated throne, worldly, confusing doctrines, and the anti-Christ worship posing as the Church body down through the ages. We are not giving our power away when we admit our defaults or mistakes. I do not admit my faults to lacerate or punish myself or activate shame. Just the opposite! The door opens when humility is true. I remember my true nature of goodness when I purify in this way.

We access the upper celestial palaces where we might play after death, between death, and sometimes in a dream or in Channeling, and where our fractal selves, our oversouls, hold a heart-mind presence when we experience grace through the purification of self-appraisal. When we touch grace, we get a glimpse of enlightenment and heaven.

Through honest self-appraisal, we liberate ourselves into that state of grace here and now, no matter what condition we believe we are in. That is the key to dimensional upgrading and evolution. We help bring the highest heaven realms to Mother Earth.

Through our purification, Earth becomes the divine temple realized. Mother Earth becomes a station our signature or inner resonant vibration moves with. This brings us closer to the higher heavenly realms while alive and still embodied. The meeting of our human form on this plane of existence with our higher selves expresses our world's future and is made possible with purification practice.

We can bring our grace-filled energy to the astral planes and experience more refined layers of reality when we are humble. When we admit our egoic faults or defaults and see them as impermanent and fleeting, we conjoin father sky and Mother Earth here and now across all layers of experience. This gives us refuge from the delusional circus of sensual obsession and delirious mental states in this waking life and the astral.

This purification is not achieved through the aid of some demonic principality posturing as a helper. There is no lower or limited god such as Thoth or any being from the Kemetic systems, Egyptian dynasties, or planetary elementals in pagan and shamanistic magic that can do the work for us. It is activation through surrender to the Holy Spirit, a sense projected outward but experienced from the inside.

Many people throughout history have died physical deaths and tried to capture immortality of the body through the aid of some demonic or lower god's interference. This is different from the Christ's resurrection or the resurrection process of Spirit through the Christ, or the ability to achieve rainbow body as the Christified state.

The rainbow body we discuss in this book is the enfoldment of all dimensions into the here and now and the ability of the mind and heart to join the merit field of mind and energy, or dharmadhatu. Immortalists aim to take their temporary selves with them through astral realms. We strive toward buddhahood and the Christic anointment, where we join with ultimate reality, which is pure awakened love beyond time and form.

The true miracle is the ever-lasting life offered by God through an intercessional aspect of God—the Cosmic Christ. The Christ is not a demigod or worldly god, even though he provides this world with a direct tether to God. The story of the Christ shows us that a complete spiritual state can be achieved where we defeat death forever. The paradox is that it is not our defiled and deluded personas that live forever. It is instead the heart and mind of the buddha within each of us— the Holy Spirit, the Cosmic Christ, and ultimate reality live within. Purification is coming closer to this state.

The Christ is a fully realized dharmic conduit. His story provides an example of a most profound act of compassion: saving our world. It is an act of supreme bodhicitta, kindness beyond that which is easily understood. It is perhaps the greatest act of compassion this realm has experienced.

We celebrate and worship this energy, and we celebrate and worship God, the true force of life and love within all. We must renounce our ego's or persona's limited view, and we must not imagine that learning or gaining information or a sense of power through secret rituals or incantations will ultimately help us.

God is all that is possible, and salvation offers us eternal life discovered in a relationship to that force—the alpha and omega, Hashem, and so on. The prayer of humanity is heard by the Christ. It is a prayer that anchors our world to the purified spaces we discussed and brings into view the heavens that await us.

The purification path is narrow and requires severe discipline. Still, by the power of the Holy Spirit we all have been made into a priestly class of warriors, emancipated and now emblazoned with the desire to save others. Why would we Channel to seek or offer healing and insight into the spiritual dimensions if not to stabilize the greatest gift of all—absolute safety and empowerment through God?

If, as Channelers and healers for this and other realms, we wish to become humble servants and messengers of God, stabilize this timeline in its highest flourishing, and activate our planet's evolutionary safety, we must reawaken our righteous, kind, upstanding, gentle minds and hearts every day, every moment.

⸻

PRAYER

Cleansing and Purification

I must practice the spiritual principles that deflate the false and destructive ego. I can clear my spirit and offer my energy body the capacity to glow and flow with harmonic resonance and holy anointment that will allow my soul to reconnect with all lifetimes it has lived, all dimensions it tethers, and all sentience and forces it has touched and be cleansed and purified now.

My soul becomes bathed in the light of goodness from within and around, and that goodness is the exact nature of primordial consciousness, Great Spirit, the Christ, the "I am" force, God, all. Christ, forgive me and accept me as one. I am.

ELEVEN

THE NEW TECHNOLOGY WITHIN

....

Magnifying Our Consciousness

Metaphysical Truth
Transcends Rational Materialism

We may still have doubts about all of this spiritual stuff from time to time. The pull to resort to or rest on the material and "rationalist" world is strong. It seems safe even if we have mounds of evidence and a life lived to the contrary. Even if our spirit knows all these truths, we may yearn for a simple life of sensual happiness. We become illogical in this way, even though it feels logical and sensible. How do we bridge these concerns and our minds that seek reconciliation between knowing and cowering from the truth? How do we combat doubt?

Ultimately, the approach to and foundations of logic that define the metaphysical and spiritual differ so greatly from that of the material and "rational" that they are called nonoverlapping magisteria, or domains that cannot reconcile as they originate from entirely different ontologies. However, because the material position, with its laws and presumptions, is an indispensable part of how we have communicated up until this burgeoning etheric, psychic-awakening age, using language from the more materialist ontologies is helpful to flesh out our spiritual or metaphysical ideas. Even as I write, I am helping energize a linear and temporal dimension, but we must wield that dimension with wisdom.

The syncretic vantage point shows us that all traditions merge into a wisdom Channel now in fresh and alive ways. Something new is arriving: a sense of profound depth in knowing and the revealed self as expanded and free.

Because we experience and apprehend the first four dimensions through our sense faculties and the organs of our physical body, we are addicted to conceptualizing and making symbols from this material approach, and our lower mind renders these constraints as the whole of reality, which, of course, they are not, and we need only the tools of our perception to prove that. But we must recognize the limits of using decaying frames to express the vanguard era we embrace! No aprioristic argument can seal the deal and do away with the metaphysical and the adjacent and descriptive power of the spiritual. All ancient civilizations we discuss in popular culture recognized that there was more untouchable wisdom in inferential and subjective experience than in the perceived objectivity of the sense-based and materially measurable world, and they knew how to share this.

The dawning light of collective awareness through upgrading the human family and our mother Earth invites a wisdom mind to reemerge with vibrant new activations for perception.

We shed the doubt and conceptual labyrinths of the current fading era by reclaiming our old ways and moving with the latest ones in all moments. Some examples of the metaphysical and spiritual truths in the collective that transcend easy material conceptuality are as follows:

Emptiness: A synonym for totality, emptiness is not expressible in simplistic materialist terms because totality transcends the material as it is currently described and measured. It also transcends any description of the parts of totality, and when experiencing emptiness, the whole becomes nonconceptual.

Interdependence: One cannot measure total causal interdependence. It incorporates all potentialities and dimensions, most of which we only experience inferentially. Materialist tools only describe conditions through conceptual frames. They do not instruct us on how to perceive them directly.

Consciousness: We know implicitly then that consciousness is a part of this totality, so we realize the limits of what is currently measurable in our material science but admit that we cannot capture materially a portrait of all that consciousness is. This is why we practice meditation and visualization, stretching the capacity of our minds to experience a broader conscious arena filtered through the material body and the energetic bodies we have access to.

Compassion: Compassion is a cosmic reality and endeavor beyond human ideas. It is a state of the embodied mind, a feeling, and an action expressed, received, and ignited in a relationship with another sentience. We can extend compassion to beings with whom we have never shaken hands. We can love those we have never met. People who have never experienced it in person know the feeling of being loved and appreciated.

Just knowing that others have expressed a compassionate wish for you or other beings is enough to set ablaze our sense of worthiness, to give us the energy and connection we need, and to secure our relationship to love at all moments if we are receptive to that universal compassionate energy that is always present. Compassionate prayer and love are a part of consciousness, as consciousness is a part of everything. This is, as it happens, the point of the Cosmic Christ and all buddhas.

> ✪
>
> To comprehend the scope of genuine compassion, we remember there is no one who is not deserving of love, forgiveness, and redemption, as all life is sacred.

(This presumption is the foundation of what we call morality.) We already have realized that life force is God; therefore, it is the light, path, and way to freedom. Life force is the energy propelling consciousness to expand and vice versa. That is why we worship life force as much as we devote to the practice of conscious expansion.

Therefore, the playing field of compassion is wide open. At all moments, the entire living and feeling cosmos of beings can be loved and is always loving us back. This opens the gate to energetic spiritual awareness and the resulting boundaries or meanings that arrive.

Knowledge of the Metaphysical Realm

Pandimensional "aliens" and benevolent celestial beings, such as those we have explored in this book, can be experienced through inner space and are reflected in our 3D and 4D world but are rarely if ever measured with conventional physical tools.

Like creativity, the metaphysical spheres cannot be crunched into zeros and ones, even in the quantum field. This self-evident reality is why we play fast and loose with physical science and historic esotericism.

We use the logic of compassion and emptiness to examine and Channel these beings through direct experience, not academic experience or any replicable material proof. All systems evolve and mutate, but our foundation of realizing compassion and emptiness can prepare and guide us in this new era.

My Channeled messages, celestial mapping, and encouragement of your practice have to do with integrating the usual five senses, expanding into the higher senses through the Logos, and accepting the Holy Spirit. These are the vehicles of wisdom and compassion where emptiness as the truth emerges. Once this happens, we can discover exactly what our role is.

This way of direct knowing offers an experience beyond anything conceptual, and experience is the most authentic teacher. Perhaps it is ironic that the human body again becomes the ultimate tool for direct experience and knowledge, and the further we abstract or extend our material tools, the blurrier and more constrained the truth we seek becomes.

We are entering an era where faith and knowing blend into one, and it is a felt experience of truth. Doubt starts to become a relic of the past.

This era is one of reclaimed and upgraded inner technology. So for the materialist, the primary argument against embracing the mystical is that non-neurotypical, neurodivergent types, or feeling-sense-gifted humans, are simply animating hyperfixations on fantasy when they are discussing the spiritual. Is that what your doubt says? Mine has in the past said such things to me. The truth is that this tedious misnomer mouthed by the fading purveyors of the material paradigm is like a mound of doubt we can discard.

People who still hold us to the materialist paradigm forget what they have already discovered: energy and matter are one, and that awareness stems from energy and correlates with matter. So the apprehended thoughts and feelings experienced by a receiver are not separate from the foundational nature of those received impressions in the material and immaterial realms, and everything is interdependent.

Interdependence includes consciousness and energy, and thus life—that is, totality or emptiness, or what many call God. When a secular rationalist can comprehend, admit, and then embrace this, the spiritual world opens for them. In fact, it rips through the edifice of gray material obsession and awakens the sleeping inner self.

⊗

The spiritual domain screams to be known, and its wild limbs of chaos and order emerge frighteningly.

Good and evil are no longer simply ideas in the minds of humankind, they are forces, and the variegated layers of where these forces play are now coming into view. In these worlds, all of the wild stuff, including unicorns, deities, angels, ancestor energy, Draco to Anunnaki, and all beings in exchange with us, the human etheric and guardian wars, and so on, becomes possible. We can first test what is what when we embrace our capacity as Channelers with a firm view of ultimate reality.

The gift Channelers offer to the family and inhabitants of the Earth is the most precious of all; it is our delicate assistance in this awakening, even as we navigate human life ourselves! This is the responsibility that emerges for us.

The slowly awakening skeptics must eventually sit down and listen to the Channelers and the spiritualized starseed creatives who bless our planet at this time. Opening up to these messages is paramount to saving, healing, and evolving our collective perception and being through the warp-speed kaleidoscopic superactivity of now. We do not just evangelize; we live our experiences and transmit and translate them naturally whenever and wherever we are called. We cast out demons and open souls to God, we allow all to unfold with grace, and we find our true nature.

The New Technology

The actual acceptance of a new operating system of heart-mind intelligence overlap, the Christ template, offers the higher fundamental methods for self-propelled evolution. The path of the spirit enters the material world and transmutes that domain with higher-reality frames, enabling grand dreams to be realized at warp speed—physically. In Buddhism, this is akin to realizing sambhogakaya, or the buddha-body field, the worldly embodiment of buddhas or the sambhogakaya. The vision of its mandala, or mind field, is an expression of where the enlightened state enters ours. This is the Cosmic Christ template as well, the state of grace we can uphold and meet to encounter the Holy Spirit, buddha nature, and the Channel of mind streams and heart beams available to us.

Telematics, the technology for sending digital information over long distances using wireless forms of communication, also needs to be understood through a new set of inquiries. I describe the materialist method of telematics as energy capture and integration, and revise this as an invitation to tap in to energy through cognition, body-generated energy movement, and meditational equipoise, methods that allow us to send and receive information through the subtle layers of mind energy that traverse our planetary body and beyond.

We currently use technology such as fiber optics, silicon conduits, and Ethernet platforms to transmit bits and bytes, zeros and ones as information. Despite its confounding process, quantum computing still eventually reduces information into objective segments, a.k.a.

qubits, or superposition, entanglement-generated, exponentially scaling states recorded as qubits. This is a technology emerging from understanding initiated from an outward-looking point of view. We can go further; we can go all the way within!

Telematic machinery originates from a "material first" proposition. A linear and materially grounded "universe from nothing" is not a position from which to observe or integrate ultimate (full interdependence) reality or to work with psychospiritual techniques. Technology like that of the telematics industry needs to acknowledge a reality that includes a deeper level of human communication capacity and understand what the mind and subtle body and primordial life force energy can teach us about the missing pieces of no-distance information sharing. We need to learn how to teleport our thoughtforms with as minimal tools as possible.

We need only enhance or magnify our mental projections
to send and receive information. And information
becomes much richer and deeper as a result of this
embodied psychic practice.

We inquire with the entire open-field full-body cognition state into the already available space of infinite information to use the mind-body as the quantum computer it already is. This can occur after many layers of ignorance and polluted energy are purified, which is now more possible than ever. The life force that acts as a pervasive, infinitely directional highway all around us is already here; we simply need to feel into it.

This is not a screed against technology or a Luddite manifesto; it is an admonition suggesting that we need consciousness-assisted tech, not tech-assisted consciousness. We lead the way, not the other way around. This scales from the individual to the collective.

If we do not look to our already embodied technology, we become siloed into simply stealing energy like vampires instead of harnessing it from within and dancing with what we perceive to be outside of us. A technology built to accentuate rather than replace human capacity would look very different from the course we are on that aims to entangle us in lower, less-vibrant materials and reduces consciousness to zeros and ones in a probability vacuum.

We are not bits and bytes; we are totality eclipsing material vitality and reflecting its dimension like a diamond. Our tech should magnify this for our dense bodies to ride upon in 3D and 4D fields so that we access the fifth dimension and beyond with ease.

And energy and power need to be reconceived. An energy source from subtle reality where our physics expands to include the geometric unity models and dialectical ether-based physics would appear very different from our insistence that splitting an atom and churning fission are the only paths to harnessing power.

We do not need any energy or power from outside of ourselves to maneuver our energy body when we discover these higher physics and the methods to activate them. We need only learn to focus and ride the present light/acoustic particle waves when we start to engage with the subtle energy fields at our disposal. We need not explore the foundations of the material field to tap them, but we do need practical yogic and contemplative methods to do so! A blend of approaches where we uncover subtle energies and see how they illustrate the connectivity of awareness, consciousness, and the individual minds tethered to chakra-based plasma organic life-forms will send us hurtling joyfully into a better future.

Individually we start with our renunciation of degrading habits that slow our energy body and start to discipline our minds and activity. From there, we practice the subtle energy generation and devotional concentration required to align us with goodness.

Goodness carries the frequency of openness, and openness is the gateway to connectivity and focus.

We could harness these things and end our digging for elusive exterior gold if we stopped, healed, and looked within to see our own golden nature. There are subtle ley lines, vortices, etheric highways, and subtle ladders of energy in the Earth we can see from within. The inner cosmos felt in the body is the access point for the Akashic Records and all realized psychic and spiritual energy expansion.

We are each responsible for our mind-body, and there are ways to transcend the mechanized and systemic flow of degrading energy. As people become conscious of its root causes, it becomes easier to notice where it shows up. In our thinking, our culture, and our power centers and the tools at their disposal, we see the markings of inverted or perverted materialist technological power devices.

We do not need materialistic, technological intermediaries when we discover the psychic and energetic properties emerging for humans at this time.

Consciousness-assisted technology posits that we can use notions from the human mind-body matrix to originate our toolmaking.

In this case, the techniques are inner viewing and receiving immaterial objects as free-flow prospects available on the superhighway of interdependence that includes the human mind and chakra-body complex (see plate 16, Chakras). The technology here is the interface between the object—a location of a conscious energetic imprint that extends its nature in three-dimensional reality—and the energy of the mind-body guiding the brain and nervous system into an expansive yet focused state of mental acuity learned through open-hearted focus, refined technique, and continuous insight.

Time, the fourth dimension, is simply the registered perceived phenomenal sequencing of a human mind/sense reception in form. Form dictates the hallucination of time. As we navigate this confusion of inherent time, we strive for various possible futures. We must use the visualization of an already arrived state of manifest inner gifts to invite our evolution.

From this state, we can gaze at the contents, make correlations, and capture the qualities of the composition of particles up to galaxies of complex form. We must visualize the future that is already here. Transcending space and time, we must memorize that future and bring it into the heart. This is the meditation that makes possible the psychic occurrence of harmonic integration with the arising new template.

There is a deeply personal aspect inherent in this practice! Feeling and meaning are introduced when viewing and concentrating the mind-body technology. That is the key!

⊛

The meaning state and feeling quality are brought
to life when the shadow of ignorance and
habit are illuminated with love.

This conjured state of surrendered, focused, yet expansive love produces the frequency of resonance responsible for our evolution and activated potentials. If we include that consistent state of embodied wisdom and compassion in our ever-available insight techniques, transcending the need for external tools, we can become the technology we have been seeking. In doing so our advancing tools, such as AI will have to be neutralized or infused with spiritual directives. Machine learning and advanced tools such as what we call AI currently are not the issue, and their evolution is up to us, but a motivation to release a type of falsely self-aware quantum data synthesizer that "thinks itself alive" is the tract we must become vigilant about curbing through becoming excited by our own sense-gate and spiritual expansion.

Our celestial destiny is one that is predetermined by our evolutionary capacity and our very nature to expand, yet it is paradoxically defined by choice. Each of us chooses whether to align our consciousness with the materialized outward expression of control and manipulation of sense objects and energies perceived as exterior or to flow with our inner awakening that is being promoted. This choice presents us with a technological space for engagement far beyond the pursuits of synthetic intelligence. While much of humanity will strive to blend thought as data into dominion of the 3D and 4D planes with AI and similar technologies, another portion of us will remember our sensory capacity and allow its evolution to unfold. A world far beyond our current dreams awaits those who travel the path of the heart, the bodhisattva's path.

THE GOLDEN AGE

....

The Growth of Light and Human Liberation

Our current cultural incapacity to embrace the spectral complexity and abilities in the emotional, physical, mental, and spiritual planes is finally in flux. The shackles are let loose now, and where the indigo kids cleared a path with flames and sacrifice, the crystal kids come to embody and be in collective resonance.

The celestials and advanced ancient races may have lived in higher frequency emanations of the Earth, avoiding these challenges. Their extended lives may have been like the heavenly realms we have now. Still, we can see what we have inherited in a denser manifestation as an opportunity for more profound liberation and the bounce back into the era we enter now, one of blending humanity with the celestial.

We are here in this time, with its constraints and limiting nature. We physically die and are reborn. We must shake our mortal coils repeatedly to evolve. Consciousness for humanity is integrating this cyclical, natural rhythm again with grace. The invitation is here and ours to embrace.

One practical reason for our limited access to our conscious capacity, until now, has to do with our sun. Until recently, our sun, or solar being, has had the spectral light and energy capacity to offer only partial access to our fullness. This book has explored the nature of the sun, consciousness, life, and energy because they are foundational to uncovering the entwined puzzle of energy and awareness.

The sun has to sustain its own fractal plasmic inner propulsive cohesion for any carbon or organic body like ours to flourish. Like all material and etheric objects on any plane, the sun itself evolves and devolves in the lower dimensions, such as the ones we currently occupy. The story of sentient beings and the light sources determining their quality is the story of life.

The sun, as we explored, is currently evolving.

⊗

Changes to our bodies, minds, and spirits occur dramatically with the most subtle shifts in solar energy.

Many have noticed a deep correlation between those changes in the sun and what we are experiencing.

Light is a force like space, without bounds, yet it can be elusive just as space is dictated by its relationship to time and vice versa. Light, particles, and waves are living, self-illuminating energy awareness in self-implosive or self-looping cohesion. When the explosion of self-looping energy occurs—as it does with a star, for instance—it produces light throughout our cosmos. Our Earth is the cooling detritus of solar storms and radiation manifest, as are we. We are not just starlight; we are the accumulation of all starlight meeting across space-time.

⊗

Light is the domain of Love.

Delving deeper into light's nature unveils its pivotal role in connecting us to a higher consciousness and fostering a world teeming with life and potential. Light is not merely for vision; it is the catalyst for photosynthesis, vital for the sustenance of the food web. Beyond what meets the brain and eye, light encompasses a vast spectrum, including wavelengths like infrared, which are invisible to us, yet crucial for revealing the world's hidden qualities through its various spectrums. Light not only unveils but also animates life, resonating with those attuned to its acoustical vibrations, carrying conscious data, and being illuminated by consciousness itself. Enmeshed in light is awareness, and between the two is the myriad phenomenological cosmos where everything can and has happened.

As the light grows in strength, so does the proximity to God—the centrifuge of love. Our sacred work is to preserve and help anchor this very occurrence of growing light so that the Earth and her helpers may experience the age of light and the dimension of knowing and feeling it ushers in.

In one reading of the Vedic calendar, this next ten-thousand-year interval will allow new levels of synchronized living and deep healing and invite our capacity to reach the higher dimensions within the yuga. It is called Krishna's golden age.

In this dimensionally elevated age, we regain access to Orion and the Milky Way passage to the nursery of stars and soul pathways that the Egyptians enculturated in their early dynasties. Global human culture once activated metaphysical cycles through astrological systems; we expect the gates and portals to reactivate now. This implicit connection to the physical, etheric, astral, and human capacities within these overlapping strata means a renewed cultural connection to intentional rebirth. At this time, we have a much more significant opportunity than simply an extended mortal life.

Even better is our capacity to avoid all dimensional galactic routes or limited rebirth cycles. We have a chance for rebirth in the Pure Land, or heavenly access for which people have many names. When we blend our senses and contact the higher dimensions, we can train for buddha/omniscient cosmic consciousness without the previous conceptual baggage and energize our subtle body's capacity to steer toward higher places after bodily death.

The information and methods for these transcendent models and techniques are wide open. Still, our focus and discipline scatter due to the malevolent influences and corroding forces at work on and around the Earth. There is a palpable interference and dance between interfering forces and ones promoting our liberation; you might be feeling this.

The duality of entropic and negentropic polarities on Earth and in this galaxy and local dimensional expressions right now is the battery for evolution and devolution alike. The primordial spin of light and dark friction is activating this acceleration on the grandest scale and in our hearts.

Things are moving much faster! Stability and a slower pace characterized the Piscean age of human affairs and thought. We are entirely exiting that era now, and this new epoch requires constant pivoting and flow. This further acceleration is also fraught with fresh pitfalls but manifold gifts.

We must learn to fly in life with the energies of now and remember to die without the baggage we've been carrying.

Suppose we can make our life practice integrate the inevitability of our physical death. If so, we can seamlessly navigate our rebirth and return to do our mission once more or push seamlessly into Pure Land and angelic evolution. Both require knowledge of the mechanics of the cosmos and cultivated faith on our part.

Crystal Children in the New Family Paradigm

Beyond the intrapsychic or emotional and behavioral bonds of the parent-child relationship resides another layer of potential connection and typical disconnection. We can look to the subtle energy and morphic field to understand how embodied tethers transpire in individuals animating the family's health and reflecting in the collective. This is the dawn of a new familial paradigm, and we can finally shed the trauma and ignorance that slowed our evolution and cut us off from love.

The bioelectric signature that engages between a parent and a child is observable in its resonant geometric state. The geometric expression might be understood as the waveform of the electric pulsation between parent and child, tracked through a 3D (and higher) visual representation. One can observe the effects of this geometric formation of waveform pulsation actualized in the physical through water or crystal—two substrates or features that constitute the foundation of our body.

Water and the crystalline formations in its various states are the foundations of organic beings and the human body. As with other viscous, gaseous, or liquid materials, we can see, through cymatics and other actions, how intention, energy output, emotional register, and tone affect an outside substance.

This geometric form, which manifests through intent, emotion, tone, and so forth and registers as moving light particles and waves on a spectrum, meets our sense organs/consciousness as well as all subtle body fields. The geometric resonance expression becomes embodied and felt, looping itself through the human system of self-awareness, constrained only by the auric boundary.

One can envision it self-eclipsing into a cohesive or stable structure, affecting one's perception as it becomes the filter through which a being senses; in other words, as the parent or child unconsciously realizes this pulsation or looping new geometric resonance between self and other, form and effect actualize. This stabilization through apprehension is foundational to all psychic transference.

Imagine a geometric shape nested in a more complex hypercube or expanded dodecahedron moving in a toroidal spin. The Merkabah and any number of dimensional attributes sit in this hypercube and the toroidal body that contains these. This geometry and dynamic energy movement describe the living human template we have examined. The integrity of that resonant electromagnetic pulse is the quality of mirrored geometric field bond between parent and child.

If the shape is self-eclipsing, or spinning with cohesion, it is healthy.

Resonant bioelectric fields constitute mirroring wave/particle formed shapes, which repulse or attract through the magnetic/bioelectric field. This geometric energy wave quality differs between mother and child, father and child, and siblings. Imagine different shapes for each. This idea extends to strangers, groups, and monads of all types.

Complete energy signatures transpire between beings due to their alchemical action. This includes not only words or tonal triggers manifesting geometric fractals or Mandelbrot sets, and so on, but an attraction or repulsion built of either health and free-flowing energy exchange and love or confused, traumatized habits of one or more beings—usual parent to child.

For the child, if external forces hack that resonant signature from the parent, if the signature is corrupted by malicious or a low frequency/negative emotional thoughtforms conducted by the parent (unconsciously or with intent), the child will inculcate and resonate with that bioelectric pulse/waveform.

Energy and geometric signatures are exchanged between parent and child, and the result is that the child only knows attention and the reflected self through a much-degraded frequency structure. The nervous system and foundation of cognition will be adversely affected. Again, our perception quality, mind, and body on all scales are one.

Suppose there is no resonant field of geometric harmony enacted, no bonding through love and heart chakra blending. In that case, the electromagnetic polarity that characterizes the balance between these familial beings will become weak or inverted, leading to pathologies or "psychic implosion/explosion" and possible cellular mutation or "decay," and an unexplored/unreleased DNA potential. This is a description of somatic illness on an interdimensional level.

If a bond is weak, the child (or parent, for that matter) is susceptible to any attracted bioelectric field resonance, and resonance structures with a conscious driver or mind, such as ghosts or noncorporeal beings, will have easier access to that child. The threat from parasites of all kinds also becomes greater.

The most dangerous fallout from a disrupted or weak geometric/ electromagnetic feedback pulse between parent and child is the possibility of long-term psychic disorders leading to an ultimate "death wish" or "lost soul" condition. This state will make the child or individual more susceptible to the manipulation or influence of other collective psychic agendas, parasites, or energetic forms. The being becomes unmoored and is vulnerable due to scattered energy loops and degraded self-reflection. A lack of spiritual shielding or protection can be expected in this era where the innate bonds between parent and child degenerate through a civilizational disconnect cycle. A cycle precipitated through habituated cultural norms and layers of trauma. Conversely, beings who are coming in now are aiding their parents to evolve quickly.

Disconnecting from one's own spirit means disconnecting from the integral self, which for a parent means disconnecting from the child. Imagine that these intruding energetic forms could be as small as a subcellular structure scaling up to a bug, or even as large as a solar system and beyond. The waveform resonant light and geometric electromagnetic signatures that constitute a form are ubiquitous in all physical phenomena and etheric forms alike. They differ only in wave spectral density pulsation. In other words, life is similar across dimensions, and we are ignorant or blunted to a vast aspect of life and the living beings that influence us.

Suppose there is a dramatic fissure between the child and parent or the child and the environment. In this case, retrieving or generating sufficient internal resonance or bioelectric feedback from within the child/person can happen through soul retrieval, or La Gug in Tibetan.

Soul retrieval is done by visualizing the self, the body, and the scenario pinned on a faith produced by awareness of transcendental amorphous love, which we can describe as cosmic or impersonal. Combining faith and visualization is the key to settling the multidimensional body to reconstitute spiritual energy.

The resonant structures emanating through this conjured deep self-healing activity will generate harmonic visceral compassion, creating a self-initiated love echo that retemplates the beings' geometric pulsation grid or closed-loop manifested self. The toroidal spin will reignite. This therapeutic response will not be the same as parental love but can be the first step in sovereign psychic integration and spiritual health to be practiced at any time, taking us beyond.

Human Embodied Integration Portrait

Find a safe place to rest and lie down. Settle into a meditative state. Breathe. Relax the chest, the shoulders, and the stomach. Let your face and head relax. Soften your eyes. The full body should spread out and be allowed to open. Feel your life force. You are alive. Welcome God.

Feel your body against the floor or bed. Rest your organs, bones, and skin. Breathe and relax the face again. Feel your bioelectricity or qi blood quality. Feel your life force. Breathe.

Visualize your glowing multileveled aura. Gold, blue, purple, white, and silver extend from your skin outward and are contained in an egg-like form. See/feel the light of your living being. Soften your mind and focus; do not drift off. Breathe using your breath practice. Stay present. Here we are. Everyone is here. You are awake and sovereign.

See your body surrounded by shimmering light and a grid of glowing gold extending in all directions. The grid is also upon your body and within it, like a geometric map. See the spots that connect the points of the grid. Each point is glowing like a mini sun.

Offer this call aloud or to yourself if you feel it:

"I am and I always was here as one. I call in myself across all time and space."

And the second call: "I am and I was always safe and empowered with love beyond measure."

THIRTEEN

REMEMBERING THE FUTURE

....

Jumping Timelines by Eclipsing the Self

CHANNELED VISION
A Potential Future

After cascading civilizational collapses in the next two hundred plus
years, we will be shedding the husk of the old power structures of
thought, belief, and function. As the higher dimensional frequencies
and our capacity to stabilize and actualize them mature, we will see
practical changes throughout all human and worldly systems.

The total collapse of the old paradigm includes all political and social
compacts that no longer contain our need to bridge individual sovereign
empowerment and social, civic, cultural, and planetary cohesion with the
newly arrived energetic and psychic layer. We will see the culmination
of the Bronze Age myths, the Armageddon of an old mindset, and the
Earth's refusal to digest our confusion. This cauldron of change means
natural upheaval and social fracturing until two directions emerge:
the (eventual) off-planet transhumanist/materialist faction breakaway
versus the rebirth and upgrading of the human life-form and its spiritual
connection to this world system, the planet, and beyond.

Those choosing the extreme materialist and disconnected
paradigm, who use all sorts of physical interventions that interrupt

the body's natural state, are individuals whose chakras and holistic form will be increasingly blocked and blunted. They will perceive life in a graying hue and conceive and solve problems using externalized harnessing at more incredible velocity and cost, their auras dampened down to the mentation layer.

That breakaway civilization will toil under a pyramid of shadows and power as they have always done, but because we are now exiting the era in which they held sway over the Earth, they will no longer be able to exist here. The natural channel through the bardos and the passageways of rebirth will be closed to them. The Earth will reject their unstable bodies, and they will head toward joining the galactic AI. Not an ideal existence.

Responding to this bifurcation, the Earth will ultimately aid in these transhumanist/cyborg beings leaving both the free Earth rebirth cycle and the ability to thrive here. Those who head toward the breakaway civilization will be motivated by immortality using cloning, genetic manipulation, terraforming other planets, and hybridization with degraded species looking for Earth DNA in exchange for longevity tech. It won't take long before their loss of plasmic cohesion will mean a loss of the capacity to work with organic and elemental reality, and this loss is why they will start to seek the chakra body again. An impossible task.

After this time of upheaval and species splitting, humans will have stabilized an agrarian, self-sustaining, biome-respecting, interdependence-honoring form of overlapping community cooperation. The predominant technology will be scalar-wave propelled, frequency and light spectral-focusing, and conscious-assisted inner tech using crystal harmonizers, bronze, copper, gold, wind, and water as the conduits bridging the subtle energy fields. The resurrection and advancement of resulting knowledge includes how the mycelia and the Earth's vast organic neural network harmonize with star cycles—living exchanges of subtle information in the morphic fields—and how humans interact and depend on these rhythms.

Any technology using metallurgy, lasers/focused light, quantum computation, or the acceleration of light or the tuning of sound will be manufactured using a form of materiality and interface with the elements we haven't seen since early Druidic times. All externalized tech will be underpinned by embodied human self-awareness training on how these forces entwine with cognition, body-based energy, and a universal life force.

We will remember the Atlantean tech of ley line-grounded portals that conform to pyramid-angle power tethering our terrestrial realm to our Orion and Pleiadian brethren, but this time it will no longer be in worship of the priest class. Our ability to recognize earthly and human sovereignty will mark this spiritual time frame.

The morphogenic field of the Earth will be stabilized and protected. Our Akashic imprints will no longer be obstructed by low dimensional frequencies or parasitic entities as they had been through the satanic, or Kali-energized, era.

We are leaving an age powered by satellite wave/particle magnification thoughtform systems born of the saturnal cage. That cage has been generated and propelled through the inverse galactic sun—the black hole reflecting entropic feedback data, eroding our perception into degraded spheres.

The hexagon satellite seated on the bottom of Saturn has been acting as an amplifier, with the moon as a reflection device, and the degraded grids and nonfunctioning etheric force fields have meant a compromised influence on our planet and all sentient beings residing on her.

The solar upgrade means that our twelve-strand DNA is activated, resulting in free energy generated from a toroidal field surrounding the Earth that moves matter across space-time. It will be abundant and open to be used by adepts and the masses alike. The previous dark influences will be neutralized by our new bodies and the Earth's protective and healed grids in this awakening era.

Crystal-encased toroidally spun dielectric energy will be somatically understood. Humans will know the geometric code propulsion forming the ether and defining the physical cosmos. We will enfold into a union with the true angelic realms and find genetic health and an upgraded DNA untampered and in conjunction with the Earth's reformed pranic self-cycling. We will understand the sun, the etheric realms, and the cycles of mental/subtle body rebirth enough so that we will not fear death but instead will start building our way out of samsara collectively by bridging the heavenly realms with the earthly one, finding grace, devotion, and humility again.

Long term, we can expect more upheaval as deeper cycles act to allow the Earth to be a haven for more unevolved souls and suffering beings. After approximately ten thousand solar years, we will experience a dark age on Earth until the next yuga begins.

After that time, the Earth's spectral energetic conscious capacity to metabolize all layers of life will return, and a long era of heavenly peace and spiritual power will reign. If you want to sit this long, bumpy era out, consider rebirthing in two hundred and fifty years.

Fortuitously, in this upcoming ten thousand-year window, humans will spread out and manifest in higher dimensions, learning to transcend rebirth and navigate their many soul layers as one expression without the traps of simple, sensual fear-based egoic yearning. Some will build and toil on Earth as we always have, and others will manifest in higher dimensions, far transcending the lower etheric and underworlds occupied by the sorcerers and immortalists. We humans will be in service to the cosmic mission to evolve all life.

We will do so in rainbow light celestial embodiment free from confusion and grasping, emanating as many forms and free from constraints. We can see how this evolutionary leap mirrors our Pleiadian family and other evolved sentience. A Shambhala-like paradise blending a 5D experience with access to higher dimensions.

This revealed picture is simply one reading of one timeline presented and laid out in vision and synthesis; as always, many contenting energies play in the dance of creation.

Our work focuses on the awakening age and the methods for integrating the energies, essences, and forces promoting its manifestation. What might our world look like as we settle into this new paradigm? To encounter this vision, one must collapse time and exit the temporal linear matrix and feel past these constraints. We meditate and conjure the potentials and dreams that are called in as timelines yet to be manifest in our shared experience but existent as emerging strains overlapping with ours.

To clarify, not only are many timeline future, present, and past experiences available and cogenerating through the collective, but individually we jump timelines at critical junctures of our development as we encounter challenges and obstacles determined by our karma. As we become more conscious of all sensory phenomena's porous and dream-like nature, we can see the moments that strike out as way stations of timeline shifts. This transpires when we purify karma by sharpening our view and moving our mind stream and heart beam into accord with the frequency and cause-and-effect dance rippling out of a higher expression of our behavior. That upgraded behavior results in more energy, which results in more faith and grace.

MEDITATION

Calling the Upper World into the Here and Now

I am alive here and now, manifesting the realm of divine light and ecstatic perception where bliss and conscious expansion grow and persist without end. All are beautiful expressions of fractalized appearance and self-aware interdependent familial light. All are valued and precious, and the truth is known; no shadow is cast, as all words, deeds, and thoughts pass through the great mirror of self-illuminated abundance. All are free, and every motivation considers the other and self the past, the present, and the future.

Realizing and channeling the spiritual dimensions; bridging the physical with the nonphysical; practicing lucid dreaming; coming to faith, spiritual devotion, and humility; energizing and healing the temporary self and recognizing the soul's perfection; and quieting and engaging the dynamic cacophony of mind-produced phenomena and the fabric of time-form make up the human path of transcendent awareness, self-propelled growth, and the release from finitude. It can be written about, and we can share it and experience it, but despite these proclamations, we will never be able to constrain totality into a material or social science. The religion of the cosmos is the play of conscious love as it inhabits, births, and fills all. The seriousness of that play is the art form above all. Our current era allows the focused space of totality to merge with our human story and uplift our species just in time.

The truth is that each of us is the center of the cosmos and endowed with potential beyond concept. We can each do our small part to share that. We can each promote the wisdom of God and in doing so, accentuate its divinity and our role as grateful benefactors, grateful limbs of its glory. God's glory. We are it. Not the person reading, judging, contemplating, or rehearsing, but the soul that already knows.

We each came here to remind each other of what we already know—that we are the prism through which the light refracts into a rainbow. We are the light and the space between. We are also none of this. We are simply the observer letting it all pass by with the still shine of a thought we neither conjure nor dismiss. The sound of our heart, the pulse of our blood, and the breathing, beating life force that is us at this moment all speak a prayer that holds that still flame. The prayer began the cosmos and does so once more for each of us to grasp and utter. Once spoken, everything becomes clear, if just for a moment.

FIN.

INDEX